The Complete Guide to the Learning Styles Inservice System

Related Titles

**Teaching Elementary Students Through Their Individual Learning Styles:
Practical Approaches for Grades 3–6**
Rita Dunn and Kenneth Dunn
ISBN: 0-205-13221-9

**Teaching Secondary Students Through Their Individual Learning Styles:
Practical Approaches for Grades 7–12**
Rita Dunn and Kenneth Dunn
ISBN: 0-205-13308-8

**Teaching Young Children Through Their Individual Learning Styles:
Practical Approaches for Grades K–2**
Rita Dunn, Kenneth Dunn, and Janet Perrin
ISBN: 0-205-15271-6

The Complete Guide to the Learning Styles Inservice System

RITA DUNN
St. John's University

KENNETH DUNN
Queens College

ALLYN AND BACON
Boston London Toronto Sydney Tokyo Singapore

Series editor: Frances Helland
Series editorial assistant: Bridget Keane
Manufacturing buyer: Suzanne Lareau

Library of Congress Cataloging-in-Publication Data

Dunn, Rita Stafford
    The complete guide to the learning styles inservice system / Rita Dunn,
Kenneth Dunn.
       p. cm.
    Includes bibliographical references and index.
    ISBN 0-205-27441-2
    1. Teachers—In-service training.   I. Dunn, Kenneth J.
II. Title.
LB1731.D86 1999
370'.71'5—dc21   98-30269
                                                    CIP

Printed in the United States of America

10 9 8 7 6 5 4 3 2 1   02 01 00 99 98

___ DEDICATION ___

This book is dedicated to those St. John's University doctoral students who have:

- contributed to the extensive research on learning styles with attention to detail, diligent persistence, expertise, and scholarly concern
- served as cutting-edge pioneers
- reported their findings in regional, national, and/or international publications
- worked devotedly toward sharing their data with administrators, citizens, educators, researchers, parents, teachers, and students
- helped to build the vision of a better education for all students by acknowledging, and teaching to, students' learning-style strengths

Among those outstanding professionals who have contributed uniquely are the following:

Drs. Elizabeth Bauer, Ann Braio, Eric Brand, Susan Brand, Patricia Brennan, Jean Bruno, Karen Burke, Elizabeth Burton, Roger Callan, John Catugno, Mona Ciarletta, Marie Carbo, Sam Carpentier, Marianne Cholakis, Mary Ellen Cirelli, Thomas DeBello, Christina DeGregoris, Joan DellaValle, Muriel Drew, Heather Dunham, Dolores Febres, Anita Ferdenzi, Edmund Frazier, Mary Ellen Freeley, Audrey Gallucci, Barbara Gardiner, William F. Geiser, Antigone Giannakos, Mary Cecilia Giannitti, Betty Gould, Fran Greb, Christina Gregoris, Jack Gremli, Francine Guastello, Stephen Guinta, Stanley J. Hanna, Helene Hodges, Joanne Ingham, Pengiren Rachma Pengiren Jadid, Fatimeh Jalali, Agatha P. Kelley, Angela Klavas, Jeffrey Krimsky, Marcia Knoll, Dennis Kroon, Miriam Lenehan, Barbara Lewthwaite, Alice Listi, Peter Lynch, Harold MacMurren, Maureen Martini, Wayne Merkling, Barbara Miles, Joyce Miller, Diane Mitchell, Peggy Murrain, Ralph Napolitano, Barbara Knapp Nelson, Patti-Ann Orazio, Janet Perrin, Jeanne Pizzo, Terrence Quinn,, Patricia Raupers, Anne Roberts, Theresa Santana, Thomas C. Shea, Joan Silver, Susan Smith, Mary Sullivan, Larry J. Svreck, Rhoada Tanenbaum, Rita Taylor, Sue Tendy, Paul Trautman, Elizabeth Van Wynen, Joan Virostko, Roberta Wheeler, Regina White, and Frederick Wenberg.

CONTENTS

5 Small-Group Techniques for Inservice Workshops Kenneth Dunn 46

6 Designing Tactual Resources Kenneth Dunn 57

7 Designing Kinesthetic Resources for Inservice Kenneth Dunn 72

**8   Designing Contract Activity Packages for Inservice
Rita Dunn   85**

PREFACE

More than ever before, it has become increasingly evident that those of us responsible for expanding the knowledge and instructional skills of pre- and inservice teachers require a totally revised system of staff development. What was done in the past barely worked then—and is likely to be even less effective in light of recently established new state standards for all students regardless of their academic standing or ability.

If students are to be examined in light of demonstrable increases in achievement, teachers will need to know how to *produce* those increases. To produce increased student achievement, teachers will need to appreciate the process of achieving through their learning styles. To achieve through their learning styles, teachers will need to *experience the process themselves.*

Why Consider a Learning-Style Inservice Approach?

1. Academic failure has been reversed through learning-style strategies for previously failing elementary, secondary, and college students throughout the United States.
2. Academic achievement has been significantly increased through learning styles among average elementary and secondary populations in the United States.
3. Academic achievement has been significantly increased through learning styles among adults. Experts have recommended that learning-style strategies be used in inservice training.
4. Experimental research with adults has demonstrated significantly higher achievement test scores when participants were provided inservice through their learning-style strengths.

Why Choose the Dunn and Dunn Learning-Style Model for Inservice?

1. Researchers at more than 115 institutions of higher education have conducted research with this model.
2. More research has been published with the Dunn and Dunn Model than with any other educational model.

3. The experimental studies conducted with inservice participants verified that:
  - Only motivated teachers succeed in conventional inservice, but all teachers gain more knowledge through a learning-style instructional approach.
  - In contrast with how participants perform during traditional teaching, those taught through their learning styles achieve statistically higher achievement and attitude test scores.

The strategies described in this text will enable staff developers and consultants to provide inservice that produces a positive and lasting effect in teacher support and implementation.

Acknowledgments

We want to express our continuing appreciation to the following:

  - St. John's University administrators, who have supported both the theory and research involved in developing our learning-style construct (1970–1998)
  - The eighteen university professors and seventy-nine doctoral graduates at St. John's University who have contributed so extensively to the research that serves as the cornerstone of our learning-style model
  - Other professors and students from more than 115 institutions of higher education who have published studies that they conducted using this learning-style model
  - The following reviewers for their comments on the manuscript: Kathleen Fite, Southwest Texas State University; Patricia Raupers, Northern Valley Schools; and Robert Felipczak, *Training* magazine.
  - Madeline Larsen and Angela Klavas for their loving support—always—to Dr. Rita Dunn
  - Laura Shea Doolan and Andrea Honigsfeld for their loving support on this book
  - The practitioners throughout the United States and abroad who have published stories of the success their schools experienced when using learning-style-based instruction.

We ask only that persons responsible for teacher inservice experiment with providing instruction through teachers' learning styles and then compare the results with those of their previous efforts.

Rita Dunn
Kenneth Dunn
www.learningstyles.net

1

Required: A Totally New System of Inservice

Rita Dunn

Problems with Teacher Education and Inservice Programs

Preparation for teaching has been ongoing through formal and informal experiences in state-certified programs for decades. And for decades, school administrators have perceived *retraining,* within a year or two of graduation from a licensed teacher education institution, as a requirement for quality classroom performance. At least part of the need for continuing teacher reeducation lies in one or more of the following problems.

1. Lack of Research-Based Instruction

The need for periodic retraining would be understandable if experimental research had shown that new instructional practices produced better results than older practices. But few instructional practices have been subjected to experimental studies with the populations currently in school (Dunn, 1991c). Furthermore, of those studies that have been published, many represent the interests of a single advocate in a single organization—suggesting possible bias in favor of the strategy.

2. Widespread Acceptance of Fads

Instead of new practices emerging from research laboratories or field-based school settings, professional and commercial groups periodically develop and promulgate new educational notions. They then employ charismatic consultants and Madison Avenue–type brochures to tout the latest theory. Few supervisors or teachers ask:

- Where can I read the results of experimental studies completed with this program?
- Have results been published in a refereed research journal?
- Has this program significantly increased standardized achievement test scores for academic underachievers in this discipline (or at this grade level)?
- May I have the names and addresses of teachers who have used this method?

Consider just a few of the recent theories that have been popularized and adopted widely. What do you know of the research behind authentic assessment, brain-based learning, learning through chaos, constructivism, critical thinking, cooperative learning, emotional intelligence, integrated or thematic curricula, multiple intelligences, problem solving, thinking skills, whole language, and—in 1997—the "well-rounded classroom"?

The U.S. government knows equally little about the theories and practices on which it spends taxpayers' dollars. Through Title I, special education, and multicultural education programs, it has allocated billions specifically for the improvement of poorly achieving populations. Those taxpayer dollars often have been used to implement theories devoid of research verification. Because every school has some failing students, and many schools have many failing students in serious academic trouble, administrators jump onto each new bandwagon in the hope that it will improve test scores. They do so with little concrete knowledge of what actually happened when the new strategy was implemented in other schools similar to theirs. As a result, their efforts rarely produce statistically higher standardized achievement tests scores (Dunn, 1997b).

Why do so many professional educators accept and support new approaches without examining their research bases? One answer may be that few teacher education programs teach future teachers to appreciate, feel comfortable with, or conduct research. As a result, when those future educators become experienced and tenured teachers, and later when they become teacher trainers, they have not experienced the excitement of monitoring the effects of their own teaching on diverse students.

Another reason that professional educators accept and support new approaches without examining their research bases is that many institutions do not require their faculty to engage in, experiment with, or publish research. These faculty remain relatively unsophisticated in terms of research, and their students cannot reap the benefit of original cutting-edge knowledge.

3. Lack of Support and Follow-Through after Inservice

Rarely do administrators offer on-site coaching, classroom demonstrations, or feedback when teachers begin experimenting with a new strategy. Rarely do they build the teacher's classroom results into an evaluation that rewards for successful implementation. Thus, there is little payoff other than personal satisfaction for teachers who struggle with the difficult task of interpreting what the inservice consultant recommended so that it becomes an effective instructional practice.

Few districts develop cooperative plans for implementation over a one- to three-year period. Rather, many districts arrange for a consultant's one-time presentation with little follow-through. Then the consultant departs, and teachers are required to undertake the difficult task of translating what was said into practical applications. That is no easy task for a hard-working teacher with thirty or more students, each with a unique set of problems, learning styles, and instructional requirements. Furthermore, district and school administrators sometimes require teachers to initiate two or more new practices at the same time.

4. Reliance on Individuals Rather Than Groups

When teachers become inspired during inservice, want to address a new approach, and then form a group or committee to work out implementation strategies cooperatively, they have a fair chance of success—with one disturbing prediction. Regardless of the approach that is being initiated, *nothing* works well with everyone. Because of individuals' unique learning styles, a strategy that is extremely effective for one student may be only acceptable to another, appropriate—but not necessarily interesting—to a third, irritating to a fourth, and devastating to a fifth. That is why one reading method produces academic excellence among certain youngsters and failure among others. Even when teachers experiment with an innovation, they need to analyze for which students it is effective and for which it should be discarded. Such decisions may be more easily made with colleagues.

5. Lack of Sufficient Time

To add to the problem, administrators rarely provide time for interested teachers to meet and plan for the implementation of a new approach. Schools, student populations, and disciplines are so different that ensuring quick and easy success is difficult. Furthermore, administrators neither require nor request feedback on the effects of new implementations, and they rarely provide advance or continuing exposure to the same approach. Thus, teachers' enthusiasm and efforts dissipate gradually. Before long, however, a newer innovation is being advocated, and the pattern repeats.

6. Teachers' Lack of Research Skills

Classroom teachers have seen so many approaches initially lauded and then discarded by supervisors that they may be reluctant to devote energy and time to experimenting with this year's popular strategy. If they knew of easy and efficient steps for determining how effective each new strategy actually is, they might be more willing to try it. Then they would know what works—and with which students. Unfortunately, few practitioners have been taught how to judge the effectiveness of different instructional approaches with a diverse student body.

7. Limitations of Certain Teacher Education Programs

The need for ongoing inservice also may be due, in part, to the inadequacy of the knowledge base provided to future teachers. At certain institutions, methods courses have remained essentially unchanged for years. New practices are added from time to time, but only to provide an overview of the more recent buzzwords being addressed at conferences and in journals. Rarely is the focus on the innovation in depth. Rather, whatever the approach, it is presented as appropriate for the entire class—without attention to the differences between the ways global and analytic processors absorb information or how strongly auditory, visual, tactual, and kinesthetic learners remember new and difficult information.

For example, in different college courses, future teachers are advised . . .

- . . . to teach with multisensory resources. This information disregards the many healthy youngsters who cannot tolerate multiple stimuli simultaneously or who prefer patterns and routines.
- . . . that learners can absorb only one thing at a time and that multisensory resources distract them from learning. This information disregards the many healthy youngsters who cherish variety and change.
- . . . that learning style is flexible and children need to learn how to adapt in the "real world." This information disregards evidence that more than three-fifths of learning style is biologically imposed and suggests that children can alter their minds and bodies at will (Restak, 1979; Thies, 1979).
- . . . of the biological nature of individual differences (Restak, 1979; Thies, 1979). These teacher education students are taught to teach students how to teach themselves in ways that respond to their unique traits.

These mixed messages also appear in professional journals.

8. Lack of Teacher Training Responsiveness to External Agencies

Many public and private commissions, state education departments, university committees, and legislative and citizen groups have suggested revised practices for teacher training. These external agencies apparently have been unable to make substantive changes from without. It may be that only well-focused determination over time can help an entrenched bureaucracy to change from within (Dunn & Nelson, 1996).

9. Lack of Respect for State Education Department Personnel

- For some time, many state education departments have been expensive to run and understaffed. Perhaps as a result, they have been the targets of uncomplimentary humor. These agencies also have been accused of imposing statewide mandates without providing funds for implementation; of being unable to provide leadership for what they have mandated; and of encouraging widespread use of across-the-board practices, regardless of their appropriateness.

10. Quality of Teacher Applicants

A contributing factor to the need for ongoing inservice may be the quality of some of the students admitted into teacher education programs. Although many inspired and enthusiastic candidates have enrolled, others are spelling-impaired, grammatically illiterate, and content-deficient.

University registrars in higher education institutions indicate that the highest academic achievers rarely apply for admission to schools of education. Worse, when faced with either teacher shortages or political demands, state education departments and administrators have granted "emergency" certifications to inadequate persons who often are then assigned to schools with the most difficult to teach students, where they do little other than try to "control" behavior. The phrase "a warm body" means something very different to educators than it does to other citizens.

11. Disparate Criteria for Determining Teaching Excellence

Despite the statements in the previous section, grade-point average or IQ may not assess adequately a person's potential for excellence as a teacher. An alternative might be to consider other traits, such as continuing personal growth; devotion to students; creativity; the ability to develop innovative resources for youngsters for whom conventional approaches have proved inadequate; or the willingness to work with young people without concern for hours, energy, or competitive salaries. If these are to be the criteria for identifying teaching excellence, however, we need to establish ways of identifying and measuring such characteristics.

Another characteristic of excellent teachers is that their students achieve well on standardized achievement tests. Many educators, however, criticize teacher evaluation that is done on the basis of student achievement. These critics suggest that teachers assigned to academically proficient groups inevitably will be rated higher than teachers assigned to poorly achieving groups, regardless of the quality of their instruction or their devotion to the task.

It is possible to design an efficient and objective system for identifying teacher effectiveness in terms of students' past and present achievement, attitudes toward learning, and attendance. Such an instrument could be weighted to favor those teachers who voluntarily teach failing students who, in turn, evidence academic breakthroughs. Such a system would justify rewards for teachers whose previously underachieving students were provided instruction that helped them reverse past failures. There are many instances of such breakthroughs nationally (Andrews, 1990; Brunner & Majewski, 1990; Dunn, Bruno, Sklar, & Beaudry, 1990; Dunn, Della Valle, Dunn, Geisert, Sinatra, & Zenhausern, 1986; Klavas, 1993; Lemmon, 1985; Quinn, 1993; Stone, 1992).

12. Urban Schools and Minority Students

There is always the possibility that the quality of teaching is inadequate only in urban schools attended by poor children who are members of minority groups. If you believe that, you should do the following:

- Visit affluent suburban schools in any part of the nation and identify the number of students classified as eligible for special education, learning disabled, and emotionally handicapped.
- Ask parents whether all their children enjoy or do well in the school they attend. Which of their children like their teachers, understand their homework assignments, and perform academically as well as the parents believe they should? Chances are good that, in any family with three or more children, one will do well, one will perform adequately, and the third will be either bored or frustrated on an almost daily basis.

13. Special Education and the Need for Inservice

Educators have effectively persuaded many parents and other citizens that special education (SE) is a legitimate classification for students who are unable to learn. One such category, the learning disabled (LD), is stipulated by federal guidelines as appropriate for students of normal intelligence who do not perform at grade level. But if certified teachers cannot teach students with normal intelligence, whom can they teach? Furthermore, the standardized achievement and attitude test scores of classified LD and emotionally handicapped (EH) students increased statistically when the traditional teaching with which they had been failing was changed to learning-style-responsive teaching.

Furthermore, significantly higher test scores were reported for special education students in these learning-style programs:

- A four-year, federally sponsored national study (Alberg et al., 1992)
- Taught by school practitioners for whom no other approach had reversed underachievement (Andrews, 1990; Brunner & Majewski, 1990; Elliot, 1991; Gadwa & Griggs, 1985; Klavas, 1993; Lemmon, 1985; Orsak, 1990; Quinn, 1993; Stone, 1992)
- In urban schools (Miller, 1997; Quinn, 1994; *Buffalo Experience,* 1995)
- In suburban schools (Brunner & Majewski, 1990; Elliot, 1991; Gadwa & Griggs, 1985; Lenehan, Dunn, Ingham, Murray, & Signer, 1994; Mickler & Zippert, 1987; Nelson, Dunn, Griggs, Primavera, Fitzpatrick, Bacillious, & Miller, 1993)
- In rural schools (Koshuta & Koshuta, 1993; Neely & Alm, 1992, 1993) throughout the United States

If future teachers were being taught to identify and teach to their students' learning styles during their initial training, the need for frequent retraining would be drastically diminished (Dunn, Griggs, Olson, Gorman, & Beasley, 1995).

14. Lack of Student Discipline and/or Motivation

Educators often conjecture that today's students are not as well disciplined or as highly motivated as students used to be. Nevertheless, teachers need to teach those students for whom they accept responsibility. Table 2-1 in Chapter 2 reveals that motivation is one of the 23 Dunn and Dunn learning-style elements. Motivation is not biologically imposed; it results from students' experiences and interests. Teachers who are unable to motivate and teach their charges need to learn how to do so, and improvement should be a requisite for maintaining employment and tenure.

More students are motivated than teachers believe (Dunn & Buchanan, 1996). If certain children still appear unteachable, however, then entirely different types of instructional programs and professional instructors should be available to them outside the regular school system.

15. Children Taking Prescription Medications

Most people have no idea of the number of children who attend school while taking daily doses of prescribed drugs. Instead of requiring teachers to teach in the ways that these children are best able to learn, educators often recommend that children be drugged to enable them to conform to the way their teachers teach. Physicians may not understand that active and nonconforming children learn differently from the way passive, conforming children do, and may prescribe drugs for active children in the erroneous belief that these youngsters are better off medicated so that they will conform to traditional expectations.

Why do parents permit their children to be drugged rather than demand that boards of education mandate instructional approaches responsive to how their children learn? Perhaps these parents are unaware that their children *can* learn. How much better it would be to use the money spent on prescriptions to develop teachers' skills through effective inservice.

16. Cultural Diversity and Immigrant Populations

Some believe that earlier European immigrants to the United States were genetically more intelligent than the minority populations who currently constitute a virtual majority among many urban populations. Does culture contribute to school achievement?

Milgram, Dunn, Price, and their colleagues (1993) studied almost six thousand gifted and nongifted adolescents in nine diverse cultures and found that opportunity influences individuals' ability to develop specific areas of talent that may eventually lead to giftedness. For example, if access to creative activities, information, or role models were not readily available in a specific culture, then relatively few adolescents would develop talent in that domain.

Thus, in cultures that respected art, higher percentages of artistically gifted students were found. The same findings held firm across other giftedness domains—athletics, dance, mathematics, literature, music, and science—when Brazilian, Canadian, Greek, Guatemalan, Israeli, Korean, Mayan, Filipino, and U.S.-born adolescents were assessed. It may be important to acknowledge that most U.S. communities financially support athletics regardless of the state of the economy, but rarely hesitate to eliminate programs in music, art, drama, or science. Is it any wonder that many young American boys aspire to becoming baseball, basketball, or football players, whereas few choose science, medicine, dentistry, physics, or the arts as career goals? If culture so influences academic achievement, why not train teachers to teach reading and mathematics through students' talents and interests?

17. Lack of Knowledge about the Differences between the Academically Able and the Academically at Risk

Do the academically able and the academically at risk differ in how they learn? Seven learning-style traits significantly discriminate between at-risk and dropout students and those who perform well in school. A majority of low achievers and dropouts need the following:

- Frequent opportunities for mobility while concentrating
- Reasonable choices of how, with what, and with whom to learn
- A variety of instructional resources, environments, and sociological groupings rather than routines and patterns
- To learn during late morning, afternoon, or evening hours, but rarely in the early morning
- Informal and comfortable seating rather than wooden, steel, or plastic chairs and desks
- Soft illumination; bright light may exacerbate hyperactivity for some
- Either tactual and visual introductory resources reinforced by kinesthetic and visual resources, or kinesthetic and visual introductory resources reinforced by tactual and visual resources

Underachievers tend to show the following characteristics:

- They have poor auditory memory. When they learn visually, it usually is through pictures, drawings, graphs, symbols, comics, and cartoons rather than through printed book text.
- They want to do well in school, but their inability to remember facts through lecture, discussion, or reading contributes to poor performance in conventional schools where most instruction is delivered by teachers talking and students listening or reading.
- They learn differently from high achievers and the gifted, but they also learn differently from one another.

What Can Be Done to Improve Teacher and Inservice Education?

If inservice is to be maximally meaningful so that its effects continue for at least several years without requiring annual replenishment, educators, citizens, and legislatures need to initiate several strategies.

1. A program of staff development about learning styles–based instruction, but implemented through participating teachers' styles, should be made available and required for every educator.
2. If one-tenth of the students in a school or class achieve below grade level, all educators responsible for those youngsters should be required to attend the staff development about learning styles. That mandate would extend to administrators and supervisors who need to be knowledgeable about instructional alternatives related to students' strengths and to teachers and paraeducators who need to implement those alternatives.
3. Parents need to be educated about how each of their children learns and how their children's teachers teach. All teaching styles are effective—but not for all children.
4. Parents need to be educated concerning how each of their children should study and do homework. Homework is good, but each homework strategy is effective for, and detrimental to, different learners.
5. Administrators and supervisors need to be made aware of the successful programs that have reversed underachievement among previously failing students and need to learn how to design similar strategies for their schools (Dunn, 1996b).
6. Teacher education programs need to be revised so that professors teach prospective teachers about learning styles and model ways of using alternative approaches in teaching. This is a long-range goal, but if we do not establish it now, our great-grandchildren will still face the same problems that our students do today.
7. Regardless of the topic, if it warrants inservice, we need to provide it for teachers through their individual styles. That is the only way they will internalize the pleasure of learning easily and enjoyably through strategies that complement how they master new and difficult academic material.

How Do We Know That Inservice Conducted through Teachers' Learning Styles Will Be More Effective Than What We Currently Do?

Research conducted at more than 115 institutions of higher education revealed that teaching through learning styles produced significantly higher gains than teaching traditionally (*Research on the Dunn and Dunn Model,* 1998). In addition, a meta-analysis of 42 experimental studies conducted with the Dunn and Dunn Learning Style Model between 1980 and 1990 at thirteen different universities revealed that matching students' learning-style preferences with approaches and resources compatible with those preferences consistently produced beneficial achievement (Dunn, Griggs, Olson, Gorman, & Beasley, 1995). Learning styles–based instruction has been effective at every academic level, including inservice (Buell & Buell, 1987; Dunn, Dunn, & Freeley, 1985; Freeley, 1984; Greb, 1997; Raupers, 1999; Taylor, 1999; Van Wynen, 1997).

Some teachers consistently demonstrate increased instructional effectiveness following staff development; others do not (Dunn & Buchanan, 1996). All teachers should become increasingly effective as a result of inservice based on their learning-style strengths.

Conclusion

This book is focused on how to improve the quality of teaching through a new system of inservice. It is about helping teachers become successful learners so that, eventually, they can model alternative strategies for their students. Chapter 1 describes the problems educators face with both schooling and inservice. Chapter 2 explains the concept of learning styles. Subsequent chapters describe how inservice coordinators can use learning-style strategies to retrain professional teachers.

Receiving inservice through their own personal styles will permit teachers to experience a whole new way of learning. Gradually, they will learn how to teach their students with nontraditional learning styles because they will have observed their colleagues learn through alternative strategies and will have experienced such approaches themselves.

The immediate aim of this book is to improve inservice. Its ultimate aim is to improve education for everyone.

_2_

Introduction to Learning Styles

Rita Dunn

_Knowledge about learning styles and brain behavior is a fundamental
new tool at the service of teachers and schools. It is clearly not the
latest educational fad. It provides a deeper and more profound view of
the learner than previously perceived, and is part of a basic framework
upon which a sounder theory and practice of learning and instruction
may be built. (Keefe, 1982, Foreword)_

Individuals have unique patterns for learning new and difficult information. Those
patterns are so diverse that, without using a reliable and valid instrument, it is difficult to predict accurately how to teach anything academically difficult to people
whose abilities to assimilate and retain new and challenging facts and concepts vary
tremendously.

Some adults can master easy information without using their preferred learning style, but most perform significantly better when the environment, the methods,
and the resources are complementary to (i.e., "match"), rather than dissonant from
("mismatch") how they learn. These statements have been documented by two
decades of award-winning research (see Appendix A).

What Is Learning Style?

According to Dunn and Dunn (1992, 1993) and Dunn, Dunn, and Perrin (1994),
learning style is the way each person begins to concentrate on, process, internalize,
and retain new and difficult academic information. More than three-fifths of learning style is biological; less than one-fifth is developmental (Restak, 1979; Thies,
1979). Learning style changes over time, but only individuals' naturally evolving
maturation over years alters those elements of their style that are biologically imposed (Dunn & Griggs, 1995). Developmental aspects change more predictably and
follow a discernible pattern. Some aspects of style change in some people; others
do not. It is the _degree_ to which each person learns differently from other people that

makes the identical instructional environments, methods, and resources effective for some learners and ineffective for others.

Most people have between six and fourteen preferences that constitute their learning style. The stronger the preference, the more important it is to provide compatible instruction (Braio, Beasley, Dunn, Quinn, & Buchanan, 1997; Dunn, Griggs, Olson, Gorman, & Beasley, 1995).

Presenters involved in inservice need to use as many teachers' learning-style preferences as possible as the basis for the instruction they provide. By learning through their own preferences, teachers see how wonderful it is to capitalize on their personal strengths. They often then begin to teach their students through the youngsters' strengths.

What Are the Elements of Learning Style?

The most widely used approach to learning style was developed during the thirty-year period beginning in 1967 by Rita and Kenneth Dunn (Dunn & Dunn, 1972, 1975, 1978, 1983, 1992, 1993). The Dunns describe learning style as the ways in which five basic *stimuli* affect individuals' abilities to master new and difficult academic information and skills. Each of the five stimuli includes smaller components called *elements* (see Figure 2-1).

FIGURE 2-1

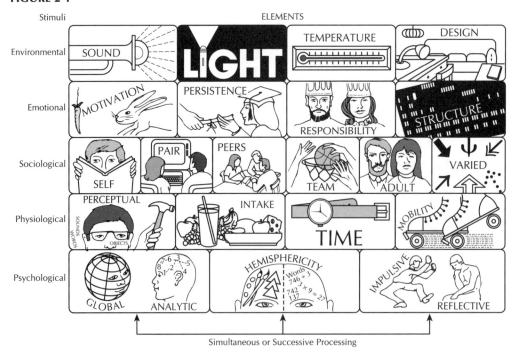

Environmental Elements: Acoustics, Illumination, Temperature, and Seating Design

Sober consideration needs to be given to *where* inservice will be conducted and *how* the facility can be adapted to respond to those elements that participants either prefer or strongly prefer (see Chapter 3). Preferences affect each person's ability to concentrate, absorb, and retain new and difficult academic material; strong preferences *strongly* affect the outcomes.

Environmental preferences are biologically imposed on human beings (Thies, 1979) and include varying needs for (1) quiet versus sound, (2) bright versus soft lighting, (3) warm versus cool temperatures, and (4) formal versus informal seating while concentrating (see Figure 2-1). Individuals who were provided a complementary rather than a dissonant environment in which to concentrate achieved statistically higher standardized achievement and attitude test scores (Dunn, Griggs, Olson, Gorman, & Beasley, 1995).

Emotional Elements: Motivation, Persistence, Responsibility (Conformity/Nonconformity), and Structure

Participants have a range of emotional reactions that influence how well they perform during inservice (see Figure 2-1). Except for persistence, emotional reactions tend to be developmental—they vary with situations and experiences.

- Are teachers **motivated** to learn the content that will be presented during the inservice? Although a simple survey could provide this information, you should assume that volunteers tend to be more motivated than staff who are *required* to attend.
- How **persistent** is each individual, and what could the presenter and administrators *do* to help teachers put into practice what they have been taught during the inservice? What can be done to get unmotivated people involved in learning? See Chapters 4 and 10 for inservice applications for this problem.
- How **conforming** or **nonconforming** are the participants? Conformists present few problems, other than that they may say what they believe you want to hear rather than share their honest opinions of the inservice content or delivery. By contrast, nonconformists are likely to say the *opposite* of what they believe you or administrators want to hear! Thus, nonconformists need to understand *why* the inservice is important and, depending on their sociological preferences, *for whom* it will be valuable—them, their students, administrators, or the community. Nonconformists also require *choices* of the persons with whom they will learn and the resources they may choose to use to learn. They need to be addressed collegially rather than authoritatively. Although the behaviors that nonconformists manifest may appear irresponsible, in reality, nonconformists defy rules only when those regulations appear to be autocratic, arbitrary, or capricious and do not permit choices.
- How much **structure**, as opposed to how many **options**, does each individual who is participating in the inservice require? Those who need structure work

well with clearly stated objectives, limited resources that are well focused, and specified times and guidelines. Participants who are strongly self-structured may resent objectives established by others and often ask for exemptions from at least some of their assigned tasks and responsibilities. They also may submit products done "their way."

These emotional elements appear to be developmental (Thies, 1979). For example, young children tend to be conforming until the age of 2, when, for the first time, many become defiant to varying degrees. In the United States, that stage is called "the terrible twos." Most children outgrow this stage and become fairly conforming again within a year. Then, somewhere between ages 12 and 14, many enter into what seems to be a second stage of nonconformity—adolescence. Many teenagers emerge from adolescent nonconformity at about the ninth or tenth grade; some adults remain entrenched in adolescent behavior well into their thirties, or even later.

The third stage of nonconformity affects some adults during their mid-forties and fifties and is commonly called "midlife crisis." During this period, many people challenge societal demands and the values they have held up to that point. Sometimes, they make rash decisions concerning fidelity, parental responsibilities, or career determinations.

That humans experience these repeated patterns at approximately the same period in their lives suggests that there is a biological aspect to being conforming versus nonconforming. Nevertheless, the nonconformist who is enrolled in inservice needs to be acknowledged and helped to respond positively to what is occurring. Without such preparation, the presenter and the participants will be required to cope with "devil's advocates" who require an inordinate amount of attention and time—to most people's irritation.

People Patterns—Sociological Elements: Learning Independently, with One or More Colleagues, or with Either a Collegial or an Authoritative Adult

Adults vary extremely in their choices of the people with whom they prefer to learn. Some—often the brightest and more analytic—learn most productively by themselves. Once they have thought things through, they can interact with others, but they really prefer working alone. When required either to listen to or to work with anyone other than a recognized authority, they become critical because they need to pace themselves and to process material uniquely—alone or perhaps with a single peer.

People who are authority-oriented prefer to learn directly with a presenter, particularly if that person is well known and well respected. Peer-oriented adults prefer to learn in small groups or teams, usually with other teachers with whom they have a collegial relationship.

Some participants like to learn with different people at different times. They function in a *variety* of groupings as opposed to just one pattern or routine. Others will work only with those colleagues they respect.

Some people cannot learn with other human beings but are marvelous with technology and can spend hours alone with their computer systems. Others, because of perceptual preferences, cannot learn with books, or through lectures, or without people nearby—not necessarily interacting, but in close proximity—"in case I need help."

Recently, inservice has incorporated some group strategies like cooperative learning. Those strategies are likely to be effective with peer-oriented teachers, but it is unlikely that most teachers who remain isolated in self-contained classrooms with their students most of each day are highly peer-oriented.

If you were unaware of these people patterns until now, perhaps you now understand that inservice cannot be effective without attention to individuals' learning styles. Sociological preferences are developmental (Thies, 1979) and some patterns are recognizable by age and achievement levels (see Appendix B).

Physiological Elements—Perceptual Preferences: Time of Day, Intake, and Need for Mobility versus Passivity

Perceptual Preferences

Perceptual preferences for remembering new and difficult information **first** by (1) hearing it (auditorially), (2) seeing it (visually), (3) handling manipulative instructional resources (tactually), and/or (4) actively participating while standing or moving (kinesthetically) may be the most important aspect of learning style. These preferences frequently either *enable* or *prevent* individuals from achieving easily. Some people can learn challenging content through more than one modality, but most people have one modality that is stronger than others. Anyone who has difficulty when learning—or who simply is not interested in specific content but is required to master it—needs to be exposed to new and difficult information *initially* through the strongest perceptual strength available (step 1). But that is only the first step toward increasing achievement through perceptual strengths.

After the initial exposure through individuals' perceptual strengths (whichever modality is strongest), most people, other than those who are gifted in a specific academic area, then need to have the same information **reinforced** through their *secondary* or *tertiary* perceptual strength. This reinforcement should follow (step 2) within a day or so. The reinforcement should then be followed by step 3— *using* that same information creatively by *applying* it, for example by converting it into a floor game, an electroboard, an illustrated booklet, or a poem. When this multiple-step sequence was followed, even previously poorly achieving or special education students performed significantly better than they did with traditional instruction (Andrews, 1990; Dunn, 1989a; Klavas, 1993; Kroon, 1985; Quinn, 1993) (see Appendix C).

Appendix E describes how some of the researchers gradually learned to increase retention with this three-step, perceptual-strength schema for (1) introducing complex content through an individual's strongest modality; (2) reinforcing that same content through that individual's secondary or tertiary modality; and then (3) requiring that the information be the basis of the content when creating a crossword puzzle, a poem, a kinesthetic floor game, a song, or some other resource designed by the learner. Creating original applications of new content contributes substantially to the retention of that information.

Three decades ago, inservice consisted of mostly verbal presentations accompanied by visual print. As an *introduction,* speeches could have been effective only for between 20 and 30 percent of teachers at any inservice session. The majority of adults are neither strongly auditory nor strongly visual. Currently, only about 20 percent of the teachers are auditory, but that percentage is *high* for any population that includes both genders. Males tend to be consistently less auditory than females (Dunn & Griggs, 1995a, 1995b). Because of that, try the following suggestions for inservice.

Inservice Application

Many males are strongly tactual or kinesthetic. Beginning an inservice session with a brief explanation of (1) what needs to be learned, (2) the choices available for learning it, and (3) how the learning can be evidenced, and following that with tactual and kinesthetic choices of resources for mastering the content, is an approach that is likely to attract many male—and some female—teachers.

Inservice Application

For teachers who are strongly visual, one week *before* the inservice, distribute a short reading about the content that will be covered—whether or not you believe that the materials actually will be read. Visual learners are among the first to skim or read material when it arrives.

Begin each inservice session with a *brief* explanation of (1) what needs to be learned, (2) the choices available for learning it, and (3) how the learning can be evidenced. Follow the introduction with visual/tactual, visual/kinesthetic, or visual/auditory choices of resources for mastering the content. This is likely to attract both visual males and females.

Inservice Application

Begin the session in the same way for everyone, but keep the objectives—what is expected of the participants—and the resources they may use to the point, clear, and brief (two or three minutes at most). Explain that all participants need to complete the identical objectives; how they do so will depend on either (1) their learning-style preferences or (2) individual choices.

If participants are not familiar with the resources—the ways in which they can learn the information, after you indicate that they are free to choose the materials and/or media through which they wish to learn—they can accompany you or others to the sections of the room, area, corridor, hall, auditorium, or building that houses the choices. Individuals then can choose to (1) listen to an explanation of the resources that are available, (2) read the directions printed on the wall next to each of the resources, or (3) examine the illustrations on the wall on the other side of the resources. Both sets of directions explain how to use the resources, but one is print-based (for analytics) and the other is picture-based (for globals). The two sets can be combined if you prefer.

Ask if there are questions about the procedures. If there are, answer one or two questions and then escort the participants to the various stations where the alternative resources for learning the content are stationed. The stations could include (1) a media room or section that houses a videotape or short film, (2) a computer room with Programmed Learning Sequenced software, or (3) a facility or room that provides resources responsive to each of the perceptual modalities and individuals' needs for working alone, in pairs, or with a small group.

As you proceed through this book, you will read descriptions of exactly how to respond to each person's strengths. For now, we are introducing one step at a time. That approach itself is analytic. Thus, if you are global, you may be thinking: "How will I put this all together? How can any single person/presenter/coordinator respond to many different participants' learning styles at one time?"

We promise to show you how to do that, and it will not be difficult. What it takes is a new way of organizing instruction and materials. When you see the results, you will wonder why you never thought to do it this way before!

Time-of-Day Preferences

Physiological preferences also include **time-of-day** energy levels for learning in the early or late morning, afternoon, or evening. Chronobiological highs and lows have more face validity than almost anything else you can name. Ask any group of people, "Are you a 'morning' or a 'night' person?" The answers will be forthcoming with virtually no hesitation. And, for this element of learning style, the answers probably are correct!

Thirty years ago, the fact that people were capable of learning difficult academic material much more easily at their "best" rather than at their "worst" time of day was unknown. School administrators did not consider whether children learned to read better at one time of day than another. Today, chronobiology is commonly acknowledged and has verified, through extensive research, that individuals with strong time-of-day preferences perform significantly better when they are matched, rather than mismatched, with their natural energy highs (Appendix F). Indeed, as one outgrowth of the research documenting the impact of energy highs and lows on achievement, the Educational Testing Services (ETS) now permits high school students to take the Scholastic Aptitude Tests (SATs) on computers at their preferred time of day.

Nevertheless, school and state education department administrators continue to mandate the administration of standardized achievement tests first thing in the morning. They remain ignorant of how few students actually are early-morning learners. They also use the guise of equity when, indeed, early-morning test administrations penalize the majority of students, whose energy levels are higher at other times (Andrews, 1990; Greb, 1997; Klavas, 1993; Lemmon, 1985; Milgram, Dunn, & Price, 1993; Stone, 1992) (see Appendix F).

Inservice, ordinarily scheduled for after-school hours when the majority of adults have energy lows, cannot continue that dismal pattern without continuing dismal results. At most, 55 percent of all adults concentrate best in the early morning, whereas 28 percent of adults function best in the evening. Others "come alive" in the late morning or afternoon, and a few during night-to-early-morning hours only. The time-of-day preferences of high and low achievers differ significantly. In addition, the majority of gifted and talented adolescents are *not* morning people (Milgram, Dunn, & Price, 1993). We offer these data because it is reasonable to think that many educators have intelligence quotients above the average.

If we were advocating the continuation of large-group inservice, both after-breakfast and after-dinner schedules would appeal to different populations; afternoon would have little appeal for most participants. Please note that our emphasis is not on finding the best time for most teachers; it is to describe a system that should work better for everyone.

Intake Preferences

The need for something to eat or drink was given little attention until the early 1980s, when it was recognized that, particularly during adolescence, many students required snacking while concentrating. Only about 6 percent of elementary school students need intake and achieve statistically higher test scores when permitted to snack while taking a test (MacMurren, 1985, 1992). However, this percentage expands to at least 25 percent during adolescence and varies substantially among adults.

Interestingly, many adult global processors perform better when eating, drinking, or chewing while learning than when they have no intake. Conversely, few analytics require intake while learning; they want it *after* concentrating, when they can relax. Thus, strongly global people use intake *to* relax *while* under pressure, whereas strongly analytic people use intake *after* pressure when they *can* relax.

Inservice Application

Provide healthful, low-fat or nonfat snacks for teachers during inservice. We recommend fruit or fruit juices, whole-grain muffins rather than cookies or doughnuts (to avoid overstimulation for the hyperactive), and tea and coffee (for those adults who require stimulation). People will tend to take what they need.

Mobility Preferences

Most presenters expect adults who attend inservice programs to be polite, sit still, pay attention, and focus on whatever is being explained. Despite that expectation, there are at least three types of people who find it difficult to remain seated for even half an hour.

1. Kinesthetic people learn *through* activity; they cannot concentrate on difficult information passively. Therefore, these teachers need to use floor games and active experiences to absorb challenging content.

2. Some adults cannot sit still for more than 10 or 15 minutes, in part because of the type of seating that is available. Often, these are people who require an informal design and, more often than not, seem to process difficult information globally—from the "big picture" to the details. Informal preferents can lounge for lengthy periods in an easy chair, on a couch, and sometimes on pillows on the floor; but when they are confined to conventional classroom seating, their minds wander, their bodies squirm, and their patience is quickly exhausted.

3. Members of the third group, those who need mobility, are able to sit and complete a task but, at designated intervals (which only their bodies predict), need to change places and move to another area, perhaps in the same room. Requiring such people to remain in the same location only frustrates them and, eventually, those around them as well.

Many males and some females need periodic mobility and cannot sit still, particularly in conventional seating. If we want restless males, kinesthetics of both genders, and those who need informal seating to profit from inservice, we should design opportunities for mobility for them as part of the learning process. These opportunities should be in addition to the breaks we normally provide for everyone at sequenced intervals. We also should provide some informal seating—perhaps a donated couch or two, or outdoor furniture that can be used for inservice when not "in service" itself.

Inservice Application

Establishing stations in different sections of the facility and directing the participants to move to the resources of their choice and engage in learning will help to focus many of them. Floor games will add activity-oriented and "fun" ways for kinesthetics to learn. However, do not get carried away and provide floor games for everyone. They will not be useful for participants who prefer to sit passively and listen, read, or remain near the presenter. But that's exactly the purpose of this guide. *Nothing* will work with everyone, and each session needs to provide appropriate options for adults who learn differently from one another.

Thus, those who want to move can learn while moving; those who want to remain in their seats can learn in that way. Have some chairs available at each station for those who want them, or encourage the participants to carry their chairs with them as they move from one location to another.

If you are analytic, conforming, or authority-oriented, you may be squirming at the thought of all those people moving from one place to another. But if you are global, you may be thinking, "Of course! This makes such sense!" Whatever you are thinking, stay with this book to the end and you will have more skills for providing effective inservice than you have ever had before!

Global versus Analytic Processing Element

Five learning-style elements increase achievement rapidly—often within six weeks. These five include the combination of light and design together, perceptual preference, time of day, and processing styles. The last describes how each individual takes in and records new and difficult academic information (see Chapter 4).

Past inservice, like traditional teaching, often was conducted in an **analytic** presentation style. Analytics learn and teach sequentially, one fact after another, each new fact gradually building up to an understanding. The *opposite* of analytic processing is called **global** processing. Globals learn in a pattern that is the reverse of the way analytics process; they also require different teaching styles. Then there are **integrated** learners—people who can shift from one style to the other. How to teach to different processing styles will be addressed in depth in Chapter 4. Although a majority of adults are global, 65 percent of teachers seem to be analytic. Thus, unless we identify the processing styles of the participants, we are likely to be doing exactly the right thing for some, and absolutely the wrong thing for others.

Perhaps you are beginning to appreciate why a totally revised inservice process is required if we hope to reach teachers and improve how they teach their students.

Theoretical Cornerstone of the Dunn and Dunn Model

The Dunn and Dunn learning-styles model is based on the following tenets:

1. Learning style is a biological and developmental set of personal characteristics that makes the identical instructional environments, methods, and resources effective for some learners and ineffective for others (Garger, 1990; Restak, 1979; Thies, 1979).
2. Most people have learning-style preferences, but individuals' learning-style preferences differ significantly.
3. Individual instructional preferences exist, and the impact of accommodating these preferences can be measured accurately (Curry, 1987; DeBello, 1990; Griggs, Griggs, Dunn, & Ingham, 1994; LaMothe, Billings, Belcher, Cobb, Nice, & Richardson, 1991; Reynolds, 1988, 1991).
4. The stronger the preference, the more important it is to provide compatible instructional strategies (Alberg et al., 1992; Braio, 1995; Ingham, 1991).
5. Accommodating individual learning-style preferences through complementary educational, instructional, teaching, and counseling interventions results

in increased academic achievement and improved student attitudes toward learning (Dunn, Griggs, Olson, Gorman, & Beasley, 1995).

6. Given responsive environments, resources, and approaches, people attain statistically higher achievement and attitude test scores in congruent (matched) rather than dissonant (mismatched) treatments (Dunn, Griggs, Olson, Gorman, & Beasley, 1995).

7. Most teachers can learn to use learning styles as a cornerstone of their instructional programs (Andrews, 1990; Brunner & Majewski, 1990; Klavas, 1993; Koshuta & Koshuta, 1993; Meighan, 1991; Neely & Alm, 1992, 1993; Perrin, 1990; Stone, 1992).

8. Most individuals can learn to capitalize on their learning-style strengths when concentrating on new or difficult academic material (Alberg et al., 1992; Dunn, Bruno, Sklar, & Beaudry, 1990).

9. The less academically successful the individual, the more important it is to accommodate learning-style preferences (Andrews, 1990; Dunn, Beaudry, & Klavas, 1989; Klavas, 1993; Quinn, 1993; Ricca, 1983).

How Do People's Learning Styles Differ?

Learning styles vary with (1) age (Dunn & Griggs, 1995b; Price, 1980); (2) achievement level (Dunn, 1989g; Milgram, Dunn, & Price, 1993); (3) gender; (4) culture (Dunn, 1989c; Dunn & Griggs, 1995b; Milgram, Dunn, & Price, 1993); and (5) global versus analytic brain processing (Dunn, Bruno, Sklar, & Beaudry, 1990; Dunn, Cavanaugh, Eberle, & Zenhausern, 1982). Dunn and Griggs (1995b) reviewed studies of culturally diverse students in many nations and reported that there were so many varied styles within each group that there seemed to be more within-group than between-group differences.

Within the same family, mothers and fathers often have opposite learning styles, and the first two offspring rarely learn in the same way as each other. Nevertheless, four learning-style traits significantly differ between groups and among individuals within the same group.

Learning Styles Differ by Achievement Levels

Although gifted people learn differently from one another (Milgram, Dunn, & Price, 1993), and underachievers have diverse learning styles (Klavas, 1993), high and low achievers are not likely to perform well with the same methods (Dunn & Dunn, 1993; Ricca, 1983). In addition, in a study of the relationship(s) between learning style and multiple intelligences, students with exceptional talent in athletics, art, dance, leadership, literature, mathematics, or music in nine diverse cultures evidenced essentially similar learning-style characteristics to other students with the same talent (Milgram et al., 1993).

Inservice Application

It is neither feasible nor necessary to subject teachers who enroll in inservice to talent or intelligence tests, but it *is* necessary to design inservice resources to respond to both highly intelligent and only average persons. To do that, the same content should be included in several alternative resources for each important inservice session so that participants can use those resources that are most responsive to their styles. After all, if teachers have not been learning in the way we have been inservicing them, let's inservice them in the way they learn (Burke, 1997)!

Learning Styles Differ by Gender

Learning styles often differ by gender. Adult males tend to be more visual, tactual, and kinesthetic and need more mobility in an informal environment than females. In addition, more males tend to be nonconforming and peer-motivated than their female counterparts.

Although less than 22 percent of adults are auditory (capable of remembering at least 75 percent of what they hear in a forty- to fifty-minute period), more females than males constitute our auditory population. Females also tend to be more conforming, authority-oriented, and self-motivated, and better able to sit passively at conventional classroom desks and chairs than males (Marcus, 1977). Females also tend to need significantly more quiet while learning (Pizzo, Dunn, & Dunn, 1990).

Inservice Application

Anything important enough to teach teachers will not reach more than one-fifth of the population if taught only through lectures, tapes, and discussions, and it is likely that many fewer men than women will learn through these auditory resources.

There also should be printed information in brief paragraphs or articles, videotapes, films, filmstrips, cartoons, and transparencies for those learners with primarily visual strengths—less than 30 to 40 percent of most adult populations we have tested.

To reach and have an impact on low-auditory and low-visual teachers, the critical information should also be delivered through hands-on manipulatives to tactual learners and through large floor games or other movement-oriented activities for kinesthetics. These groups, combined, make up the majority of males we have tested.

Two types of seating will be necessary—formal and informal—because males find it much more difficult to sit on traditional classroom chairs than females do.

Learning Styles Differ by Age

Although more than three-fifths of learning style appears to be biologically imposed, the longer children remain in school, the greater the change in their processing styles. Most young children are global, but, as they move from elementary to middle to high school, more become analytic—although the majority of adults appear to remain global. We do not know whether those changes are maturational or an outgrowth of students' ability to respond to conventional schooling. Learning styles continue to change as people grow older and mature (Dunn & Griggs, 1995b; Price, 1980).

Parallel Elements

Sound and intake preferences   The need for sound and intake can be observed as early as second or third grade and remains fairly consistent for many until about sixth grade. At that time, preferences for sound and intake increase and, during adolescence, become stronger than previously. For many, at about ninth or tenth grade, these two elements begin to return to their previously "normal" levels for those individuals. Among older adults, the need for quiet increases and the need for intake decreases. Thus, depending on the ages of the teachers attending an inservice session, it will be important to provide quiet areas devoid of much activity and sound, as well as activities in which those who thrive on sound and involvement can enjoy learning.

Inservice Application

We need to provide two or more areas in which to work with the participants—an essentially quiet one for those who cannot concentrate in the midst of discussion or activity, and an action-oriented area in which those who prefer active participation and sound can learn together.

Temperature preferences   Temperature inclinations tend to remain the same throughout childhood and adulthood. They may change gradually toward needing more warmth among some older staff.

Inservice Application

Although you may not be able to control the temperature in any given facility, you could alert participants to bring a sweater or to wear a short-sleeved blouse or shirt depending on the amount of climate control available.

Seating preferences   Whereas design preferences remain stable during elementary school and gradually become increasingly informal as students reach adolescence, they then change on a highly individual basis. Many adults feel comfortable in conventional classroom desks and seats, whereas others cannot sit in them for more than 10 or 12 minutes and continue to concentrate on difficult academic material. Males, more than females, require informal seating.

Seating is one of the most important aspects of style. Arrange for some chaise or easy chair seating at any inservice session. If that is impossible, bring pillows for participants to sit on, or encourage them to bring their own. Few people realize that when a human being is seated on a plastic, steel, or wooden chair, fully 75 percent of that person's total body weight is resting on just four square inches of bone (Branton, 1966). Only people who, by nature, are well padded exactly where they need to be can remain seated while concentrating on academic matters for more than 10 or 12 minutes.

Emotional Elements

Preferences for being motivated versus unmotivated   Interest in the topic and the degree to which the presenter's teaching style matches participants' learning styles contribute substantially to motivation. Thus, motivation toward inservice changes from one presenter to another, depending on who is presenting to whom, the topic, the session, when the inservice is scheduled, and the approaches used to provide it. Motivation also is determined by the extent to which participants enjoy either the presenter, if they are authority-oriented, or the other participants, if they are peer-oriented.

Inservice Application

Participants need to believe that what is being offered during the session(s) has value to them or their students, that it will produce positive results, and that they *can* succeed.

Preferences for persistence versus breaks   Persistence tends to be a quality more representative of analytic rather than global processors. Once analytics begin a task, they tend to stay with it to completion. They are the "on-task" learners who feel compelled to avoid coffee and conversation breaks until they have completed what they are working on. Global processors often require breaks for intake, interaction, change of focus, and so forth.

During inservice, the analytic teachers who are present expect presenters to address the topic in a direct, forthright manner. They tolerate few deviations into humor, personal history, or extraneous anecdotes. Analytic teachers prefer to deal with the content and to use any available remaining time either to go home, where they always have work to do, or to return to their students, who may or may not be covering the curriculum with the substitute. Analytics value their time and do not want someone else to waste it. Thus, during inservice, give them well-stipulated objectives for the time permitted, suggest alternative resources so that they can learn through their strengths, and be there to check their answers or materials when they have finished. If their task was well done, indicate the follow-through you require, and allow them to leave.

There are always exceptions to the rule, but globals tend to be fun-loving people. (Analytics also enjoy having fun—but "in its place," which is not during inservice.) Globals require objectives so that they comprehend what they need to do, but you can anticipate lots of peer interaction and joking *while* they are learning. Globals may need more interaction from both peers and the presenter than analytics do.

Inservice Application

At the beginning of the session, and in writing, make your expectations for the time allotted clear to all. When global teachers notice some of the analytic teachers leaving for lunch, they, too, will begin to pack up and leave—finished or not. During the opening of each session, it is necessary to establish rules for either going to lunch or leaving at the end of the day. We need to point out that the end products of those who are leaving were checked when they completed them; therefore, for them, it *is* lunchtime. Then be ready to help all those who have not yet finished to do their work.

Interestingly, as analytics age, many develop some global traits—and apparently vice versa. Once you explain the differences in behavior between the two types of processors, however, many people either will tell you, "I *used* to be that way when I was younger, but . . ." or "That's my spouse! I'm the opposite!"—for opposite processing types tend to marry—at least "the first time around."

Conformity versus nonconformity preferences In the early 1980s, researchers found that "responsible" versus "less responsible" tended to correlate with conformity versus nonconformity (Dunn, White, & Zenhausern, 1982). As indicated previously, people tend to experience at least three, and perhaps four, periods of nonconformity during their lives.

Inservice Application

Conformists need to be given explicitly stated objectives for each session, whereas nonconformists will require options and a collegial instructor who provides choices.

Preferences for external versus internal structure The older people become, the less structure they need. However, under pressure of examinations, multiple task requirements, personal problems unrelated to the inservice, or the need for recognition, many adults still require structure (Napolitano, 1986; Sawyer, 1995).

Experienced presenters have interacted with participants at various sessions who approach them for additional directions or help with a task. Instead of finding a way to accomplish what has been assigned or getting help from a colleague, participants who need more external structure than others gravitate toward someone who will provide it. If they are authority-oriented, they seek the presenter; if they are peer-oriented, they seek a colleague.

Experienced presenters also have interacted with participants at each session who pay scant attention to the directions that have been provided. They do almost everything *their* way, always finding "better," "different," and unusual methods for accomplishing what needs to be done. These registrants tend to be internally structured—they find their own way for accomplishing what has to be done—or may be creative and in need of variety.

Inservice Application

When providing options for people who enjoy variety, nonconformists, and those without the skills required for an assigned task, be aware that some participants will resist making choices. When considering resources, they may ask, "Which one is better?" The answer that the resources are equally good may not be what the person is seeking. Instead, something like, "I like this one!"—naming one of the options—may be more helpful to the person who wants someone else to make the choice. We know that people *should* decide for themselves but some prefer having decisions made for them.

Sociological Elements

Sociological preferences for learning alone versus in a group with an authoritative versus a collegial presenter, and with routines as opposed to in varied groupings, develop over time. They change with age and maturity and are developmental (Thies, 1979).

Young children want to please their parents and teachers, but by third grade many children become peer-motivated and want to please their peers. By contrast, a quarter century ago, students rarely became peer-motivated much before ninth grade.

Few analytic teachers enjoy learning in groups. They tend to focus on task completion and, if they are high achievers, are often competitive. It is the global processors who, in general, enjoy peer interaction. They are more likely than analytics to want to work with small-group strategies like cooperative learning, team learning, brainstorming, Circle of Knowledge, role playing, or case studies. Providing these instructional strategies as options adds to the number of alternatives all participants have. When given knowledge of their sociological strengths, learners become more productive and more highly achieving than when required to learn in their nonpreferred style.

Inservice Application

If we establish clear requirements for completing assignments, some will elect to work independently, others in pairs, a few in small groups, and some directly with the presenter. Permit teachers to decide how and with whom they will complete inservice requirements, but be certain that those requirements are clear.

Physiological Elements

Perceptual preferences Perceptually, the younger the children, the more tactual and/or kinesthetic they are. In elementary school, less than 12 percent are auditory (able to remember three-quarters of what they are taught through lecture or discussion during a 40- to 50-minute period) and 40 percent at most are visual (able to remember three-quarters of what they read in the same amount of time). The older children are, the more visual and, eventually, the more auditory they become. However, females generally are more auditory than males, and males generally become more visual and remain more tactual and kinesthetic than females. A previous section described adults' perceptual strengths. Female teachers tend to be more auditory than other adults, but, at best, only 22 percent currently are capable of listening to new and difficult information for a 40- to 50-minute period and remembering at least 75 percent on even a short-term basis, and certainly not on a long-term basis.

Time preferences Chronobiological preferences definitely change with age but, by the time adults are ready for inservice, their energy highs and lows are well established. Nevertheless, both young, new teachers and many getting close to retirement may be experiencing changes in their time-of-day energy patterns.

Inservice Application

Two important rules to follow are: (1) provide the same inservice at least twice at very different times (e.g., early morning and evening, or early morning and immediately after lunch), and (2) permit staff to choose when they attend. You will have takers for both schedules, and, overall, they will express more satisfaction with their choices than with an assigned session.

Length of time preference If inservice requires more than a half-day exposure, or if limited funds restrict using the same excellent presenter for two days, seek volunteers for the first day, who then will assume responsibility for exposing colleagues to the same material on another day. Granted, secondhand training cannot compete with an outstanding presenter, but participants who experience inservice at their worst time of day are getting so little from the exposure that there may not be too much difference in the outcome.

In addition, those who get to hear the expert will need to pay particular attention to the information because they will be responsible for sharing it correctly at a later date. Of course, in this technological age, we should be videotaping the expert and making that resource available to all staff, parents, and students—when appropriate.

There is one more consideration. Some teachers cannot maintain high energy levels; they *cannot* continue momentum all day. Half a day of exposure to an outstanding presenter may be the maximum they can give. If they become overtired, the results may not be what you want.

Inservice Application

Ask staff for their honest opinion concerning who wishes to attend for only half a day and be exposed to just the basics of that topic, and who wants to experience the full day and, in turn, will provide some follow-through that a few colleagues may observe. The system may save many half-days of substitute pay, and teachers may appreciate participation more.

Mobility preferences   Highly kinesthetic adults and some who simply require mobility should be permitted to move *while* learning. Some adults can learn without movement or activities, but only for a relatively short period of time. These people require opportunities to change position and location periodically. They will learn more, with greater efficiency, when permitted to move *while* learning whenever they become restless.

Inservice Applications

- If inservice is important enough to take teachers who need mobility away from their students, permit them to learn in ways or sequences that allow at least intermittent mobility.
- If inservice is important enough to take kinesthetic teachers away from their students, make it available through kinesthetic resources (see Chapter 6).
- The facility where inservice sessions are held, whether in a single room or in a larger space, should be subdivided into sections that permit teachers who need mobility to learn in ways or sequences that permit intermittent mobility.
- The facility where inservice sessions are held, whether in a single room or in a larger space, should be subdivided into sections that permit teachers who are kinesthetic to use kinesthetic resources either alone, in pairs, or in small groups without intruding on others' concentration.

Processing-Style Preferences

Investigations of individuals' global versus analytic processing styles revealed that relationships exist among these cognitive dimensions and many individuals' environmental, emotional, sociological, and/or physiological learning-style traits, and that these cognitive dimensions and specific learning-style traits often cluster together. For example, learning persistently, with few or no intermissions, in a quiet, well-lit, formal setting, with little or no intake, often correlates with being an analytic or left processor. Conversely, learning with intermittent periods of concentration and relaxation, in soft lighting and with sound (music or voices), while seated informally and snacking, correlates with highly global or right-brain processing styles (Cody, 1983; Dunn, Bruno, Sklar, & Beaudry, 1990; Dunn, Cavanaugh, Eberle, & Zenhausern, 1982). In some cases, more attributes allied themselves with one processing style than another. Although global and right-processing students often preferred learning tactually and with peers (Jarsonbeck, 1984), no clear perceptual or social pattern was revealed by analytic or left-preferred students (see Table 3-3 in Chapter 3). Practical applications for inservice activities suited to both global and analytic processing are provided in Chapter 4.

Conclusion

Given the extensive research published in refereed research and professional journals during the past three decades, widespread reports documenting the reversal of poor academic achievement after learning style–responsive strategies were substituted for traditional teaching, and our expanding understanding of how individuals learn, effective inservice requires different instructional approaches for teachers who learn in different ways (Burke, 1997; Greb, 1997; Raupers, 1996, 1999; Taylor, 1999).

3

Identifying Participants' Learning Styles

Rita Dunn

Identifying Adults' Learning Styles

The concept of adult individual differences has widespread support in several professions—education (Dunn, Bruno, Sklar, & Beaudry, 1990; Lenehan, Dunn, Ingham, Murray, & Signer, 1994; Nelson et al., 1993); nursing (Dunn & Griggs, 1998; Griggs, Griggs, Dunn, & Ingham, 1994); business (Dunn, Ingham, & Deckinger, 1995; Ingham, 1991); and the law (Boyle & Dunn, in press; Ingham & Dunn, 1993). Because of this widespread interest in how adults learn effectively, many instruments purport to measure individual learning styles (DeBello, 1990). Examination of the instruments that Curry (1987) considered reliable and valid revealed that many of those used in nursing studies *failed* to have an impact on instructional improvement when apparently complementing nurses' styles. Those, however, were different from the instruments used in studies in which significant gains were reported. Apparently, different instruments yield different results. Therefore, it is important to consider how these instruments differed and whether their differences accounted for the disparate results.

Curry's Onion Model of Learning and Cognitive Style

Curry (1987) conceived a theoretical framework in which learning-style models and their related instruments could be examined. Her "onion model" encompassed approximately twenty-five different learning-style instruments and identified four different layers.

Personality Dimensions

At the core of the onion were relatively stable traits of basic personality, such as those measured by the Myers-Briggs Type Indicator (MBTI) (Myers, 1962). Each of the MBTI types incorporated multiple elements of the Dunn and Dunn model.

Information-Processing Models

The next layer of the onion addressed the individual's preferred intellectual approach to assimilating information, as operationalized in Kolb's (1976) Learning Style Inventory and Schmeck's Inventory of Learning Processes (Schmeck, Ribich, & Ramanaiah, 1977). Studies with the Kolb instrument tended to employ correlational rather than experimental designs. However, the experimental studies conducted with nurses failed to provide evidence of significant achievement gains (Griggs, Griggs, Dunn, & Ingham, 1994).

Social Interaction Models

The next layer of the onion addressed *how* students functioned in the classroom, as measured by Witkin's (1971) Embedded Figures Test, which identified field-dependent versus field-independent learners.

Multidimensional and Instructional Preference Models

This final layer of the onion, as assessed by Dunn, Dunn, and Price's Productivity Environmental Preference Survey (PEPS) (1982) for mature adults and versions of their Learning Style Inventory for nontraditional adults, encompass all the constructs of the three previous layers to assess comprehensively between 21 and 23 elements of learning style. The number of elements assessed varies with the form of the instrument and is based on the age and achievement level of the population for which it is intended.

Curry proposed that (1) each layer represented separate and discrete constructs, (2) very few instruments assessed more than one level, and (3) the PEPS was one of the few instruments with good reliability and validity at that time. Curry's position was endorsed by DeCoux (1990), who observed that the innumerable learning-style instruments were strikingly dissimilar and that the theoretical constructs on which they were based contained only tenuous connections (Griggs, Griggs, Dunn, & Ingham, 1994).

Instruments for Identifying Adults' Learning Styles

It is an almost impossible task to identify learning style accurately without a reliable instrument (Beaty, 1986; Dunn, Dunn, & Price, 1977; Marcus, 1977); some traits are not observable, and others lend themselves to misinterpretation. For example, if two persons sitting next to each other during a presentation whisper, squirm in their seats, and pay little attention to the speaker, and if you had not assessed their learning styles, you would not know whether those people were (a) not interested in the topic, (b) antiauthoritarian, (c) nonconforming, (d) unable to sit in the available chairs, (e) in need of mobility, (f) kinesthetic, (g) peer-oriented, (h) in need of an informal design, or (i) just rude.

To identify how individuals learn, it is necessary to use a comprehensive instrument—one that diagnoses many different learning-style traits. Only three comprehensive models exist, and each has a related instrument designed to reveal individuals' styles based on the variables included in that model (DeBello, 1990).

In addition to being comprehensive, an instrument also must be reliable and valid. A reliable instrument provides consistent information over time; a valid instrument measures what its research manual says it does. Instrument reliability and validity are crucial because it is impossible to obtain reliable and valid data from an unreliable or invalid assessment.

Instrument #1: The Productivity Environmental Preference Survey

The most frequently used learning-style instrument in experimental studies with adults has been the Dunn, Dunn, and Price Productivity Environmental Preference Survey (PEPS). PEPS reports how strongly the following learning-style elements affect each person (see Figure 3-1).

Instrument #2: Building Excellence

A new, recently field-tested instrument, Building Excellence (BE) (Rundle & Dunn, 1996), was specifically designed to identify the learning styles of adults in corporate and industrial firms. Developed cooperatively by St. John's University's Center for the Study of Learning and Teaching Styles and Performance Contracts, a business firm, BE can be administered and hand-scored on site within a 20- to 30-minute period and has the advantage of permitting presenters to identify either one, several, or all of its 21 learning-style elements—including global versus analytic cognitive processing styles. In addition, BE includes a brief global introduction to each element and provides short descriptions of how to increase productivity based on the analyses of each person's style.

What does BE identify?   BE reports on each individual's:

- Environmental preferences for sound or quiet, low versus bright light, warm versus cool temperatures, and informal versus formal seating designs while concentrating on demanding tasks
- Emotional preferences concerned with high or low motivation and structure, persistence as opposed to needing frequent relaxation breaks, and responsibility levels (which correlate with being either conforming or nonconforming)
- Sociological preferences for learning alone, in pairs, with peers, in a small group, with an authoritative versus a collegial presenter, or in varied ways as opposed to in a pattern or routine
- Physiological preferences, such as the perceptual modalities through which individuals best remember new and difficult information—for example, by hearing versus by reading, or by manipulating materials with their hands versus by experiencing; the time of day or night during which each person concentrates best; and individuals' preferences for intake or mobility while concentrating
- Processing-style preferences as required by analytics and globals (see Figure 3-2).

FIGURE 3-1 Productivity Environmental Preference Survey Elements

Environmental Elements	Bipolar Continuum
1. Noise level	Silence vs. sound
2. Light	Dim vs. bright light
3. Temperature	Cool vs. warm temperature
4. Design	Informal vs. formal seating

Emotional Elements	
5. Motivation	Self-motivated vs. requiring periodic breaks
6. Persistence	Remaining on task without breaks
7. Responsibility	Conformity vs. nonconformity
8. Structure	Internal vs. external structure

Sociological Elements	
9. Alone/peer	Learning alone vs. peer-oriented learning
10. Authority figures	Authority figures absent–present; requiring vs. not requiring feedback
11. Several ways requiring variety	Requiring patterns and routines vs. variety

Physiological Elements	
12. Auditory	Remembers 3/4 of what is heard
13. Visual	Remembers 3/4 of what is read/seen
14. Tactile	Remembers 3/4 of what is written/ manipulated
15. Kinesthetic	Remembers 3/4 of what is experienced
16. Intake	Learns best while eating/drinking
17. Evening–morning	Evening vs. morning energy highs
18. Late morning	Functions best in late morning
19. Afternoon	Functions best in afternoon
20. Mobility	Learning while passive vs. while mobile

FIGURE 3-2 Research Concerned with Learning Styles and Processing Style

Researcher and Date	Sample Examined	Subject Examined	Aspect	Sig.
Dunn, R., Bruno, J., Sklar, R. I., & Beaudry, J., 1990, St. John's University	College students	Remedial Mathematics	Processing Styles	$(p < .0001)$

Continued

FIGURE 3-2 *Continued*

Researcher	Date	Subject	Aspect

Findings: In this experimental study, the learning-style preferences of underachieving community college minority students enrolled in remedial mathematics classes were identified. Most underachievers were found to be global processors. Alternative chapters of their analytic mathematics book were designed to respond to global (rather than analytic) styles. When students were taught with instructional materials and strategies that matched their processing style, they achieved significantly better. In addition, significant relationships were revealed between students' hemispheric processing preferences and their diagnosed learning style. Right processors preferred an informal environment, sound, and intake. Left processors preferred the opposite: formal design, quiet, no intake, and bright light.

Researcher	Date	Subject	Aspect
Bailey, G. K. University of Southern Mississippi	1988	N/A	Hemisphericity and Environmental Preferences

Findings: This study investigated the relationship(s) between hemispheric processing and environmental preferences that influence learning style. It also determined which of the PEPS variables in combination would successfully discriminate among right, left, and integrated hemispheric preferences. Eight variables were related to left hemispheric preference, five to right hemispheric preference, and seven to integrated processing.

Source: Table created by Andrea Honigsfeld.

Which Learning-Style Elements Must Be Accommodated?

Of the 20 or more elements that PEPS and BE identify, most people are affected by somewhere between 6 and 14 elements. Some adults are affected by as many as 16 (or more); many have fewer (1–6). However, every element that is revealed as a preference or a strong preference for an individual is likely to increase the ease and enjoyment with which that person concentrates. The combination of these elements that makes up an individual's preferences constitute that person's "learning style."

All learning-style elements are important and contribute to how well each adult concentrates, processes, internalizes, and retains new and difficult information. Processing style, perceptual modalities, the combination of light and seating design, and time of day have an impact on approximately 70 percent of all people. Sound, mobility, and sociological preferences also affect large clusters of people. These elements vary by age, gender, achievement level, and ethnicity (Dunn & Griggs, 1995a, 1995b). Figure 3-3 summarizes research on adults' learning styles.

FIGURE 3-3   Research Concerned with Learning Styles and Adults in College or Business

Researcher	Date	Subject	Aspect
Clark-Thayer, S. Boston University	1987	Mathematics	Achievement Homework

Findings: This study examined relationships among first-year students' learning styles, study habits, and college achievement. Both study habits and learning styles correlated significantly with achievement. Successful students were Motivated, Responsible (Conforming), Learning Alone rather than Peer-Oriented preferents, and required Varied instructional experiences rather than routines and patterns. Successful students were not Tactual learners. High achievers also engaged in specific study habits and had positive attitudes toward their educational experiences.

Researcher	Date	Subject	Aspect
Dunn, R., Deckinger, E. L., Withers, P., & Katzenstein, H. St. John's University	1990	Business	Achievement

Findings: The learning-style preferences of college business students were identified. Students were taught how to study and complete assignments using their individual learning-style strengths. Students who applied the information about their learning styles to study achieved significantly higher grades than those who did not. A comparison also was made between the group who received exposure to learning styles and a control group who was not introduced to learning styles. The learning-styles group performed better than the control group.

Researcher	Date	Subject	Aspect
Dunn, R., Bruno, J., Sklar, R. I., & Beaudry, J. St. John's University	1990	Mathematics	Processing Style + Hemisphericity

Findings: This experimental study identified the hemisphericity and processing-style preferences of community college students enrolled in remedial mathematics courses. All students were exposed to four lessons, two with a global approach and two with an analytic one. When these underachieving students were taught with instructional strategies that matched their processing style, their achievement scores were significantly higher, especially for the global learners.

Researcher	Date	Subject	Aspect
Ingham, J. *Human Resource Development Quarterly*	1991	Truck Drivers	Improving Safety Records

Continued

FIGURE 3-3   *Continued*

Researcher	Date	Subject	Aspect

Findings: This experimental study examined the effects of teaching male truck drivers safety information through resources that were congruent and incongruent with their perceptual preferences as revealed by the PEPS. Drivers scored statistically higher scores when taught through their perceptual strengths than when taught through their secondary or tertiary modalities. Subsequently, the number of accidents was reduced. In addition, the drivers' learning styles differed statistically from the styles of executives and salespersons in the same company.

Jenkins, C. The University of Mississippi	1991	Generic Fresh- man Studies	Learning Style Preferences

Findings: This study identified the relationship(s) among selected demographic variables—entrance examination scores, gender, grade-point average (GPA), and major or career choice—and the subset of environmental preferences preferred by most first-year students of Alcorn State University. Results indicated that only the element of design was significant (Design) in discriminating among students' scores on the college entrance examination, Females' preferences were significantly different from male students' preferences in the areas of Motivation, Persistence, Structure, Authority Orientation, and Kinesthetic Preference. However, males had a higher preference for learning with peers and in the evening versus morning. Students with a high GPA preferred Tactile instructional resources more than low achievers did. There was no significant difference among the learning-style preferences of first-year students based on their major or career choice and the cluster of learning-style preferences preferred by most first-year students included Afternoon, Structure, Authority Figure Present, and Auditory Perceptual Modality.

Nelson, B., Dunn, R., Griggs, S. A., Primavera, L., Fitzpatrick, M., Bacilious, Z., & Miller, R., St. John's University	1993	Across- the-board GPA	Achievement Retention

Findings: This experimental study compared the GPA and retention rate of three groups of first-year students in a Texas community college. Experimental Group 1 was introduced to learning styles and had its Productivity Environmental Preference Survey (Dunn, Dunn, & Price, 1987) printouts interpreted. Experimental Group 2 was exposed to learning styles and also taught how to study in congruence with individuals' learning-style strengths. The control group received no information about learning styles. Students also were identified as probationary and nonprobationary.

Students who received the most exposure to learning style and were shown how to study on the basis of their learning styles achieved significantly higher GPAs during the spring semester than did those who did not receive instruction. These students also demonstrated significantly higher retention rates then expected, whereas the retention rates of those

FIGURE 3-3   *Continued*

Researcher	Date	Subject	Aspect

having no or limited exposure were statistically lower than those of the learning-style groups.

Lenehan, M. C., Dunn, R.,	1994	Anatomy	Nursing Students'
Ingham, J., Murray, J. B., &		Physiology	Achievement
Signer, B., St. John's University		Bacteriology	Anger

Findings: Students in the experimental group were shown how to study by capitalizing on their identified learning-style preferences. All students in the control group were shown how to study with conventional study-skill guidelines, tutoring, and advisement assistance. Students in the experimental group achieved statistically higher science grades *and* grade-point averages than students in the control group, suggesting that homework prescriptions for use in one subject affected grades in other subjects positively. In addition, the experimental group evidenced significantly lower anxiety and anger scores and significantly higher curiosity about science. The control group was significantly more anxious about, and angry with, their science course(s) than the experimental group, and were less curious about science at the end than when the term began.

| Raupers, P. M. | 1999 | Traditional versus learning-style-responsive staff development | Effects on long-term memory and attitudes |

Findings: Teachers in the learning-style-responsive experimental group achieved statistically higher long-term retention scores on technology content ($p < .0004$) than teachers in the comparison treatment. Both groups revealed similarly positive attitudinal scores.

| Taylor, R. G. | 1999 | Traditional versus learning-style-responsive staff development | Effects on knowledge, achievement, and attitude test scores |

Findings: All teachers in the learning-style-responsive staff development experimental group ($n = 45$), regardless of their learning style, revealed significantly more knowledge ($p < .0001$) about the content, higher achievement ($p \leq .001$), and higher attitude ($p < .05 - p < .0001$) test scores than the teachers in the traditional comparison group ($n = 39$). Motivated teachers in the comparison group had statistically higher gains ($p < .05$) than teachers in the same group with other learning-style preferences. Thus, when teachers are exposed to traditional staff development, only motivated teachers can be expected to evidence significant gains.

Source: Table created by Dr. Rita Dunn and Andrea Honigsfeld.

4

Global and Analytic Approaches to Inservice

Kenneth Dunn

In any adult group, as many as 50 to 60 percent of the participants may be global or holistic in their processing styles for assimilating and applying knowledge. Between 25 and 30 percent will be analytic or sequential in their approach. The rest are integrated and can shift from one style to another. However, after testing thousands of teachers for their individual teaching styles, more often than not, as many as two-thirds tended to use sequential, analytic strategies. The likelihood is that instructors teach the way they were taught. In addition, analytic learners were successful in college with analytic instructors, while others, who were integrated learners, adapted their learning to the college instructor's style. Many of the global learners struggled and passed with lower grades than the other two groups unless they were fortunate enough to be assigned to global professors.

Identifying Processing Style

After testing more than three million adults and students for their learning styles, the following five elements appear to correlate directly with individual processing styles:

Global (X)	*It Depends* (—)	*Analytic* (√)
Low light		Bright light
Food, drink, intake		No intake
Sound, music, conversation		Quiet
Informal design		Formal design
Breaks		Persistence
Many projects simultaneously		Single project at a time

Ask participants to think about how they prefer to concentrate on, internalize, and remember new and difficult information and concepts with respect to these five elements of learning style. Have them place an X in the middle of this chart if they prefer low light, a √ if they prefer bright light, and a dash (—) if it doesn't matter to them or if the amount of light varies depending on the nature of the material. Participants should do the same for the other four elements. Then have them count the number of X's and √'s. Three X's indicate that a participant tends to be global, three √'s indicate an inclination to process analytically, and three or more —'s suggest neither strong global nor strong analytic tendencies. This latter trait describes those who can master any content that interests them. If not interested in what they are learning, however, such people "turn off," "tune out," and do not concentrate. If motivated, those adults with three or more —'s probably can respond to either global or analytic approaches; their processing styles are "integrated."

Obviously, four X's or four √'s indicate strongly global or strongly analytic adults, respectively. Five or more of either would signify an extremely global or analytic processing style. Following are descriptors of several opposite characteristics of analytic and global processing styles:

Analytic	Global
Sequential	Simultaneous
Successive	Holistic
Inductive	Deductive
Left-brain processing	Right-brain processing
Specifics	Generalizations
Details	Themes
Discipline focus	Multidisciplinary
Field-independent	Field-dependent
Linear	Overall
Analyze	Synthesize
Out-of-context concentration	Within-content concentration

It is easier to identify the strategies required to respond to strong analytic or global processors by referring to this list of processing-style characteristics. For example, analytic participants prefer step-by-step, *sequential* materials to meet detailed specific objectives. Global adults attending inservice sessions tend to respond to an integrated, overall view of the objectives; they want to hear about concepts and long-range goals first, details later. Obviously, the higher the score (five X's or five √'s, or even four of each), the more likely it is that those individuals will tend to complete inservice objectives if materials are presented in their processing styles initially.

After testing for analytic, global, and integrated processing styles, ask everyone about their interactions with their families—children, spouses (and ex-spouses). Did one go to sleep early and the other late? Who pushed the thermostat up—or down? Who asked for the air conditioner in the car to be turned on, to the dismay of the other? Who is the risk taker?—"Let's buy the car now and pay later" versus; "Oh no, we have to save it all up first—we're not going into debt again!"

These real-life situations will be recognized by participants and aid in matching strategies to processing styles. It's a realization that might even help prevent divorce as people recognize how a team of global and analytic partners can be positive as each offers perspectives to problem solving and important decisions.

Listening to the Words of Global and Analytic Processors

Presenters and inservice colleagues often can recognize processing style by listening to what "Globals" and "Analytics" say.

1. *Analytic:*   Everything has a place!
   Global: My desk is a mess but don't touch anything—I won't be able to find it!
2. *Analytic:*   What room is it in and how do I get there?
   Global: Do I turn right or left? Just point the way.
3. *Analytic:*   Where are the specific directions? I need them now!
   Global: I'll figure it out when I have time.
4. *Analytic:*   Don't put off for tomorrow what you can do today!
   Global: What does it matter in the big scheme of life?
5. *Analytic:*   I can't stop now. I'm right in the middle. I have to finish.
   Global: O.K. Let's go. This can wait!
6. *Analytic:*   Would you check this before I hand it in?
   Global: I need a break!
7. *Analytic:*   It's important to complete this project on time!
   Global: Will it make the world a better place?
8. *Analytic:*   Electroboard Questions: Should the shiny side be up?
   Global: Why do we have to cover each one with tape?
9. *Analytic:*   He's very directive!
   Global: What a tyrant!
10. *Analytic:*   Her frequent reminders help me to get things done.
    Global: Nag! Nag! Nag!
11. *Analytic:*   If isn't broken, don't fix it!
    Global: Let's see what else it can do.
    Super-global: **BREAK IT!**
12. *Analytic:*   What did you order from the menu? Add them up and add 8 percent for the tax and 15 percent for the tip . . . Yes, do the 15 percent first.
    Global: What's the total and divide by 5.
13. *Analytic:*   I'm so frustrated. I can't make the checkbook balance.
    Global: Why worry? Are you close?

General Inservice Approaches

Whatever the goals and objectives of an inservice program, at least two different approaches should be prepared. If possible, the presenter should match the processing style of the audience: analytic to analytics and global to globals. This is not always possible, but the solution lies in understanding how each group works best and, more important, how each individual processes. Then the presenter can reach both types of learners.

What Is Needed for Analytic and Global Learners

Analytic		**Global**
Scope and Sequence	*(begin with)*	*Fantasy or Story*
Steps		*Steps*
1. Prerequisites		1. General goals
2. Objectives		2. Optional resources
3. Directions		3. Clues or mystery
4. Process steps		4. Multiple approaches
5. Specific outcomes, then conclusions or decisions		5. Generalizations, then specific knowledge

Inservice Directions for Analytic Processors

Step 1. Prerequisites   Most analytic processors respond well to detailed needs assessment questionnaires and rating scales for what they believe would be useful to them. They would like to know what will be required of them at the outset. What do they need to know? What should they bring to the sessions? What will they do first? What will happen at each succeeding step?

Step 2. Objectives   Each objective should be spelled out in detailed, concrete terms—for example, "By the end of Session 2 on Tuesday afternoon, you will have completed and decorated a flip chute and set of flip chute cards that will give complete directions for accessing the Internet on your computer."

Step 3. Directions   Materials should be prepared and ready for distribution before the inservice sessions begin. These should include words, numbers, and diagrams or pictures that are labeled in great detail. Taped cassettes and videotapes are useful for those analytic learners who require review, repetition, or checking "to be sure" they are correct.

Step 4. Procedures   Briefly review every step verbally while pointing to words, numbers, and directions on the screen or chalkboard. Highlight all key items, and suggest the participants do the same on their materials. Provide finished examples of all techniques, strategies, and devices for them to handle, look at, and ask questions. Place large posterboards with directions, steps, diagrams, and pictures on the walls near the tables where they are working.

Step 5. Outcomes   Check all items as they near completion. Some participants will finish ahead of others; if they are correct, use them to help and check the others. Encourage participants to share well-done finished products. Solicit specific suggestions about how they will use the materials for themselves and for their students. Ask how these specific strategies build toward general goals.

Inservice Directions for Global Processors

Step 1. General goals   Begin with humorous stories and real-life anecdotes about the strategy to be learned or materials to be completed. Allow participants to ask questions and to challenge what you are proposing. Show them the finished product right at the beginning, and relate the anecdote to what you are holding or showing them—for example: "Do you have older students who seem "dead all day"? The homework disk and scheduling later in the day could really help.

Step 2. Optional resources   Many globals may prefer to copy your models or skim the directions and then help one another (or work alone) to design and develop their own version of the objective for the session. Some may ask for a text or look at your wall charts first. A few will not ask for help directly. Be patient and positive—"Have you tried this?"

Step 3. Clues or mystery   Provide clues in envelopes with pictures or diagrams on the outside. Use large question marks and perhaps a picture of Sherlock Holmes and a magnifying glass to indicate solutions to problems they may be having—"Is the flip chute card 'flying' out? If not, open this mystery clue envelope!" Inside you can list all items that could be wrong during construction of the flip chute: (a) Check to see if tape or clear contact paper extends above the bottom line of the lower slot; (b) measure the distance from the top of the back slide to the top of the rear wall—it should be $\frac{5}{8}''$ and can be adjusted slightly up or down to adjust the pathway; (c) is the flip chute card $2\frac{1}{2}'' \times 2''$, and did you put it into the slot sideways?

Step 4. Multiple approaches   Many globals will vary the strategy, change the size, or find other ways to do the same thing. If what they devise is successful, praise, recognize, and share what they have created.

Step 5. Outcomes   Discuss one or more general goals that globals believe have been reached for them or that can be achieved with their students. List them and then solict an analysis of categories and then of specific knowledge learned and possible applications.

If both extreme analytic and global approaches are planned and prepared, those participants who easily can shift between analytic and global processing styles may use directions and processes that they prefer. Obviously, at times, even extreme analytics or globals may benefit from elements of approaches used for the other group. For example, some analytic learners want to see a sample early, and some globals may read the directions (when all else fails). Also, creativity is not limited to globals; many analytics and those who are integrated may be inspired to design variations and innovations as they go through the various steps.

What Analytic and Global Processors Respond to and What Demotivates Each Group

This list may be helpful in preparing inservice sessions.

Analytics usually respond to:	*Globals usually respond to:*
Facts	Humor
Numbers	Anecdotes
Explanations	Stories
Words	Pictures
Paragraphs	Diagrams
Details	Color
Specific directions	Fantasy
Course outlines	General goals
Complete modules	End products

In this regard, when we have asked global participants what made them unhappy at sessions, they complained about the same things over and over again.

Circles of "Unhappiness" for Global and Analytic Learners

Negatives for Globals

Research has indicated that global processors prefer a different learning environment from that provided by the traditional arrangements. Therefore, these items create unhappy global learners:

- Successive teaching
- No intake
- Tactile instructional resources *after* listening for a long time
- Hard desk and chair

- No music or happy working sounds
- Bright light
- Minimal peer activity

Negatives for Analytics

A parallel list from analytic inservice participants usually includes the following:

- Humor and stories without objectives
- Lighting poor or too low
- Too much noise and distraction
- Forced into groups when they like to work alone
- Disorganized, no clear directions
- Left on their own without handouts

It is wise, therefore, to poll future participants about which inservice arrangements or materials build interest and motivation for them after discovering what has made them unhappy or unmotivated.

Helping Globals to Get Organized

Vivian Porcu and Iris Sweig, two St. John's doctoral students on Staten Island, New York, described exactly what happens to "global" check balancing:

> Did you really write all those checks last month?
>
> Uh-oh! It is the 28th of the month and the fat, brown envelope has arrived in the mail. It has come from the local savings institution and contains the checking account statement. We now have to psych ourselves up for a few days so it can be checked against my so-called "record keeping."
>
> Gathering all the papers to get ready to check the statement is a good idea provided you are an organized person. Where did you put that almost used up checkbook with the stubs? Are the yellow deposit tickets all in one place? No—some are left in the wallet, one got scrunched up in your pocket, and I don't recall where the last one went. You kind of remember the figure, so you'll wing it.
>
> Are the deposit slips in chronological order? Get the cashed checks inside the brown envelope, and put them into numerical order. You stop for a few minutes to look at the backs. Who signed them? Where were they cashed? Which dates? That's enough.

Using a More Analytic Approach

> Open the statement. There are three pages this month. Gosh—how many of these did we write? Did we really have that much money available? Or were most of them for ten dollars or less? Take a deep breath and start.

Look at the numbers on the checks. Hunt up and down the statement to find them. Check them off. Wait—you must get a red pen. That will make the marks stand out. Be sure all the deposits are reflected. Also, check them off, but this time use a green pen. This is important; the bank has to have a record of monies put in.

If a check never comes back, so much the better. But then there will be holes in your checkbook and an asterisk will show up on your statement, declaring "not in numerical order." Every couple of years a check fails to make it onto the statement. What happened to it? Did the post office not deliver it? Did the recipient get it and put it away somewhere? Was it discarded with the recycle papers? After six months, the amount of the check, which is now stale, is gleefully added back to the balance.

Sum up all the outstanding checks that are not stale. Subtract that amount from the grand total of the subsequent deposits and the statement balance. This should be the figure in your checkbook. Uh-oh, it's not! Oh well, go back and do it all over again until one figure is the same as the other.

Look, no green light balance (overdraft) this month. We must have been prudent and didn't overspend. That's a relief.

This description could be a model for all inservice sessions conducted by global presenters who may have talent but need to learn how to organize and plan just a bit more analytically for all inservice participants—especially the analytics.

On the other hand, analytics who have purchased checking account and income tax software for their computers and enter all information every day (and sometimes several times a day) are so organized that any disruption to their computer systems, such as a virus that corrupts data for certain months in 1996 or 1997, or the bank's failure to put items in the correct sequence, may cause undue stress and even lead to failed marriages—once the arguments are over. Both extremes in your inservice group can disrupt or reduce the effectiveness of the program. There are two basic solutions:

1. Respond to individual needs.
   and
2. Explain global and analytic processing styles to all and have them discuss and analyze their own styles and what they observe in order to be more tolerant and supportive of the opposite style.

Conclusion

Here are some principles for global and analytic participants:

1. Match materials and arrangements to the processing styles of those in attendance.
2. Identify their styles so that all may share, understand, and support one another.
3. Design step-by-step sequences with analytics, and begin with the end results followed by overall patterns for the globals.
4. Reach the same outcomes through opposite pathways.

5

Small-Group Techniques for Inservice Workshops

Kenneth Dunn

Many adults respond best to a learning situation that involves from two to five peers, but some prefer to work with a single partner. We have observed teachers and other professionals behaving as if they were bored, resentful, or anxious when attending sessions conducted by authoritarian presenters. These participants relax, become stimulated, and often are motivated when part of a team. Their levels of responsibility increase through the sharing process, and their brain activity is elevated as suggestions and challenges flow within the group. For these adults, productivity rises sharply, and interaction brings fun and effective learning. Remember, however, that many adults prefer to work alone or will join groups only on some occasions or for a few specific tasks.

Workshop Outlines

Teachers across the nation complain about one-day inservice or superintendent's conference days. Too often these result in one-day presentations without involvement, interest, or follow-through. Most instructors would rather work in and prepare their rooms and materials for the imminent arrival of their students at the beginning of the year, or they need to plan for midterms, new semesters, or improving reading and math productivity at various levels in the school system. At the very least, staff should be involved in assessing priority needs and in planning choices for individual instructors to acquire practical techniques that they can use immediately. Recent topics might include integrated curriculum, small-group techniques, positive inclusion strategies, multiple intelligences, student research, homework options, alternative assessment, course portfolios, matching teaching strategies to learning strengths, and so forth. Teachers may select three and vote 3, 2, or 1 point for suggested topics and those that they add to the list.

Assuming a topic or topics have been selected by staff and the suggestions in Chapter 10, "Managing the Implementation," have been incorporated in planning, sample one-day and one-week outlines follow for teams, pairs, and individuals.

One-Day Outline

8:00–9:00 A.M.	Registration; breakfast snacks, juice, coffee and decaf; outlines, schedules, and handouts distributed; time for friends to meet and greet one another
9:15–10:30 A.M.	Keynote presentation by experienced expert on the staff-selected priority topic, for example, multiple intelligences, integrated curriculum
10:45 A.M.–12:00 noon	Multiple sessions (teams assigned by grade levels and subject areas)—for example: • Diagnosing individual intelligences • Examples of productivity in a specific area • Building interest and motivation
12:00 noon–1:00 P.M.	Lunch
1:15–3:00 P.M.	Development of specific strategies by teams for each of the identified intelligences at various grade levels and subject areas; sharing and group evaluation of designed techniques
3:15–4:00 P.M.	• Questions and answers • Team plans for continuing development and trial lessons and strategies • Team plans for evaluation and sharing

One-Week Outline

Day 1

8:00–9:00 A.M.	Registration; breakfast snacks, juice, coffee and decaf; outlines, schedules, and handouts distributed
9:15–10:15 A.M.	Greeting, overview of program, and objectives for the week on staff-selected priority topic, such as "Teaching Students through Their Individual Learning Styles"
10:30 A.M.–12:00 noon	Selected teams complete exercises that provide knowledge of the introduction to learning styles, its elements, and basic research (teams assigned by grade levels and subject areas)

12:00 noon–1:00 P.M.	Lunch
1:15–3:00 P.M.	Participants review their own individual adult learning-style profiles and suggested study techniques, and compare their individual differences.

Day 2

8:00–8:45 A.M.	Breakfast, schedule organization
9:00–10:30 A.M.	Teams review sample student learning styles profiles and use *group analysis* on key questions:

    1. Which elements are key to learning success for each of the two students in the exercise?

    2. Is each student global or analytic in his or her processing style?

    3. Is each student a problem in a traditional classroom? Why or why not?

    4. How would you design the correct set of instructional strategies for each student?

10:45 A.M.–12:00 noon	Team Learning on Team Learning to introduce new and difficult material
12:00 noon–1:00 P.M.	Lunch
1:15–3:00 P.M.	Small-group strategies: Brainstorming for Instruction
	Brain Writing (three variations)

Day 3

8:00–8:45 A.M.	Breakfast, schedule organization
9:00 A.M.–12:00 noon	Small-group strategies
	Group analysis (*sample:* Visual Literacy)
	Circle of Knowledge (review technique)
12:00 noon–1:00 P.M.	Lunch
1:15–3:00 P.M.	Role playing
	Simulations

Day 4

8:00–8:45 A.M.	Breakfast, schedule organization
9:00 A.M.–12:00 noon	Team workshop on tactual strategies:
	Electroboards
	Flip Chutes
	Pic-A-Holes

	Puzzles
	Task Cards
	Board Games
	Other
12:00 noon–1:00 P.M.	Lunch
1:15–3:00 P.M.	Team workshop on kinesthetic strategies

Floor games	Group substitution of inanimate objects
Relay races	
Sports games	Team parody
Body sculpture	Yellow Brick Road of Learning Inventions

Day 5

8:00–8:45 A.M.	Breakfast, schedule organization
9:00 A.M.–12:00 noon	Team introduction to varied teaching strategies
	Programmed Learning Sequences
	Contract Activity Packages
	Multisensory Instructional Packages
12:00 noon–1:00 P.M.	Lunch
1:15–3:00 P.M.	Club Improv(isation)
	Team inventions and innovative tactual, kinesthetic, auditory, and visual learning strategies
	Sharing and questions and answers

Advantages of Small-Group Techniques

Adults report many advantages to the use of small-group techniques for reaching inservice objectives. These include but are not limited to the following testimonials:

1. Interaction and sharing increase productivity.
2. Camaraderie, joint ownership, stimulating debate, and teamwork build a positive tone.
3. Quiet, reserved individuals are more likely to participate in this setting.
4. Review sessions or evaluation of previously learned information becomes interesting and informative.
5. Focus and intensity are targeted toward one task at a time.
6. Creativity and innovation are more likely to result from the challenge of questions and tasks posed to the group.
7. Boredom disappears in a climate of fun.

Designing a Team Learning Assignment for Inservice Workshops

Team learning is an excellent inservice technique for introducing new and difficult material. Begin by selecting material from textbooks, encyclopedias, newspapers, the Internet, or other commercial sources. Original material prepared by the presenter can be even more valuable, depending on the topic and objectives to be reached. Pictures, diagrams, artwork, graphs, formulas, cartoons, and other images may prove useful to the groups established just prior to distributing the team learning assignment. This activity will include several types of questions about the printed reading or diagrammatic material.

The four or five participants assigned to each team should be able to select a table, five chairs in a circle, pillows on the floor, a carpeted area, or another comfortable arrangement in which to work. Any combination of these items is appropriate when selected on the basis of each team's seating preferences.

A strong caution: Do not require that participants assume roles and individual assignments that they resent, such as observer without talking, recorder without participating, or facilitator without having opinions. Training adults for these and other specific roles in group dynamics patterns may be useful under certain circumstances, but inservice sessions should be relaxed, motivating, and productive.

A positive climate is likely to emerge at the outset if a humorous technique is used to select a single recorder for each team who will keep a record of the group's answers and keep members on task. Some ways to select recorders might include choosing the person:

- Who has the curliest hair
- Who lives closest to the inservice facility
- Who is wearing the most red
- Whose birthday is closest to today

After the group has read the assignment, members should respond to the questions attached to it. These should include initial queries that require straightforward factual answers taken directly from the text or printed material. After the group has answered a few factual questions, higher order thinking questions of analysis or inference should be posed. These are included to challenge the group to reason from the information available in the text, to form opinions, and to reach decisions through consensus, if possible. Next, add assignments that require creative applications of what was learned. Poetry, raps, television scripts, role playing, drawings, tactual games, and so forth are options that can be posed to increase retention of what was learned. Further, the challenge of applying the new information will stimulate members' thinking and increase their brain power (see Figure 5-1).

FIGURE 5-1   Sample Team Learning: "Gray Matters"

Team Members:

1. _____   **3.** _____

2. _____   **4.** _____

Recorder: _____

Directions: Read this excerpt from "Gray Matters," *Newsweek,* March 27, l995, and answer the questions that follow.

> **No hard feelings:** Last year Penn's [the University of Pennsylvania's] Ruben Gur and his wife, neuroscientist Raquel Gur, enlisted a PET scanner in the aid of an old stereotype: Men can't read emotions on people's faces. (The pair got into the field of sex differences when they were struck by their own temperamental differences. He is more intrigued by numbers and detail; she likes to work with people. He reacts to a setback by taking a deep breath and moving on; she analyzes it.) They and their colleagues asked volunteers to judge whether male and female faces showed happiness or sadness. Both sexes were almost infallible at recognizing happiness. But sadness was a different story. Women correctly selected a sad face 90 percent of the time on both men and women, but men had more trouble. They recognized sadness on men's faces 90 percent of the time—that is, they did as well as the women—but were right only 70 percent of the time in judging sadness on women's faces.
>
> Well, of course. Evolutionarily speaking, it makes sense that a man would have to be hypervigilant about men's faces; otherwise he would miss the first hint that another guy is going to punch him. Being oblivious to a woman's emotions won't get him much worse than a night on the sofa. The Gurs can't understand why men find it so hard to be sensitive to emotions. According to the PET scans, women's brains don't have to work as hard to excel at judging emotion. A woman's limbic system, the part of the brain that controls emotions, was less active than the limbic system of men doing worse. That is, the men's brains were working overtime to figure out the emotions on faces.

Questions for Team Discussion

1. Although our brains evolved to meet modern challenges, describe the gender differences within the species.
2. What are some of the reasons proposed by the author to explain these differences?

Continued

FIGURE 5-1 *Continued*

---

3. What are some of your reasons to explain these differences?
4. Write a poem describing how women recognize emotions on the faces of other people.
5. Draw at least five of the signs that connote to women the sadness others feel.
6. Are women more sensitive than men?
7. Write a short television scenario demonstrating the major points in the article from *Newsweek.*
8. Role-play sad and happy situations, and assess whether males or females are more accurate in "reading" emotions.
9. Show pictures and posters of males and females with varied emotional expressions to teams of women and men, and develop a score sheet for correct responses.

Source: This team learning was designed by Patricia M. Raupers, coordinator of staff development, Northern Valley Schools Curriculum Center, Demarest, NJ.

Designing a Circle of Knowledge for Inservice Workshops

The Circle of Knowledge technique is highly motivating and an excellent activity for reinforcing knowledge or skills learned during the inservice session. It provides an action framework for review in which all participants learn more or solidify what they already have mastered.

Several small circles of four or five participants are positioned evenly around the room at a distance from one another so that whispered answers to the recorder in each circle cannot be overheard by other teams. A single question or problem is posed to all the circles, and a short time limit is imposed (two to three minutes) in which to list as many answers as possible. Each participant quietly tells an answer to the recorder, one after the other, clockwise or counterclockwise from the person next to the recorder, who also participates by contributing answers in turn. No member may skip a turn, give two or more answers at one time, or receive an answer from others directly. If a participant is unable to add to the list, others may pantomime, draw pictures, or give other nonverbal clues. At the end of the predetermined time, the presenter calls a halt to the knowledge sharing, and all recorders stop writing. The overhead transparency, whiteboard, or chalkboard is divided into columns, each representing one of the groups. The first group's recorder calls out one answer, which is written in the appropriate column. Each team recorder should cross out that answer on his or her own list to avoid a penalty for repetition later in the game. If a team does not have an answer that is called out by another team, that recorder should add it to the list to help all in the group remember it—but, of course, then cross it out.

When the last team recorder is reached, he or she should give two answers. Then, the teams give answers in reverse order, pendulum style—1, 2, 3, 4, 5, 6 (two answers) 5, 4, 3, 2, 1. Now Team 1 calls out two answers, as does the last team from then on whenever it is their turn. This method gives all teams more equitable participation in the competition than repetition of a straight sequence from 1 through 6. When a team runs out of answers, its recorder calls out "pass" but stays in the game and can challenge repetitions or wrong answers to gain additional points.

As the answers are recorded on the screen or chalkboard, any member of any team may call out "Challenge!" if an answer that has been given is incorrect or has already been called out and placed on the screen or board. A *challenge* that is incorrect is penalized one point. If the challenger is correct, his or her team gains a point. A team that gives an incorrect answer loses the chance to gain that point. At the end of the game, when all teams have called out "pass," each group may discuss missing answers, and the first team to call out a missing correct answer gains one additional point for the new response, plus one bonus point during this end round. The points—one for each correct answer, bonus points, and negative points for each incorrect challenge—are added and subtracted to determine the winner.

During the course of this strategy, some 12 to 14 repetitions—visual, auditory, and tactual—aid each participant to remember what has to be learned. The fun and intensity help, too (see Figure 5-2).

FIGURE 5-2 Sample Circle of Knowledge: Triune Brain Theory

Circle Members:

1. _____   **3.** _____

2. _____   **4.** _____

Recorder: _____

Game 1 In two (2) minutes, list as many words as you can that are associated with the triune brain theory.

Game 2 In three (3) minutes, briefly define each term.

Words	**Definitions**
_____	_____
_____	_____
_____	_____
_____	_____
_____	_____
_____	_____

Designing Brainstorming Sessions for Inservice Workshops

Brainstorming is an exciting group participation process designed to develop multiple answers to a single question, alternative solutions to problems, and creative responses. It is an associative process that encourages all involved to participate. Thus, it responds to personal motivation and does not suppress natural spontaneity.

Setting

From five to ten participants should form a fairly tight semicircle of chairs facing the leader. (Larger groups can be effective at times.) Behind the leader should be a wall containing three to five large sheets of lecture pad paper or newsprint in sets of two (one blank sheet behind the one to be written on) in order to prevent strike-through marks on the wall.

These sheets, approximately 20 to 24 inches wide and 30 to 36 inches high, should be attached to the wall with masking tape and placed a few inches apart at a comfortable height for recording. The leader should use broad-tipped, colored felt markers for instant visibility by the entire group. A timekeeper should be appointed for the two- or three-minute brainstorming segments, but he or she should participate too. It is useful to have additional sheets available and an overhead projector to permit groups to analyze, plan, or do subset brainstorming for specific aspects of general answers (see Figure 5-3).

Rules for Participants

1. Concentrate on the topic—"storm your brain."
2. Fill the silence—call out what pops into your head.
3. Wait for an opening—don't "step on" someone else's lines.
4. Record the thoughts in short form.
5. Record everything—no matter how far out.
6. Repeat your contribution until it is recorded.
7. Be positive—no put-downs, body language, or editorial comment.
8. Stay in focus—no digressions. Withhold judgment.
9. Use short time spans—one to three minutes.
10. Analyze later—add, subtract, plan, implement.
11. Brainstorm from general to specific subsets. (The reverse is also possible for strongly analytic processors.)

Procedures

The brainstorming leader also acts as recorder. His or her functions include recording all responses, asking for clarification or repetition, synthesizing large phrases into short key ideas, and keeping the group focused on each single topic.

The leader should not comment, editorialize, or contribute. His or her effort should be concentrated on producing an effective and productive session.

FIGURE 5-3   Sample Brainstorming: Three-Part Planning

After an inservice workshop, a three-part brainstorming could be used to plan and implement change and improvements based on what was learned.

What would be the climate in your school if it had high morale and total cooperation?	What would the obstacles be to reaching the goals listed in column 1?	Which actions should we take and which programs should be developed to overcome the obstacles in column 2 and reach the goals in column 1?

Sample answers for each of the three columns:

The Ideal (Goals)	*Obstacles*	*Action Plans*
Respect among all in the building	Ancient hurts	Focus groups
Very few discipline problems	Lack of trust	Open communication
Higher grade point averages	Dissolution of family structures	Student interpersonal relations committee
(and so forth)	(and so forth)	(and so forth)

Subsequent brainstorming sessions would determine the highest priorities in each column. Then the group could develop a series of steps to implement its key recommendations. Brainstorming is an excellent strategy for redesigning an integrated curriculum; planning block schedules; resolving inclusion problems; designing effective approaches to teaching multiethnic and multilingual school populations; and overcoming lack of resources, overcrowding, or poor facilities. The first column helps in establishing "blue sky" goals; the second aids in checking real-world obstacles; the third offers a framework for action. Groups become energized when they debate priorities in each column and discuss how to establish teams, task forces, and other action plans and evaluation techniques for continuing positive change.

Conclusion

These three small-group techniques and others you may use or devise are crucial in building motivation and in releasing creativity to solve problems, make decisions, and invent new approaches for applying what was learned at the inservice sessions.

- **Team learning** introduces new material, uses both factual and inference questions, and builds in challenges for creative applications.
- **Circle of Knowledge** reviews and reinforces previously learned material.
- **Brainstorming** releases creative energy and aids in planning and in solving problems.

Variations on these and other small-group techniques include case studies, simulations, role playing, group analysis, task forces, and research committees. Each technique should focus on a specific objective—learning new material, designing new approaches, making decisions, and so forth. If you select or develop these so that they respond to the learning styles of peer-oriented participants, your inservice sessions will be rewarding both for you and for them. Again, it is possible that individuals, pairs, and trios may do as well or better than the usual four- or five-member teams when that different preference is a strength.

6

Designing Tactual Resources

Kenneth Dunn

Tactual inservice strategies are essential for those adults whose primary perceptual strength involves touching and manipulating materials in order to learn critical information and concepts. For many, listening or reading does not provide initial or long-lasting retention and pathways to desired applications of presented inservice objectives. In addition, teachers who design one set of tactual materials will be able to design classroom "workshops" for students who learn tactually. Once an initial set of model games and materials is completed, students can be encouraged and challenged to design their own self-teaching strategies. They will learn as they design them and will gain praise from the instructor, recognition from peers, and improved confidence and self-image.

Advantages of Tactual Inservice Resources

The advantages of tactual strategies are many. They include:

1. Immediate self correction
2. The ability to go back and check the material
3. Active, direct involvement
4. Increased interest, motivation, and fun
5. Released creativity
6. Individual, pair, or team interactions
7. A match with individual learning styles

Beginning the Design Process

Designing Tactual Strategies

Old board games, oaktag, foam board, plastic-covered boards, and other basic materials can be used to develop inservice activities to teach and actively involve all participants. Gradually gather the following items.

Materials

- Oaktag or foam board
- Spinners, dice, poker chips, plastic figures
- Multicolored plastic or posterboard
- Old board games
- Opaque white, light-colored, and clear Contac paper
- Thin- and thick-line permanent pens of various colors
- Colored plastic tape, one-half inch wide
- Sketch pads for ideas
- Rulers
- Xacto knives
- $3'' \times 5''$ and $5'' \times 8''$ index cards
- Velcro
- Pairs of scissors
- Continuity testers
- Half-gallon juice or milk empty containers (waxed) cartons
- Plastic clothespins
- Golf tees
- Brass paper fasteners
- Aluminum foil, telephone wire, copper wire, or a role of tie-wraps (with aluminum strips inside)
- Masking tape
- Old magazines and used manuals or textbooks

Using Task Cards and Pic-A-Holes to Present New Material

The attention span of teachers who are not auditory wavers during inservice lectures. Retention may be limited and application in the classroom almost nonexistent. Several options are available.

1. Perceptual strength areas should be designed with appropriate furniture, such as tables and chairs for tactual participants; soft, comfortable theater seating for visual learners viewing films, slides, Power Point, and so forth; and tables

and a carpeted area for using kinesthetic strategies. Strong auditory learners should have comfortable chairs with table arms or tables for taking notes. Handouts should be designed to accommodate individual strengths. In this case, Task Cards and Pic-A-Holes would teach the objectives of the inservice workshop.

2. All in attendance could meet at a central location to review individual strengths, areas that match, and explanation of the objectives and procedures.
3. All participants could be given the option of moving directly to the area of their individual strength and reading the directions and using the materials designed for their preferred modality.
4. All approaches could be located in a central room, with participants moving to each of four different areas to sample one or more strategies.
5. All strategies and handouts could be distributed to participants prior to the workshop and later could be used for review and evaluation.

Objectives: The Triune Brain Theory

- Who was the scientist most responsible for developing the triune brain theory?
- What are the three separate processing systems within the human brain?
- What was their evolutionary order?
- Can you locate them on a diagram?
- Can you list several characteristics of each system?
- What are the behaviors controlled by each system?
- What are some typical human reactions during periods of stress?

Directions for Constructing Task Cards* to Learn the Objectives

1. Cut either oaktag or poster board into rectangles, or any other shape you creatively decide to use. Sets in varied shapes seem to attract interest.
2. Divide the shape into two or more sections. We suggest that you introduce participants to two-part task cards initially.
3. Print the related subject matter boldly on the face of the shape (half on each section). Add self-correcting codes through color, picture, shape, or symbols on the back of the shape.
4. Laminate the entire set of Task Cards before cutting them apart in different patterns to separate each task from the answer or match to it (see Figure 6-1).
5. Place each set into a plastic bag, an envelope, or an attractive box, with its label indicating the tasks related to that set of cards.

*Based on materials designed by Dr. Patricia M. Raupers, Coordinator of Staff Development, Northern Valley Schools Curriculum Center, Demarest, New Jersey.

FIGURE 6-1

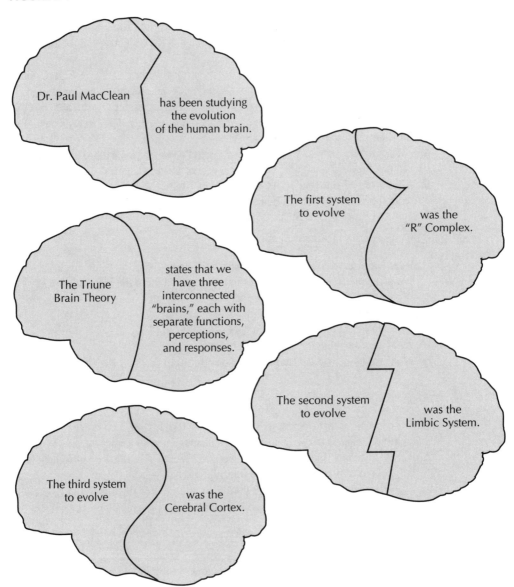

Dr. Paul MacClean

has been studying the evolution of the human brain.

The first system to evolve

was the "R" Complex.

The Triune Brain Theory

states that we have three interconnected "brains," each with separate functions, perceptions, and responses.

The second system to evolve

was the Limbic System.

The third system to evolve

was the Cerebral Cortex.

Directions for Constructing Pic-A-Holes to Learn the Objectives

1. Cut a colorful piece of cardboard or posterboard $24^3/8$ inches by $6^1/2$ inches.
2. Following the guide below, measure and mark the cardboard (on the wrong side) to the dimensions given. Use a ball point pen and score the lines heavily (Figure 6-2).

FIGURE 6-2

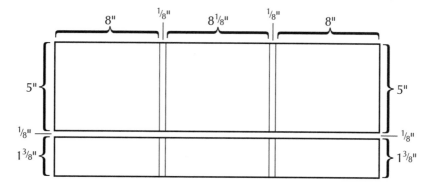

3. Remove the shaded areas. Use a ruler and razor or Xacto knife to get a straight edge. The piece of posterboard then should look like the illustration in Figure 6-3.

FIGURE 6-3

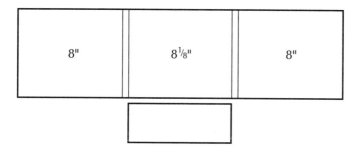

4. Working on the wrong side of the center section only, follow the measurement guide given in Figure 6-4.

FIGURE 6-4

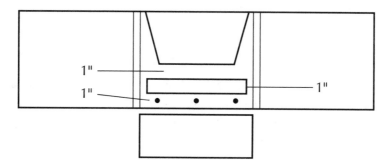

5. Remove the shaded areas with a ruler and razor or Xacto knife.
6. Fold on all the drawn lines, using a ruler as a guide to obtain sharp, straight fold lines.
7. Punch three holes, as shown in Figure 6-4.
8. Place an index card under the center section. Trace the openings onto the card. Remove the same areas from the index card. This will serve as a guide for placement of questions and answers, which can be written on 5″ × 8″ index cards in appropriate places. Punch the holes.
9. Using 5″ × 8″ index cards, mark holes and punch them out. Use as a guide for the placement of information.
10. Fold over the first side under the center section. Then fold up the bottom flap. Now fold over the last side. Paste or seal together with clear Contac paper, being certain that the bottom flap is in between (Figure 6-5).

FIGURE 6-5

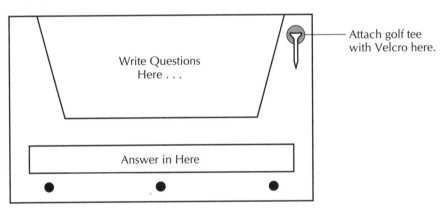

Figure 6-6 shows a sample of Pic-A-Hole 5″ × 8″ index cards on the triune brain theory. Holes are punched all the way through the cards and the folder that holds them. Correct answers are cut through once on each of the 5″ × 8″ cards, permitting that card to be pulled from the pocket when a participant selects the right answer. Correct answers should be alternated randomly among the three or four possible answers. Random selection will prevent guessing, although an incorrect answer signals the user to place the golf tee in another hole until the card pops out. The participant replaces the card in the back of the packet. When it appears again, the user invariably selects the correct answer if he or she selected the wrong answer on the first or first *and* second tries.

FIGURE 6-6

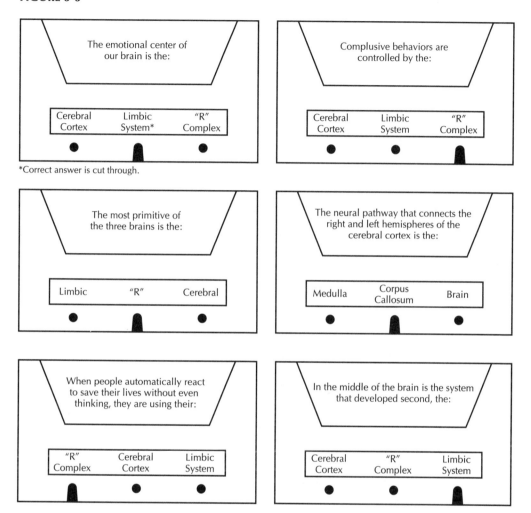

*Correct answer is cut through.

Using Flip Chutes and Electroboards to Present New Material

Flip Chutes

The options suggested for using Task Cards and Pic-A-Holes apply to Flip Chutes and Electroboards as well. Indeed, they apply to all tactual strategies, including the four described in this chapter and others such as board games, Wraparound Cards, Learning Circles with Velcro answers, and any other strategy that uses the sense of touch and the hands to place correct answers with questions or to build things that, in the making or using, will aid tactual learners to reach objectives in an inservice workshop or series.

Objectives: The Ecosystem and Its Protection

- What is ecology?
- What is a habitat?
- What is a niche in the environment?
- What are the changes in the communities of an ecosystem called?
- Explain the interaction of plants and animals in a specific ecosystem.
- Describe how a succession occurs.

Some tactual adult learners have learned a foreign language, computer language, medical terms, and other difficult materials using Flip Chutes.

Directions for Constructing Flip Chutes to Learn the Objectives

1. Pull open the top of a half-gallon milk or juice container.
2. Cut the side fold of the top portion down to the top of the container (Figure 6-7).

FIGURE 6-7

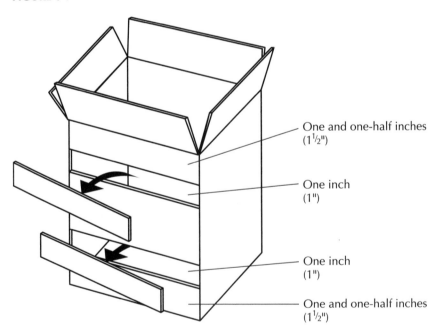

One and one-half inches (1½″)

One inch (1″)

One inch (1″)

One and one-half inches (1½″)

3. On the front edge, measure down both (a) 1½″ and (b) 2½″. Draw lines across the container. Remove that space.
4. Mark up from the bottom: (a) 1½″, and (b) 2½″. Draw lines across the container. Remove that space.
5. Cut one 5″ × 8″ index card to measure 6½″ by 3½″.

6. Cut a second index card to measure $7\frac{1}{2}''$ by $3\frac{1}{2}''$.

7. Fold down $\frac{1}{2}''$ at both ends of the smaller strip. Fold down $\frac{1}{2}''$ at one end of the longer strip (Figure 6-8).

FIGURE 6-8

$7\frac{1}{2}$ inches by $3\frac{1}{2}$ inches $6\frac{1}{2}$ inches by $3\frac{1}{2}$ inches

8. Insert the smaller strip into the bottom opening with the folded edge resting on the upper portion of the bottom opening. Attach it with masking tape. Bring the upper part of the smaller strip out through the upper opening with the folded part going down over the center section of the carton. Attach it with masking tape (Figure 6-9).

FIGURE 6-9

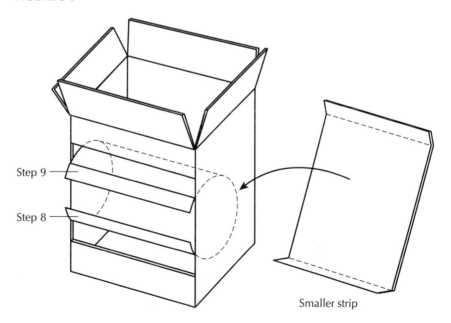

Step 9

Step 8

Smaller strip

9. Work with the longer strip. One end is folded down and the other end is unfolded. Insert the unfolded end of the longer strip into the bottom opening of the container. Be certain that the strip goes up along the back of the container.

Push it into the container until the folded part rests on the bottom part of the container. Attach it with masking tape. The top should be taped ⅝″ from top to ensure rapid movement down the slide. Slight adjustments can be made—up if the card moves slowly and doesn't "fly out," and down if the card seems stuck inside the chute.

10. Cut index cards into $2\frac{1}{2}″ \times 2″$ sections. Write the question on one side and the answer on the back—*upside down*. Please note that *cards* can be reversed; that is, definitions or answers may be placed first to teach the name or topic. For example, "the last stage of succession" could be placed in the slot, and the user must say or write "climax stage."

11. Decorate the Flip Chute to represent the topic to be learned.* Figure 6-10 shows a side view of the container.

FIGURE 6-10

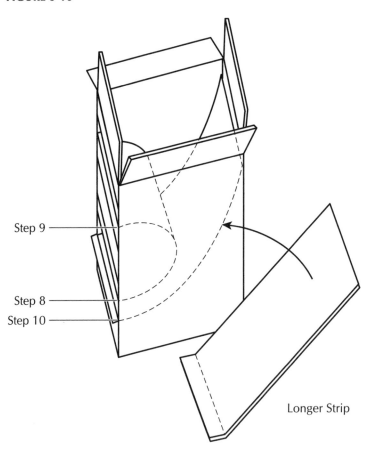

Step 9

Step 8

Step 10

Longer Strip

*Flip Chute directions were developed by Barbara Gardiner.

Sample Flip Chute Cards*

Front	**Back (written upside down)**
ECOSYSTEM •	A group of living things and their environment
SUCCESSION •	The series of changes in the communities of an ecosystem
HABITAT •	The special place in a community in which a plant or animal lives
ECOLOGY •	The study of how living and nonliving things affect one another
PIONEER STAGE •	The first stage of succession
CLIMAX STAGE •	The last stage of succession
NICHE •	The role that each living thing plays in a habitat
PREDATOR •	An animal that hunts another animal for food

*Based on materials designed by Majorie Schiering, elementary teacher, Rockland County, New York.

Objectives: The Great Depression

- What was a Shantytown?
- What was Black Tuesday?
- What were Hoovervilles?
- How long did the Great Depression last?

Objectives: Basic Bookkeeping

- What is a capital asset?
- What is a journal?
- On which side do you record accounts in an inventory?
- What is included in an inventory?

Electroboards

Tactual adults learning about new subjects that they have to teach or use may prefer Electroboards to gain initial knowledge. Designing additional questions and answers will expand knowledge and can be used with others as teaching products grow and expand during the inservice sessions.

Directions for Constructing an Electroboard to Learn the Objectives

1. Cut two identical pieces of posterboard in the shape of the unit topic. The size may vary from 8″ × 10″ to 18″ × 24″ or larger if more space for items is needed.
2. On one of the posterboards, write questions on the left side with answers out of sequence on the right side. Add a title at the top.
3. Laminate the side with the questions and answers.
4. Punch holes.
5. Insert *brass* fasteners with the "button" on the front and the prongs on the underside.
6. Connect each question with its proper answer using a 1″ strip of aluminum foil (folded twice to lend durability). Cover each strip completely with masking tape before doing the next strip.
7. Cover the back of the posterboard that has aluminum foil/masking connections with the other identically shaped posterboard when all questions and answers have been completed. Seal edges with tape, strips of clear Contac paper, or electrical tape.

Note: Telephone wire, tie-wraps, or copper wire may be used instead of aluminum foil. In any event, no part of the connecting strips should touch any others as they crisscross, nor should the brass prongs touch any other paper fasteners or aluminum foil. The masking tape protects the integrity of the circuit to prevent incorrect answers from lighting up. Telephone and tie-wraps do not need to be covered with masking tape except at the ends, where copper or aluminum are exposed.

Xacto knives may be used to cut an X whenever hole punchers do not reach items placed away from the borders—the skeletal system, maps, and so forth.

Sample Electroboards Figure 6-11 shows an Electroboard in the shape of a loaf of bread, designed by Camille Sinatra for a unit on the Great Depression.

FIGURE 6-11

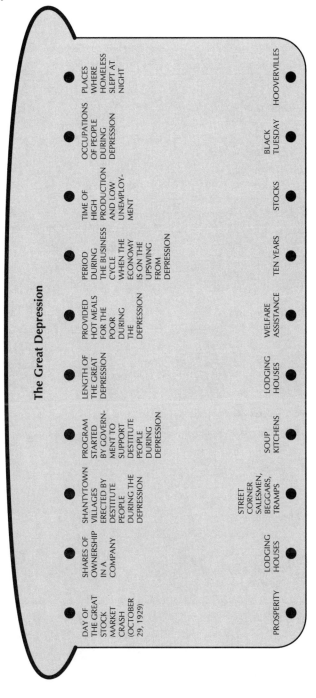

Figure 6-12 shows an Electroboard in the shape of a bookkeeper's legend, designed by Karen Robinson.

FIGURE 6-12

Bookkeeping	
● Land is an example	What customers owe. ●
● Long-term notes payable	is the dollar value of the stock on hand. ●
● Debits	Borrowing to be repaid after one (1) year. ●
● Credits	are on the *left* side. ●
● Initial capital	Any business deal that involves money. ●
● Journal	is the money and assets the owner contributes to start a business. ●
● Transaction	Capital. ●
● Accounts payable	is money owed to outsiders. ●
● Inventory	Basic tool for recording. ●
● Accounts receivable	are on the *right* side. ●

Generic Electroboards

Questions and answers printed and illustrated on posterboard may be designed to be attached with Velcro or dropped into pockets in the center of Electroboards that are fully completed as described, but left blank. In addition, if the Electroboard is turned upside down, new patterns of answers evolve, which is useful in the event that students memorize the pattern of connections that light up without retaining what they are learning. Number these circuits **I, II, III,** and so forth.

Board Games

Old game boards from Monopoly, Scrabble, stock market games, and other games are easily adaptable to any new subject or topic to be learned by adults who are tactual and enjoy learning with one or more other adults. Light-colored Contac paper may be used to cover an old or inappropriate game, and a completely new one can be created.

Conclusion

Tactual teachers at inservice sessions usually are pleasantly surprised by the interesting variety of tactual resources described in this chapter. Motivation increases as they begin to learn and then decide to construct and use the ideas for their tactual students as well as themselves. Teaming, for those who prefer to work that way, promotes social interaction, sharing new ideas, and motivation through productivity and fun. New topics for inservice sessions, such as the multiple intelligences, inclusion, integrated curriculum, block scheduling, and peer mentoring, can all be converted into tactual strategies to offer alternatives to a lecture format.

7

Designing Kinesthetic Resources for Inservice

Kenneth Dunn

Kinesthetic inservice strategies are likely to be the most neglected, but they are among the most important approaches for upgrading inservice instruction. Indeed, kinesthetic activities, as opposed to listening or reading, should be used in many initial learning experiences. Kinesthetic teaching actively involves whole-body movement and/or real-life experiences. In addition to John Dewey's concept of "learning by doing," we would add *retraining by becoming the thing that you are learning*.

Kinesthetic participants *require* action to learn easily and enjoyably. Many others may enjoy this kind of learning, but it is essential for kinesthetic adults. Further, some of the kinesthetic activities in this chapter may seem aimed at student learning, not at adults. In our experience, however, many teachers, especially first- and second-year "beginners," need to *experience* kinesthetic techniques before introducing them to students.

As indicated earlier, inservice techniques translate into many models for use with students as well as for the teachers experiencing them. Indeed, once teachers develop two or three kinesthetic instructional resources, their students can be encouraged to create and design additional floor games as homework assignments. Not only will these contribute to the students' own learning, but students also will gain confidence, motivation, and a better self-image as they share their good ideas and receive credit, recognition, and praise.

Advantages of Kinesthetic Instructional Resources for Inservice

The many advantages of kinesthetic inservice approaches include:

1. Active, direct involvement
2. A match with individual learning styles
3. Immediate self-correction
4. Individual, pair, or team interactions
5. Released creativity
6. Interest, motivation, and fun

Beginning the Design Process

Shower curtains and liners, old bedsheets, tablecloths, and plastic rolls all can be used to develop inservice activities to teach and actively involve all participants. Gradually gather the following items for the inservice session, or ask participants to bring them.

Materials

- One large sheet of plastic or shower liner in the four- or five- by five- or six-foot size range
- Multicolored plastic or posterboard that can be cut into patterns, decorations, and illustrations and then glued onto the sheet
- Permanent thin- and thick-line ink pens of various colors
- Glue that adheres plastic to plastic
- Interesting discarded game items and other plastic figures
- Sketch pads for ideas
- Colored plastic tape ½″ or ¾″ wide
- Oaktag or foam board
- Bean bags
- Cardboard boxes
- Spinners or dice
- Xacto knives
- Yardsticks
- Velcro
- Scissors

Objective: Improving Computer Skills

Many adults (and students) first learn the computer keyboard by reading and following directions in a manual. Those who struggle may need kinesthetic or whole-body involvement in order to absorb, retain, and apply skills and knowledge.

Some teachers can learn and enjoy new strategies through kinesthetic games, materials, and assignments. Remember, however, that teachers who are not kinesthetic may feel uncomfortable when participating in role-playing activities and floor games. Everyone should be given options, as explained in other chapters.

Kinesthetic Game Example: Computer Keyboard Floor Game

This sample involves an IBM keyboard but a Macintosh keyboard could be substituted.

Keyboards for IBM computers vary. In Figure 7-1, keys are shown as they are displayed on the IBM Personal System/2 Model 25 Space. This drawing, or a similar one, can be enlarged with an opaque projector and drawn with permanent markers on large labels that then can be laminated and glued on or attached with Velcro. Removable patterns have the advantage of being replaceable with other model keyboards or other games.

Several kinesthetic variations can be achieved with the use of this floor game pattern. Develop a set of printed and illustrated directions for each game.

FIGURE 7-1   Sample of Computer Keyboard Floor Games for Kinesthetic Participants

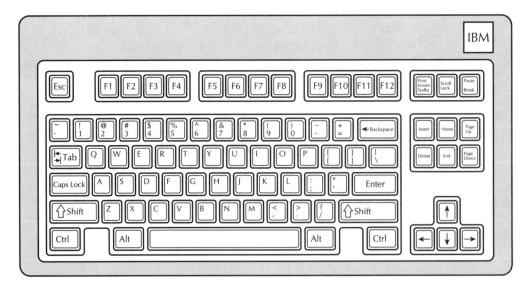

Objective: Learning the Placement of Keys on the Computer Keyboard

1. Step on one key at a time. Look at the letter or number, say it, look up, say it again, and look down again.
2. Cover the letters and numbers. Repeat step 1 without the visible clues until you achieve 100 percent.

or

1. Toss bean bags with matching letters and numbers onto each matched key.
2. Remove the bean bags and cover the letters and numbers.
3. Toss the bean bags onto the correct keys.

This game may be played alone, in pairs, or in small groups until the objective is mastered.

Objective: Learning the Function Keys

1. Read function key cards standing up next to each key.
2. Remove function key cards, mix them up, go back, and place them next to the correct key.

or

1. Cover function keys after reading them.
2. Place a duplicate set onto the covered ones correctly.

Designing Facts Games: Baseball and Balloon Race

Objective: Teaching Key Communication Phrases to Students Who Have Limited English Proficiency

1. Cut four pieces of oaktag or foam board into 18″ squares. Number them with large black designations, **1, 2, 3,** and **H,** representing first base, second base, third base, and home plate (see Figure 7-2).

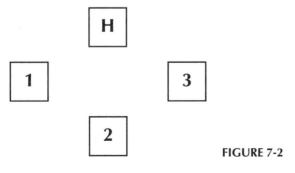

FIGURE 7-2

2. Design "base-hit" questions of varying difficulty to achieve "singles," "doubles," "triples," and "home runs."
3. When ready, place the bases in an empty space in the inservice room and conduct a tryout with other participants. Simulate what you would do in your own classroom by selecting two teams of four or five participants each. Select an umpire/scorekeeper and design an actual inning score sheet using baseball rules, with three outs per side for each half inning (see Figure 7-3).

FIGURE 7-3

	1	2	3	4	5	6	7	TOT.
A								
B								

Objective: Learning about the Cultural Differences of New Immigrants

1. Write a series of cultural differences questions on slips of paper. Number them and designate all the correct answers on a "monitor" board.
2. Fold and place each slip in an individual balloon. Blow up and tie the balloons so that they stay inflated with questions still secured inside.
3. Set up two teams of four participants each who must hop with a balloon between their knees without dropping the balloon. When each participant reaches a designated line about ten paces away, they drop the balloon, stomp on it*, pull out the question, and give the correct answer to the monitor. The first team to complete its balloon answers correctly wins. (Each participant runs back to tag the next player to begin his or her balloon hop to the answer line.)

Designing Role-Playing Strategies

Objective: Teaching Practical Spanish

1. Enlist other participants in the inservice workshop to design a "bodega." Use cardboard boxes, paint, and markers to designate counters, products, and sale prices.

---

*A variation of the "stomp" is to have each relay racer place the balloon on a chair at the finish line and try to break the balloon by sitting on it—hard!

2. Design place cards with string to label customers, salespeople, cashier, manager, and so forth.
3. All signs and cards should be printed in Spanish.
4. Conduct business for twenty minutes with "translators" available to keep the role playing going.
5. Have two record keepers note all correct and incorrect responses. Have large cards with the answers printed on the back of each item and provide the record keepers with numbers and number combinations, with English and Spanish versions side by side.

Objective: Making Shakespeare Real

1. Bring pictures of the main characters of Romeo and Juliet or any Shakespeare play under study to the workshop.
2. Have participants re-create the costumes with old clothing, painted cardboard, and other materials to represent the time period in the play.
3. Designate roles with place cards and give the players set dialog from the play.
4. Act as the director, and elicit a modern exchange of words portraying the same events and emotions.

Releasing Creativity—Club Improv(isation)

After designing a few successful kinesthetic strategies by following the directions described here, individuals, pairs, and groups can be challenged to improvise their own games and techniques. Again, once these are practiced, teachers then can inspire their own students to release their creativity and, in this way, empower student self-teaching.

Learning by Doing

Objective: Room Redesign

One of the most successful hands-on kinesthetic strategies for inservice involves helping teachers redesign their own classrooms based on the types of learners assigned to them. If the inservice sessions are held in a central location or in a school at a distance from their own classrooms, a model room may be established that begins as typically representative of the usual design (see Figure 7-4).

Printouts of individual learning styles and summaries of percentages of students who prefer (or do not prefer) bright light, warmer areas, soft chairs, working

FIGURE 7-4

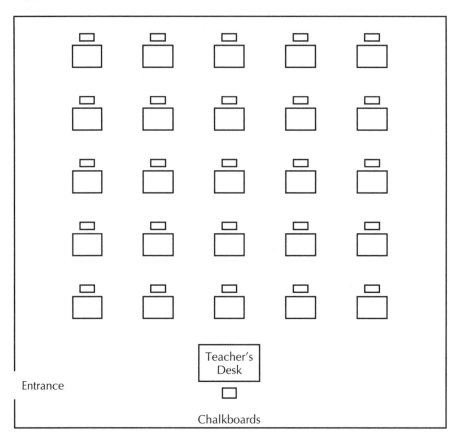

alone, and so forth would be very helpful, but even if these are not available, almost all classrooms require the following areas:

- Places where several students may meet to discuss what they are learning
- Well-lit reading areas
- Warmer areas
- Desks or tables and chairs
- Sections that permit responsible students to work without direct supervision
- Sections that permit students to work alone, with a friend or two, in small groups, with an adult, or in any combination thereof, provided they show academic progress
- Essentially quiet, screened study areas for individuals or pairs
- Darker sections for media viewing, photography, or dramatizations
- Cooler areas
- Carpeted, informal lounge sections with couch and easy chairs
- Sections that permit close supervision of less responsible students

- An area where snacking may be available (preferably raw vegetables and fruits, nuts, and other nutritious foods)

Teachers at the inservice session can begin to move furniture and dividers to provide more room and learning areas that match student styles. Figure 7-5 shows a possible first step.

FIGURE 7-5

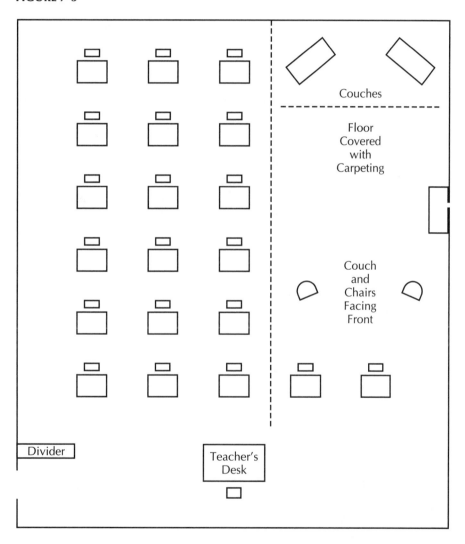

This design maintains full frontal control for the teacher but provides informal and formal learning sections for those students who work best in each of those areas.

Speaking of control, here is a list of concerns expressed by many teachers when considering redesigning a classroom to improve productivity and motivation:

- I have too much material to cover. I will never finish if students are all over the room doing different things.
- I could lose control. These students are difficult enough when I can see all of them in rows.
- The principal would never let me do this.
- The parents will be upset if I don't lecture to the students every day.
- How could I possibly address the whole group in this setup?
- I have wall-to-wall students now. Some of them almost have to hang their feet out the windows as it is.
- We have no money, no resources, no bookshelves . . . I'm fortunate to have a tablet arm-desk for each student.
- I am a traveling teacher. I have five classes in five different rooms.
- I might be able to do this, but the teacher who follows me will complain.

Ironically, control through self-control, productivity and "accelerated learning," receptivity by parents and students alike, and involvement by students all increase, as demonstrated by thirty years of practice and the prize-winning research described elsewhere in the text.

Further, as part of the inservice session students can demonstrate how to reestablish the classroom of rows (see Figure 7-1) in one minute or less. Perhaps of even greater importance is the good news that room redesign does not require a huge budget and unattainable resources. Indeed, donations of carpeting, couches, lawn furniture, and so forth, in addition to existing furniture and free dividers, can provide all the resources any teacher needs without large expenditures (see Figure 7-6).

FIGURE 7-6

Examples of Waist High Dividers Used by Teachers

Cardboard boxes	Cardboard carpentry
Bookshelves	Homosote
Filing cabinets	Closets
Wooden crafts	Colored yarn
Bulletin boards	Fish nets
Coat racks	Fish tanks
Boards on wheels	Long tables
Plastic six-pack holders	Voting booths
Shower liners	Shower curtains
Wire and posters	Bed sheets
Burlap	Plastic wall covering
Styrofoam	Piping
Planters and plants	Drop cloths
Display cases	Cutting boards
Art easels	Awnings

Dividers can be painted or covered by leftover wallcoverings. Discussing how to involve students and parents in room redesign should take place at this session to prepare for closure and an inviting learning area.

Some teachers are willing to try but are reluctant, at first, to relinquish control of the whole class and to allow students to follow prepared work assignments without the instructor leading. Initial large-group instruction could begin each session, with students moving out to other appropriate learning areas at the teacher's directions (see Figure 7-7).

FIGURE 7-7

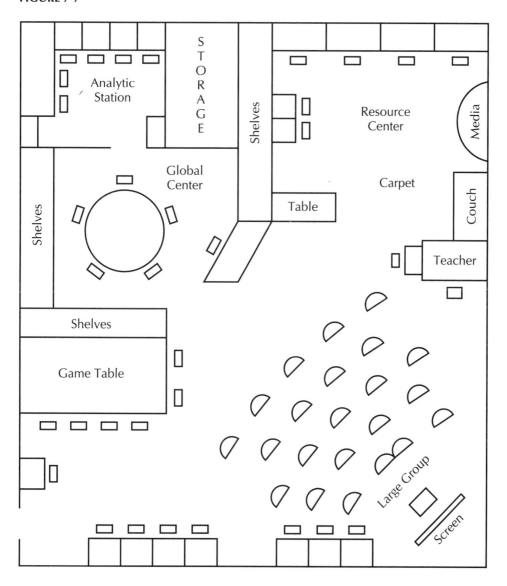

Finally, an infinite number of variations can be designed during the inservice session or back at the home school. It's usually wise to begin slowly, with constant evaluation. One teacher completed her design as depicted in Figure 7-8.

Obviously, teachers can begin with small sections of the room and increase re-design efforts as each area proves successful.

FIGURE 7-8

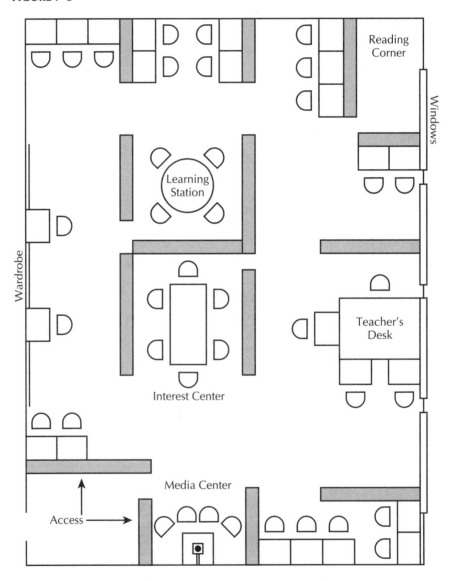

Objective: Adding Variety

Tossing Games

Ring toss, rubber horseshoes, or tossing Ping-Pong balls into boxes, poker chips into plastic glasses, bean bags onto numbered squares, and so forth, may appeal to some participants. Teams of colleagues can answer questions of ascending difficulty cooperatively, with appropriate point scores given to the participants. Higher scored questions should be placed at greater distances to build competition and interest.

Racing or Track Games

Nascar auto racing, horse racing, and track and field events can be ways of keeping score as participants answer questions correctly. Shower liners or plastic sheets can be used to draw oval tracks or straight tracks. Participants may add illustrations of their scenes and drivers. Miniature race cars, horses, and track figures with numbers can represent the players.

Competitive Sports

Miniature golf, basketball, football, and other sports can be designed to move plastic miniature figures across a field designed on a Floor Game sheet with permanent markers or plastic colored tape. Participants may answer questions directly from cards or begin with kinesthetic movement, such as "scoring" with miniature basketballs into a net, or getting a hole-in-one in a miniature golf game.

Relay Races

Participants can line up and run, walk, or dance to question cards attached to a bulletin board with Velcro. As they answer the questions, other participants can act as scorekeepers. When correct, runners return to their team as quickly as possible to tag the next participant, who then repeats the process. Velcro darts can be used to increase competitive interest.

Generic Floor Games

Plastic shower liners can be designed in a variety of ways, to be used for any subject area.

1. Create boxes of different sizes and decorate them with colored plastic tape. Numbers can be added and changed with Velcro. Bean bags, plastic poker chips, or other materials that do not bounce can be used to obtain question cards with varying points to gain scores on a chart.
2. Draw target designs with the higher points in the more difficult smaller circles.
3. Use tic-tac-toe as a competition between two teams. Large O's and X's are added as individuals answer questions correctly.
4. Develop story sheets such as "storming a castle with a moat," climbing Jack's beanstalk, or adding leaves to a tree with different colors for different teams.

5. Design generic wall games
    a. Duplicate "Jeopardy" with pockets to change question cards.
    b. Build a Wheel of Fortune to complete answers.
    c. Use Velcro balls to gain high-point questions.

Becoming Part of the Thing to Be Learned

1. Demonstrate how parts of a machine work—for example, an automobile engine, with participants acting as the pistons.
2. Create living sculpture or ballet in which participants become the thing they are learning—for example, the earth rotating on its axis and revolving around the sun.
3. Design a huge electric circuit on benches, platforms, or chairs placed side by side. Participants become electrons, encounter resistance, and are "pushed off" the circuit.
4. Create a fantastic journey in which participants draw and travel through huge arteries and veins to learn the heart and circulatory system.
5. Build an underwater scene with cardboard or papier-mâché. Model undersea life hanging from the ceiling and growing up from the floor, with pathways to discover ecosystems. All items are labeled, and participants can "walk" on the ocean bottom.
6. For early childhood teachers, design a rainbow with primary colors above the floor. Use a ladder with safe seats to sit on the rainbow and literally "eat" the colors by using colored sherbet or ice cream. Show them how their children can say, eat, and point to the words that spell out the colors.
7. Living history can be achieved by researching, designing costumes, creating scenery, and reenacting, for example, the Boston Massacre (or another event), with children pelting the hated "lobsterbacks" with foam "snowballs" until the anger leads to soldiers firing on a crowd.

Conclusion

Kinesthetic teachers at inservice sessions will no longer be bored or unmotivated if given choices based on their personal learning-style strengths. Kinesthetic strategies are exciting and stimulating, and they inspire creativity in those who enjoy this approach. Teachers, in turn, can bring excitement to their classrooms for students who respond to kinesthetic learning and who actively become involved in creating similar strategies for their classmates to use. Designing and practicing kinesthetic strategies at the inservice session also can impart knowledge and improve teaching and learning in the classroom.

8

Designing Contract Activity Packages for Inservice

Rita Dunn

A Contract Activity Package (CAP) is an instructional strategy that allows motivated people to learn at their own speed. A CAP consists of several components:

1. Simply stated objectives
2. Multisensory resources that permit choices of materials that match individuals' perceptual preferences
3. Activity Alternatives in which adults apply newly mastered information by creating original resources to show that they have learned what was required or selected
4. Reporting Alternatives so that the completed Activity Alternatives can be shared with others in the workshop
5. At least three small-group techniques to permit persons who enjoy working or learning with colleagues to do so
6. A performance or written test so that the participants can show their working knowledge of the material they have mastered

Van Wynen (1997) used a CAP in a managed-care project for training nurses in New York (see Figure 8-1). Based on each nurse's Productivity Environmental Preference Survey (PEPS) profile, she issued study guides that capitalized on each participant's unique learning style (see Figure 8-2). At first, the participants were surprised that they were permitted such choices; they had not experienced assignments like those during their entire college career. Van Wynen, instructor of nursing at Dominican College, reported that the nurses "loved having the choice of how to proceed with an assignment. Their grades were equally positive. In addition, they reflected critical-thinking skills, quality written work, and creativity" (p. 48). She concluded that "one size doesn't fit all" (p. 44).

FIGURE 8-1 Course Assignment: Patient Care Delivery Models/Managed Care Project

---

Patient Care Delivery Models/Managed Care Project

You may select *one* of the following suggested activities for submission of your patient care delivery models/managed care project to *Liz Van Wynen on or before April 22, 1996:*

CHOICE 1: Learning Exercise (textbook, page 195, #9.1):

(Based on a given scenario, this exercise provides an opportunity for the learner to evaluate various types of patient care delivery systems. Learner analysis should include an examination of many methods of care delivery, a diagram of a new patient care organization, rationales for positions affected by the reorganization, and an explanation of implementing a planned change.)

CHOICE 2: Case Study:

Assume that you are a director in a home health agency. You primarily employ RNs, although there are some LPNs on your staff. Most of the nursing care that your agency provides is done on a contractual basis with clients in their home. Although your nurses provide care for a wide variety of patient needs, there seems to be a high incidence of patients who have cancer, irreversible spinal cord injuries, or who are recovering from a CVA. Because many of these patients require nursing care on an extended basis, you believe there is great potential for your nurses to form therapeutic relationships with these patients and to implement a holistic nursing care plan. Currently, patient assignments are rotated among the staff.

Assignment:

Decide whether an alternative method of patient care management or a modification of the current method would be appropriate. Be sure you consider the makeup of your staff in terms of the motivation nurses need to care for the same patients on a long-term basis. How would you guard against having an inadequately prepared or undereducated nurse assigned to a patient on a long-term basis? What evaluative check points can be constructed to guard against this happening?

CHOICE 3: Group Project:

If you work/learn better in a group, arrange for three (3) of your classmates to work together on this *assignment:* Design and write a pamphlet describing the nursing care your "group" of nurses administers. Describe the functions of each member of the healthcare team for the client according to the type of care delivery system in your "group's" institution (case method, functional, team, primary, or case management). Be certain that it is in terms that your clients will understand and that it will attract them to the setting for which you are producing this pamphlet/brochure.

CHOICE 4: Individual Project:

Please refer to the handout on "Mindmapping" distributed in class. Design a mindmap that incorporates the related concepts of different care delivery systems and differentiated practices of nurses. Incorporate how management decisions may vary with differing care delivery systems.

CHOICE 5: Build a Collage:

1. Collect news articles, magazine articles, photos, advertisements brochures, etc. regarding local healthcare services, or services in some identifiable region. List your article titles.
2. Organize them into time frames or developmental stages. Highlight new agencies and services within the time period(s) you select. Identify geographic areas with the newest developments and expansions, perhaps with a creative visual or map.

Source: E. A. Van Wynen, "Information Processing Styles: One Size Doesn't Fit All," *Nurse Educator,* Vol. 22, No. 5, 1997, pp. 44–50. Used with permission.

FIGURE 8-2 Excerpts from Nurses' Homework Study Prescriptions

---

Learning Style Inventory Homework Guides

Name: SENIOR #1 (ANALYTIC PROCESSOR)
Occupation: STUDENT NURSE Date: 02/17/96
Affiliation: NURSING

Sound—37; Light—28; Temp—76; Design—55; Motivation—60; Persistence—56; Responsible—64; Structure—57; Alone—32; Authority—44; Variety—51; Auditory—35; Visual—59; Tactile—57; Kinesthetic—50; Intake—34; Time of Day—64; Late Morning—60; Afternoon—38; and Mobility—39.

Sound: You often need quiet when learning something new or difficult and when working on a challenging project. It would be productive for you to find a quiet area at home or at the office where you can concentrate on your work.

Learning Alone: You often prefer to work and learn new and difficult information by yourself. You are usually more productive when you alone are responsible for specific tasks. When working with a committee or team, assume specific responsibilities to complete by yourself and then contribute the product to the group.

Intake: You usually do not eat, drink, smoke, chew or require intake while you are learning something new or difficult and when working on a challenging task.

Name: SENIOR #2 (GLOBAL PROCESSOR)
Occupation: STUDENT NURSE Date: 02/17/96
Affiliation: NURSING

Sound—70; Light—66; Temp—37; Design—34; Motivation—44; Persistence—61; Responsible—54; Structure—57; Alone—67; Authority—57; Variety—30; Auditory—76; Visual—48; Tactile—57; Kinesthetic—47; Intake—70; Time of Day—28; Late Morning—40; Afternoon—79; and Mobility—69.

Sound: You usually work with some type of sound present in your office or study, whether it is the radio, TV, or tapes. You find it disconcerting to learn something new or difficult and concentrate on a demanding project when it is too quiet in your environment.

Design: You often concentrate most efficiently in an informal work area. Your office or workspace should be relaxing and might include a soft chair or couch. When learning something new or difficult and when working on a challenging task, an informal work or study space will maximize your productivity.

Peer-Oriented: You often prefer working on challenging projects and learning new and difficult information with someone else, rather than alone. Working and learning as a team or with a colleague enhances your ability to concentrate.

Intake: You usually have some kind of intake, such as something to drink or snack on when learning something new or difficult or when working on a challenging task. Intake enhances your ability to concentrate.

Source: E. A. Van Wynen, "Learning Style Inventory Homework Guides," *Nurse Educator,* vol. 22, no. 5, 1997, pp. 44–50. Used with permission.

Just as tactual resources are effective with adults who enjoy learning with their hands, and kinesthetic resources are effective with adults who enjoy learning *while* they are actively involved in the process, small-group techniques are effective with adults who enjoy learning with other people. CAPs, however, work best for an entirely different type of learner. Each strategy teaches exactly the same content, but each teaches it differently. That is why, when you are planning inservice, it is important to assign adults whose motivational levels differ to the instructional strategy that best accommodates their unique learning styles.

For Whom Are CAPs Effective?

CAPs are most effective with *independent* and *motivated* participants because they provide self-pacing for individuals who want to achieve, improve, or be among the best in their field. They also are effective for nonconformists because CAPs provide multiple options and allow creative individuals to demonstrate mastery of the inservice requirements *their* way. Caps can be used by the learning-alone preferents, who enjoy working by themselves, and by peer-oriented preferents working in a team. This approach reduces much of the frustration and anxiety often experienced during inservice by motivated and very competent teachers who are required to progress at the larger group's pace. Indeed, CAPs can be used flexibly to accommodate a variety of learning-style characteristics. Some examples follow.

Sound

When quiet is important to an individual, earplugs can be used to block out unwanted noises. Conversely, when sound is desired, earplugs can be used to provide recorded music to block out the environmental sound distractions that disturb certain adults. Others may not notice such sounds; not only do they not *hear* them, but sometimes they unconsciously *make* them—by breathing loudly, speaking to themselves, tapping their fingers or pencils, and/or humming to themselves while thinking!

When discussion and interaction are important to one group of individuals, a work area, similar to a classroom Learning Station or Interest Center, can be established in a corner of the facility—whether that be a room, corridor, or office. Cardboard or available furniture such as tables, file cabinets, or bookcases can be placed perpendicular to the wall to form dividers and to create a sanctuary for occupants. Simultaneously, these created spaces, "offices," or "dens" protect colleagues who require quiet to avoid distraction because of the movement or conversation that occurs when other people are actively engaged and interacting.

Rules for participants' discussions need to be posted on a large oaktag surface mounted to the wall within that area so that no one, either inside or outside the instructional area, is distracted from concentrating and doing his or her work. These rules could include the following:

- Your learning style may not distract anyone with a different learning style.
- No participant, either inside or outside this area, should be able to repeat the exact words being used by any member in this group.

- Each participant needs to master the objectives for this session.
- Evidence of classroom use of what was mastered during this inservice should be observable within three weeks.

Light, Temperature, Seating, Intake, and Sociological Preferences

Participants who elect to use a CAP are encouraged to work on it anywhere in the immediate environment as long as they do not interfere with anyone else's learning style and respect the rules that have been established for that area. They can adapt the available illumination, temperature, and seating to their personal learning-style preferences. In addition, participants may work alone or with a colleague or two when using a CAP and may either snack or not, as they choose.

Structure, Mobility, and Responsibility (Conformity/Nonconformity)

The CAP system itself provides a great deal of structure through the itemization of specific objectives, Activity and Reporting Alternatives, small-group techniques, and a related self-test assessment. By permitting choices of these items, CAPs provide "breathing room" for nonconformists who often resist direction or structure from others in authority.

Processing Style

As indicated previously, a CAP provides an outline of what needs to be learned and how to learn it, while simultaneously providing options for those with different learning-style preferences and for nonconformists. CAPs tend to respond to analytic processors. However, through multiple illustrations, graphics, and Activity Alternatives, CAPs respond easily to a variety of perceptual and sociological preferences in addition to individual interests. To that extent, they can respond to the preferences of global users.

Designing a Contract Activity Package (CAP)

Designing a CAP requires the designer to organize the content (topic) to be addressed into logical, easy-to-follow objectives. In truth, no inservice should be provided without that type of organization and planning. If you begin with step 1 and gradually move through each of the remaining steps until you have completed your first CAP, the one you design will be well structured and sufficiently inclusive to enable all participants to address the objectives you establish. In addition we assure you that each consecutive CAP will be easier to develop and increasingly professional in style and scope.

Experiment with the first CAP you create. By their comments during its use, participants will provide feedback on potential improvements you can incorporate into the next CAP you design. Inservice assignments and the participants themselves can be enlisted to create and share additional CAPS until you have a full arsenal.

Inservice Applications

If you need to keep all inservice participants in attendance during the specific amount of time allocated for the session or program, use a CAP just as you would an assignment for a small group. If you have some leeway, a CAP permits people to self-pace themselves at the time of day they are best able to concentrate. Thus, some participants may elect to complete the CAP at home, whereas others may do so during the time officially established for the inservice. *Present the option of home completion to motivated, conforming, selfstructured* participants (those with scores of 60 or above on the PEPS or as similarly defined by BE).

Step 1: Identify the Content and Develop an Analytic Title

Begin by identifying the topic, concept, or skill that you want participants to master as a result of the inservice. Then choose a straightforward, analytic title for the CAP. The analytic title can be the same as or adapted from the title of the chapter in the textbook you use on that topic.

Step 2: Develop a Humorous or Clever Global Subtitle

Learning needs to be interesting or fun to global people, or they will not concentrate on whatever it is that someone else wants them to learn. To develop an interesting or humorous subtitle to attract the attention of global participants, brainstorm, either alone or with a global friend or spouse, a global counterpart to the analytic title. Strive to make it a funny play on words that illustrates or relates to the straightforward analytic title. Here are some examples:

- Coping with Depression: Changing Your Mind and Your Life
- The Triune Brain Theory: *Three* for the Price of One
- Teaching Aerobics: Don't Hold Your Breath!
- Teaching Inference: They Don't Have a Clue!
- Numismatics: *Money* Talks!
- Teaching Decimals: What's the *Point*?
- Teaching the Addition of Two-Digit Numbers: Growing by Leaps and Bounds!
- Philately: Don't *Stamp* on Me!
- Paper Making: The Cutting Edge

- Graphing: Get the *Point*?
- Bubble Gum in the Classroom: A *Sticky* Situation!
- Teaching Division: The *Long* and *Short* of It!
- Learning Style: It *Suits* You!
- Teaching Mitosis: Breaking Up Is Hard to Do!
- Your Arteries: Getting Back into Circulation!
- Nonverbal Behavior: Your Body Speaks for Itself!
- Explaining the Need for Orthodontia: Get It *Straight*!
- Travel: A *Moving* Experience!
- Photography: *Picture* This!
- Our New Dental Plan: The *Cutting* Edge!—or Getting to the *Root* of Things!—or A *Crowning* Experience!—or A *Filling* Experience!

How to develop a global title analytically   After a few experiences with it, global processors have little trouble developing global counterparts for their analytic titles; it comes easily to them, and they usually don't mind helping others to develop subtitles for their CAPs. Analytics, however, often need to identify a key word in the analytic part of the title and then extrapolate from it—or an idea—to develop the global second half of the title. If you are willing to try, here is a format that worked for this analytic CAP developer.

1. Make the analytic part of the title simple and direct. For example, for a session on new ways to teach electricity through a tactual/kinesthetic approach, the key word would be *electricity,* which also would be the focus of the content.
2. Brainstorm all the words you can think of that have something to do with electricity—for example, *shock, bolt, charge, watt, static,* and *lightning.*
3. Associate any of those words with the key word of the title by using it in a phrase. The funnier the phrase (and the title) or the more it can be associated with a phrase with which they are familiar, the more the participants will relate to it. For example:

- Electricity: The *Shocking* Truth!
- Electricity: A *Bolt* Out of the Blue!
- Electricity: The *Charge* of the Light Brigade!
- Electricity: *Watt's* Happening?
- Static Electricity: Snap! Crackle! Pop!
- Electricity: *Lightning* Strikes!
- Electricity: I'm Really *Wired*!
- Electricity: *Watt a Circuit Breaker!*

These titles did *not* come easily and *did* take lots of time, but, gradually, they helped me to develop a pattern or format for creating additional global counterparts to the analytic halves of both CAP and Programmed Learning Sequences (PLSs) (see Chapter 9).

Step 3: Decide on the Purpose of the Inservice—What Do You Want Participants to Learn?

Identify and list exactly what inservice participants need to learn during the session or program for which this CAP is intended. Keep the list simple and direct, but include each item that is important to either you or the administration. The purpose of inservice is to educate; thus, specifically outline exactly what the participants need to learn.

Step 4: Translate What Needs to Be Learned into Straightforward Objectives

Convert the list of what you want participants to learn into *objectives*—clearly stated goals that clarify the purpose(s) of the inservice. Objectives are written for the participants and always should begin with a verb. For example, if you were alerting staff to some of the things they should consider before purchasing a new computer system, you might include some of the following:

- *Describe* the questions you need to ask of the salesperson before making a decision about purchasing a new computer system.
- *Differentiate* between the items you *require* and those you may *enjoy* having in a new computer system.
- *Identify* the problems concerned with adapting to a new computer system.
- *Explain* the differences between analytic and global software packages.
- *Compare* the advantages and disadvantages of the Microsoft Word and Corel Word Perfect software packages.

Inservice Application

These objectives are related to factual knowledge and seek specific responses—"correct" answers. These objectives tend to be analytic, discrete facts or pieces of information. Although it is appropriate to require that factual information be learned, those who *only* seek specific information tend to ignore other kinds of thinking strategies. Thus, consider adding a few higher level cognitive skill objectives to encourage participant discussions and to provide opportunities for answers that are not necessarily "right" or "wrong." Here are two examples:

- *How* would parents who recognize the need for early computer literacy but are on a limited budget provide computers for their school-aged children, all of whom need to do homework and would profit from ongoing access to a word processor?
- Angela has been teaching for almost 23 years and is eligible to take early retirement within the next two years. She has always wanted to write and

recently submitted a manuscript to a major New York publishing house. She received a telegram from the publisher stating that the review of her manuscript had been extremely positive. Furthermore, the president of the company offered her a three-year contract as editor on staff at a salary roughly equivalent to her present income. On the one hand, this is Angela's "dream come true"; on the other, she is concerned about succeeding. What are the pros and cons of Angela's situation? If her decision were yours to make, what would it be—and why? What other questions should she ask?

Objectives clearly indicate what needs to be mastered during the inservice, but *how* they are mastered is determined on the basis of each participant's learning style.

Step 5: Establish Diverse Activity Alternatives and Permit Choices

Objectives should indicate clearly what needs to be learned. They allow participants to show that they have mastered the information in ways that respond to their learning-style preferences. Thus, consider the objective that requires participants to compare the advantages and disadvantages of the Microsoft Word and Corel Word Perfect software packages. After individuals have identified the advantages and disadvantages of each, when using a CAP, they then choose *how* to demonstrate their mastery.

Mastery of the CAP content is revealed by completion of *one* of at least three or four activities aligned with each CAP objective. Individuals may choose the single activity they like most. They then demonstrate mastery by completing that Activity Alternative. For example: in a CAP titled "Teaching Aerobics: Don't Hold Your Breath," Sue Tendy (1998) used the Activity Alternatives shown in Figure 8-3 (page 94) for one of the objectives.

By making a video, writing a brief paragraph or song, or constructing a chart, people evidence their mastery of the content. By *applying* the recently mastered content in a creative way, participants will increase their retention of it substantially. By *sharing* that completed creative activity with one or more colleagues or the instructor, they again review and reinforce the information for both colleagues and themselves.

Step 6: Establish Diverse Reporting Alternatives and Allow Choices

Using new and difficult information by *applying* it creatively in completion of an Activity Alternative is an excellent way to increase long-term memory. Sharing that creative Activity Alternative with colleagues reinforces the content again and permits recognition for the creator (see the Reporting Alternatives posed previously).

FIGURE 8-3 Sample of CAP Activity Alternatives

OBJECTIVE: Identify at least four (4) different ways to monitor your exercise intensity.

Activity Alternatives	*Reporting Alternatives*
1. Make a videotape showing at least four (4) ways to monitor your exercise intensity.	**1.** Watch your completed video with two (2) colleagues and ask them to comment in a two (2) line poetic statement.
2. Write a brief paragraph describing four (4) or five (5) ways to monitor your exercise intensity.	**2.** Have two (2) or three (3) colleagues read your paragraph and initial it if all the information is correct. If the information is not correct, revise it and *then* seek their initials.
3. Construct a chart explaining four (4) or five (5) ways to monitor exercise intensity.	**3.** After a brief warmup, have three (3) of your classmates exercise with you. After three (3) minutes of activity, determine the level of intensity each of you has reached using at least one (1) of these methods, and find that level on the chart.
4. Write a song that explains four (4) or five (5) ways to monitor your exercise intensity.	**4.** Share the song with three (3) of your classmates. Have them monitor their exercise intensity with you.

Source: S. Tendy, *Teaching Aerobics: Don't Hold Your Breath* (Jamaica, NY: St. John's University's Center for the Study of Learning and Teaching Styles, 1997). Used with permission.

Inservice Applications

The list of Activity and Reporting Alternatives in Figure 8-4 may be used to develop options for those inservice participants who elect to learn through a CAP. Select those that appeal most to you—or permit several options and encourage the participants to choose those that appeal most to them.

Step 7: Develop Multisensory Resource Alternatives

After you have developed the objectives and their related Activity and Reporting Alternatives, begin a new page, titled "Resource Alternatives." This page of the CAP

FIGURE 8-4 Sample Activity and Reporting Alternatives

Activity Alternatives	*Reporting Alternatives*
1. Make a poster "advertising" the most interesting information you have learned.	1. Display the poster and give a two (2) minute talk explaining how the information will be used with your classes.
2. Prepare a brief travel lecture related to this content.	2. Give the lecture before a small group of colleagues who attended this inservice.
3. Describe in writing or on tape an interesting person, character, or idea you learned about.	3. Ask two (2) or three (3) colleagues to share their perceptions of the person or idea you described.
4. Construct puppets and use them in a presentation that explains an interesting part of the information you learned.	4. Display the puppets and do the presentation.
5. Make a map, chart, or drawing representing new information you learned.	5. Display the map, chart, or drawing and answer questions about it.
6. Broadcast a book review of the topic as if you were a newspaper critic. Tape record the review.	6. Permit others to listen to your tape and tell you if they would like to learn more about this information.
7. Design a mural to illustrate the information you found interesting.	7. Display the mural and answer questions that arise.
8. Make a timeline listing important dates and events that you learned about in sequence.	8. Write a news story, an editorial, a special column, or an advertisement. Explain your views concerning any major aspect of this topic.
9. Write an imaginary letter to your principal describing what you learned during this inservice.	9. Show the letter to a trusted colleague.
10. Keep a make-believe brief diary about your experiences during this inservice series.	10. Read a portion of your diary to two (2) of your colleagues. Compare your reactions. Discuss the similarities and differences in your viewpoints. If you all agree, sign the diary and send it to either your principal or your superintendent.

Continued

FIGURE 8-4 *Continued*

Activity Alternatives	*Reporting Alternatives*
11. Search the library card index and/or locate published evaluations of the same content/topic being addressed in this inservice.	**11.** Add the information to the Resource Alternatives of this CAP.
12. Speak with colleagues from other schools or districts who also have received inservice in this topic.	**12.** Report on their experiences either with the classroom implementation of this content or during inservice.
13. Design your own Activity Alternative to show how much you learned about this content.	**13.** Obtain approval from either the instructor or the coordinator of this inservice. Then design an original Resource Alternative in which you share the creative application of the contents of your Activity Alternative.

includes a listing of all the instructional resources that participants can use to master the required objectives for this inservice session or program. Be certain to include all the tactual/visual and kinesthetic/visual resources that you designed for those participants who are likely to profit from them, such as Electroboards, Flip Chutes, multipart Task Cards, Pic-A-Holes, and Floor Games. These resources may be used by anyone who elects to complete the inservice objectives through a CAP. Chapter 9 describes still another resource—a Programmed Learning Sequence (PLS). Eventually, after you have developed a PLS, its title also should be listed on the Resource Alternative page.

Step 8: Develop at Least Three Small-Group Techniques

Teach the most difficult objectives for the staff development session with a **Team Learning**—a small-group strategy used to *introduce* new information (see sample in Figure 8-20). Reinforce the information in the Team Learning with a **Circle of Knowledge** (Figure 8-21). Use **Role Playing** (Figure 8-22) to encourage creativity through dramatization and to allow kinesthetic participants to move while learning.

Step 9: Develop an Assessment Directly Related to the Inservice Objectives

An assessment or examination directly related to the stated inservice (and CAP) objectives is called a criterion-referenced test. Questions for such a test are formed by either restating or rephrasing the objectives. For example, if the objective were,

"Describe the software compatible with the computer tasks you normally perform" (Flanary, 1997), the corresponding test statement could be, "Itemize the tasks for which you normally use your computer, and then describe the software that would be most compatible with your needs."

For an objective such as, "Compare and contrast (a) sensory memory, (b) short-term memory, and (c) long-term memory" (Raupers, 1997), the assessment question would be identical: "Compare and contrast (a) sensory memory, (b) short-term memory, and (c) long-term memory."

Step 10: Develop a Cover for the CAP

Create an outer cover that includes both the analytical and global CAP title, a space for the participant's name, the date, and an illustration representing the content.

Step 11: Develop an Informational Top Sheet

On the page directly after the illustrated CAP cover, itemize information that may be important for using this CAP—particularly for the first time. Some items that might be included are the following:

- The CAP title
- The participant's name
- The inservice title and session sequence—for example, "first in a series of two"
- The objectives that have either been assigned to or been selected by the participants
- The time or date by which the CAP—or selected sections—should be completed (to provide structure for participants who need it)
- A space where a pretest and/or a posttest grade or comments can be inserted
- The names of colleagues with whom the participant collaborated (if any)
- Directions for working on—or using—this CAP, such as which objectives are required and which are optional, how to choose the Activity and Reporting Alternative for each objective, how to form teams to engage in the small-group techniques, and which Resource Alternatives respond to which styles

Step 12: Reread and Correct the CAP

Overview all the parts of a CAP to be certain that each is clearly stated, well organized, in correct order, grammatically accurate, and spelling-perfect.

Step 13: Illustrate the CAP Pages

To each page, add illustrations related to the CAP's content so that it becomes attractive and motivating, and serves as a model for those who use it.

Step 14: Reproduce the CAP

Duplicate copies of the CAP for participants who may wish to use one during the scheduled inservice session. Briefly explain the objectives for the inservice, offer the Resource Alternatives you have collected/designed—including the tactual and kinesthetic materials and this CAP, and note that the first page under the CAP cover includes directions for its use. If you previously identified each participant's learning style, you can anticipate who will want to use the CAP as a resource. If you were unable to administer a learning-style instrument, assume that only about 13–20 percent of the participants will prefer a CAP over the tactual and kinesthetic resources. Or, if you want to be "safe," make some extra copies. Also, make extra copies of the Team Learning in the CAP, because many peer-oriented adults who may not want to work with the entire CAP *will* enjoy mastering objectives with their colleagues.

Step 15: Develop a Brief Evaluation of Participants' Reactions to the CAP

Keep it short, but ask the people who opted to try the CAP how they liked it and what you could do to improve it. You will be surprised at the range of emotions that emerge. Some will love, and others will hate this instructional resource. But that is precisely why different resources must be provided if most people are to profit from inservice designed for large groups.

Step 16: Keep a Record of Who Uses the CAP

Design an easy-to-use record-keeping form to keep you aware of which participants request the CAP and their comments. This will enable you to plan for the correct number of CAP copies the next time you design one for this group of inservice participants.

Step 17: Implement the First Inservice CAP

Introduce the first CAP you design at the next inservice session for which you are responsible. Be prepared to guide and assist participants in its usage. Don't forget the inservice reminders made in previous chapters. For example, post directions for using each of the resources on adjacent wall areas close to where they will be used, *in addition* to including them in the resources themselves.

Special Guidelines for Perfecting a CAP

The previous section includes basic tenets for developing a CAP. These next points are extra hints for developing especially good CAPs.

- Although it is not incorrect to state repeatedly, "You will be able to . . ." (when itemizing the objectives), doing so makes reading the objectives repetitious and often provokes criticism. To avoid this, you can use such a statement just once, as an introduction to the objectives. For example, you might say: By the time you have completed this CAP, you should be able to demonstrate each of the following:

  1. List two (2) types of brain cells and describe how each functions.
  2. Label the sections of the brain that are involved in the memory process (Raupers, 1995).

- Any time you use a numeral in the objectives or Activity and Reporting Alternatives, spell the entire number word and then, in parentheses, write its numeral. This strategy is used to accentuate the required number in its analytic (word) form and global (picture) form to prevent participants from overlooking exactly what they need to do. For example: Organize and demonstrate at least four (4) low-impact movements (Tendy, 1998).
- Use complete, grammatically correct sentences. Do not capitalize words that should not be capitalized, and do capitalize those that should be capitalized.
- Be certain that each objective begins with a verb.
- Use the phrase *at least* before writing a numeral that requires a specific number of responses. This will entice highly motivated individuals to do more than they really are required to do. For example, "List at least four (4) pieces of computer hardware in this room. Can you think of a fifth (5th)?" (Flanary, 1997).
- Be certain that the objective does not become an activity. The objectives state what the participants need to learn. The Activity Alternative enables the participants to show what they have learned by using the information to create an original product. Activities require that the participants *make* something, such as a map, a poem, a song, a puzzle, or a Floor Game.

Example of an objective   Identify at least five (5) nontraditional careers for women.

Example of an Activity Alternative related directly to the objective   Develop a humorous poem describing at least five (5) nontraditional careers for women.

- Have the participants share their completed Activity Alternatives with between one and three colleagues—never the entire group. Thus, reporting should occur in pairs (2), threes (3), or to the teacher, but only rarely by four (4) or more simultaneously.
- Underline each of the major parts of the CAP. For example, where they are listed, underline: Resource Alternatives.
- Check your CAP to see that you have each of the following:

  1. Both an analytic and a global title
  2. Clearly stated objectives that require no further explanations

3. A new page for each objective and its related Activity and Reporting Alternatives
4. Multisensory resources for the Resource Alternatives, e.g., audiovisual, tactual/visual, and kinesthetic/visual
5. "At least" statements to encourage highly motivated participants to respond to more than the minimum requirements
6. Numbers written with both symbols and words
7. Related Activity and Reporting Alternatives for each objective
8. Choices
9. A Team Learning to introduce each difficult objective and a Circle of Knowledge to reinforce what was taught in each Team Learning
10. Three (3) different types of questions in each Team Learning—factual, higher level cognitive, and creative
11. Two other small-group techniques, such as brainstorming, simulation, case study, or role playing
12. An assessment directly related to the objectives
13. Pictures, illustrations, graphics, and/or cartoons directly related to the CAP content
14. Easy-to-read type
15. No spelling or grammar errors
16. An evaluation

Sample CAP

This CAP on "Understanding Memory: How to Plant a FORGET-ME-NOT!" (Figures 8-5 through 8-24) was designed by staff-developer Patricia M. Raupers (1997).

FIGURE 8-5   Sample CAP Cover

Understanding Memory: How to Plant a FORGET-ME-NOT!

Name: _____

Colleagues: _____

Inservice Date: _____

Evaluation/Comments:

FIGURE 8-6 CAP Global Introduction, Objectives, and Directions

Of all the mind's capabilities, memory is definitely the most remarkable. We all recall thousands of events, images, and thoughts, but, until recently, little was known about the *process* of developing memory. During the past three decades, learning-style research has shown that matching strong preferences with responsive environments, resources, and strategies enables people to process and retain new and difficult information. Now, recent developments in the cognitive sciences are helping us to understand some of the very basic mechanisms concerned with how people remember.

As teachers, we can now begin to transfer this new information into applications that will help our students remember more of what they—and we—believe is important.

By the time you complete this Contract Activity package (CAP), you should have mastered at least nine (9) of its ten (10) objectives.

1. List the two (2) types of BRAIN CELLS and describe how each FUNCTIONS.
2. Label the sections of the brain involved in the memory process.
3. Describe the role of the HIPPOCAMPUS in the developing of memories.
4. Explain how EMOTION influences memory.
5. Compare and contrast SENSORY memory, SHORT-TERM memory, and LONG-TERM memory.
6. List the four (4) memory PRINCIPLES.
7. List and describe at least six (6) INTERNAL memory strategies.
8. List and describe at least five (5) EXTERNAL memory strategies.
9. Create a personal PLAN that you will use to help you maximize your students' memory.
10. Outline how you will EVALUATE whether your plan has been successful.

FIGURE 8-7 Directions for Using This CAP

This CAP allows you to complete the objectives for this inservice YOUR way! Use any of the resources itemized in the Resource Alternatives to gather the required information. When you have the answer to an objective, complete the Activity Alternative of your choice. Work toward accuracy rather than a finished product. After you have completed an Activity Alternative (AA), share it with others as suggested by its related Reporting Alternative (RA).

Complete any nine (9) objectives and one AA and RA for each objective. Also complete the Team Learning and Circle of Knowledge in the CAP. Choose the person(s) with whom you'd like to work. If you prefer, do these small-group activities independently.

If you know all the information cited in the objectives, take the test at the end of the CAP without using the RAs. If you are willing to go through the Resources, take the test at the end of the CAP after you have shared your AAs. GOOD LUCK!

When you have finished this CAP, please use its COVER to write your reactions to it. Thank you for trying this resource!

FIGURE 8-8   Illustration for Cover and Other Pages

FIGURE 8-9   Objective 1 and Related Activity and Reporting Alternatives

---

Objective 1: Describe how the two (2) types of brain cells function.

Choose *one* (1) of the following:

Activity Alternatives	*Reporting Alternatives*

1. Create a poster that shows the two types of brain cells and explains how each functions.

1. Display the poster in the area where you are working, and ask two (2) colleagues to check and initial it.

2. Create a graphic illustration on the computer using one (1) of the graphics programs available here at school.

2. Copy the graphic onto a computer disk, and make it available for interested colleagues.

3. Write a descriptive essay that describes how the two (2) types of brain cells function.

3. Give a copy to all interested colleagues.

4. Make a clay model of both types of brain cells, and write a descriptive paragraph on an index card for each model.

4. Present your models to several colleagues, and then show it to the presenter.

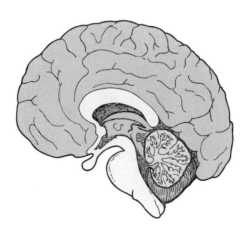

FIGURE 8-10 Sample Objective 2 and Related Activity and Reporting Alternatives

---

Objective 2: Label the sections of the brain involved in the memory process.

Choose *one* (1) of the following:

Activity Alternatives	*Reporting Alternatives*
1. Fill in the names of the sections on the diagram provided.	**1.** Present your work to the presenter.
2. Make a transparency of the diagram provided and fill in all of the names.	**2.** Show the transparency to three (3) colleagues.
3. Using the diagram provided, create a puzzle that shows the placement and names of the brain sections involved in the memory process.	**3.** Ask three (3) colleagues to complete the puzzle.
4. Create a graphic representation using a computer graphics program of the sections of the brain involved in the memory process. Make sure each section is labeled.	**4.** Make the disk available to your supervisor.

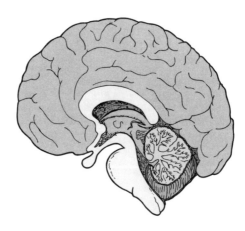

FIGURE 8-11   Objective 3 and Related Activity and Reporting Alternatives

---

Objective 3: Describe the role of the hippocampus in the making of memories.

Choose *one* (1) of the following:

Activity Alternatives	*Reporting Alternatives*
1. Write a scenario in which a memory is being formed and reaches the point in the process where it comes to the hippocampus.	**1.** Present the scenario to three (3) colleagues.
2. Write a paragraph describing how the hippocampus operates in the memory process.	**2.** Ask three (3) colleagues to read and react to your paragraph.
3. Create an attribute wheel using the hippocampus as the subject of the wheel.	**3.** Make copies for the presenter.
4. A patient, E. W., has suffered a stroke, and his hippocampus is not functioning. Prepare a prognosis report on this patient dealing with his ability to develop memories.	**4.** Present your work to the principal.

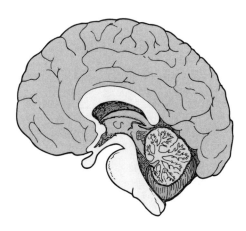

FIGURE 8-12 Objective 4 and Related Activity and Reporting Alternatives

---

Objective 4: Explain how emotion influences memory.

Choose *one* (1) of the following:

Activity Alternatives

Reporting Alternatives

1. Write a short story in which the main character experiences an emotional event that forms a strong memory. Describe what is occurring in his or her brain as the memory is formed.

2. Describe three highly memorable events from your past and analyze why they are still vivid memories. Use a diary format.

3. Create a poster that compares two memories being formed— one a theory from math class, the other the events of a first date with a "very special someone."

4. Make a tape of a "news report" explaining the discovery and explanation of the currently held theory of how emotions influence memory.

1. Make copies of the story for the supervisor in charge of inservice.

2. Present your work to the principal.

3. Display the poster in the hall outside your room or office.

4. Play the tape for two (2) of your colleagues. Submit a copy of the inservice coordinator.

FIGURE 8-13 Objective 5 and Related Activity and Reporting Alternative

---

Objective 5: Compare and contrast sensory memory, short-term memory, and long-term memory.

Choose *one* (1) of the following:

Activity Alternatives	*Reporting Alternatives*
1. Make a set of Task Cards that require the user to differentiate among the characteristics of each memory system.	**1.** Ask four (4) friends to use the Task Cards.
2. Using the "One and All" chart provided, place any characteristics that are shared by all three memory systems in the center area and unique characteristics under each individual title.	**2.** Make copies for three (3) members of the inservice group working on this CAP.
3. Write an essay analyzing sensory memory, short-term memory, and long-term memory for ways in which they are similar and different.	**3.** Submit the essay to the supervisor in charge of this inservice.
4. Write a short story in which the three main characters are the three memory systems.	**4.** Submit the story to a journal.

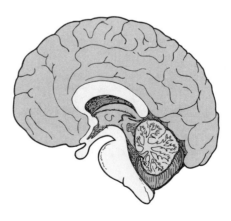

FIGURE 8-14   Objective 6 and Related Activity and Reporting Alternatives

---

Objective 6: List the four (4) memory principles.

Choose *one* (1) of the following:

Activity Alternatives	*Reporting Alternatives*

1. Write an outline in standard outline form, using the term "Memory Principles" as the main idea and the four (4) principles as the subordinate ideas.

1. Give a copy of the outline to two (2) colleagues using the CAP in this inservice session.

2. Create a web using the term "Memory Principles" as the center of the web, with the four (4) principles as the spokes.

2. Mount the web in the area where the participants are using tactual resources.

3. Make a set of Task Cards that fit together the principles and their explanations.

3. Ask two (2) colleagues to match the cards to see if your information is correct. If it is, they should initial the back of one of the cards.

4. Create a colorful poster in either outline or web format that lists the four memory principles. Create a visual representation for each.

4. Display the poster near where the participants are using kinesthetic Floor Games.

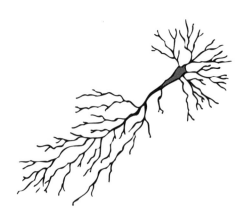

FIGURE 8-15   Objective 7 and Related Activity and Reporting Alternatives

---

Objective 7: List and describe six internal memory strategies.

Choose *one* (1) of the following:

Activity Alternatives

1. Create a crossword puzzle that uses the six (6) internal memory strategies. Write a description of each strategy and attach it to the puzzle.

2. Make a Flip Chute with a set of flip cards that list the six (6) internal memory strategies and their descriptions.

3. Develop a poster that lists and describes six (6) internal memory strategies and their descriptions.

4. Write the diary entry of a student attempting to improve his or her memory by applying the six (6) internal memory strategies.

Reporting Alternatives

1. Give the puzzle to two (2) colleagues to try.

2. Challenge at least three (3) colleagues to use the Flip Chute.

3. Display the poster in the inservice facility.

4. Submit the diary entry to the inservice coordinator.

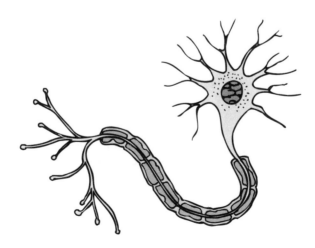

FIGURE 8-16 Objective 8 and Related Activity and Reporting Alternatives

---

Objective 8: List and describe the five external memory strategies.

Choose *one* (1) of the following:

Activity Alternatives	*Reporting Alternatives*
1. Design a set of Task Cards that fit together the strategies and their definitions.	**1.** Ask two (2) colleagues to match the cards and watch them complete the task.
2. Write a short story in which the main character "discovers" each of the five (5) external memory strategies.	**2.** Submit the short story to the inservice coordinator.
3. Prepare an overhead transparency that lists and describes the external memory strategies.	**3.** Show the transparency to the group working on the CAP by mounting it where the Resource Alternatives are.
4. Create a videotaped "infomercial" (the type that might appear on late-night television) for a product that teaches people the five (5) external memory strategies.	**4.** Ask two (2) colleagues to view the tape and write a response to your work.

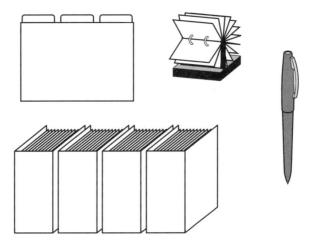

FIGURE 8-17 Objective 9 and Related Activity and Reporting Alternative

---

Objective 9: Create a personal plan that you can use to help your students to maximize memory.

Choose *one* (1) of the following:

Activity Alternatives	*Reporting Alternatives*
1. Prepare your plan in the form of a letter from a famous memory expert who has created a personalized blueprint specifically for you.	**1.** Submit the plan to the inservice coordinator.
2. Write your personalized plan in the form of a prescription.	**2.** Share the plan with two (2) colleagues.
3. Write an essay describing which memory strategies would work best for you.	**3.** Submit the essay to the principal.
4. Prepare a personal plan to maximize your memory and record the plan on a cassette tape.	**4.** Choose at least three (3) colleagues to listen to your tape.

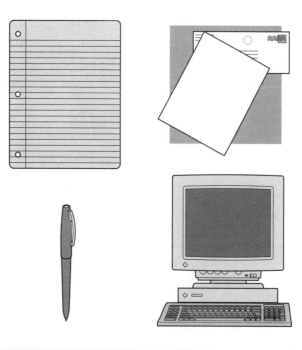

FIGURE 8-18   Objective 10 and Related Activity and Reporting Alternative

---

Objective 10: Explain the interaction among sensory, short-term, and long-term memory.

<table>
<tr><td align="center">Activity Alternatives</td><td align="center">Reporting Alternatives</td></tr>
</table>

1. Graph the interaction among sensory, short-term, and long-term memory. Label it.

2. Write about the interaction among sensory, short-term, and long-term memory for an educational journal.

3. Photograph the interactions among sensory and short- and long-term memory.

4. Have your students document with their returned test papers, stories, or tape-recorded comments the relationships among sensory and short- and long-term memory.

1. Present the graph to your principal.

2. Send the mini-article to the journal.

3. Submit the photographic essay to the local newspaper.

4. Share the students' exhibit with the PTA.

FIGURE 8-19 Diagram of the Interaction among Sensory, Short-Term, and Long-Term Memory

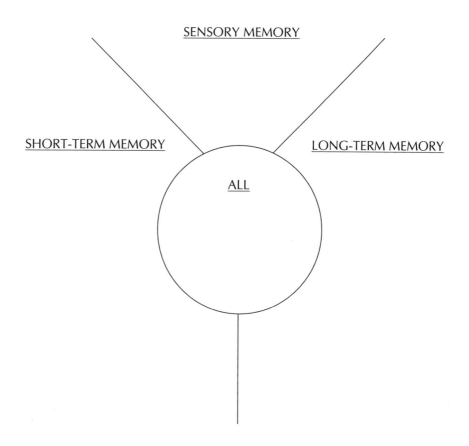

FIGURE 8-20 Sample Team Learning

Team Learning

Group Members:

1. _____   **3.** _____

2. _____   **4.** _____

Recorder: _____

Directions: Read the following excerpt from "Glimpses of the Mind"
(*Time,* July 17, 1995), and answer the questions that follow.

Building a database: We think of learning and memory as somehow separate
functions; in fact, they're not. Both are processes by which we acquire and
store new data in a way that makes them retrievable later on. The storage
takes place, says the current theory, as a pattern of connections among
neurons, the nerve cells that serve as the brain's basic building blocks. When
information—the image of a new acquaintance's face, for example—enters
the brain, it arrives in the form of electric impulses streaming from the retina,
up the optic nerve and into the cerebral cortex, the so-called gray matter that
houses the brain's higher functions.

The impulses die away within milliseconds, but their passage reinforces
the particular set of connections between this particular set of neurons,
giving them the ability to re-create the image. The more often the pattern
is reinforced by repeated sightings of the person, by the effort to remember
him or by connection with some other mental trigger ("This person is
attractive"; . . . or "This man looks unpleasant; I need to avoid him") the more
likely the pattern, or image, will not go into short-term memory, lasting weeks
or months, but into permanent, long-term memory. And from there, barring
brain injury, disease or old age, it can be re-created by inducing the neurons
to send up electric impulses in the old, by now familiar pattern.

That's the simple version. In fact, almost every memory is made of many
different patterns of neuronal connections, some for sound, some for sights,
some for smells or textures—tens of thousands of neurons firing off minute
electric impulses simultaneously. The combination of all these patterns,
says Larry Squire, a professor of psychiatry at the University of California in
San Diego, "gives you a complete perception. The persistence of the firing
patterns over time gives you the transformation from perceptions to memory
of that object." The fact that many overlapping patterns are stored together
means that a single stimulus can bring on a flood of remembrance.

FIGURE 8-20 *Continued*

Memories of concrete facts and events, which can in principle be retrieved on demand, are coordinated through the hippocampus, a crescent-shaped collection of neurons deep in the core of the brain. Other sorts of memory are handled by other areas. The amygdala, for example, an almond-size knot of nerve cells located close to the brain stem, specializes in memories of fear; the basal ganglia, clumps of gray matter within both cerebral hemispheres, handle habits and physical skills; the cerebellum, at the base of the brain, governs conditioned learning and some reflexes.

Damage to any one of these regions has an effect on the corresponding form of memory. A much studied patient known as HM, for example, lost much of his hippocampus in the course of surgery to relieve severe epilepsy. As a result, he could remember everything that happened to him before the surgery, but he was completely unable to form new memories. He was stuck forever in the 1950s. Yet HM was able to learn new skills, such as drawing while looking in a mirror.

1. Describe how the fact that memories are stored in patterns of neuronal connections influences the way we remember interrelated items.

2. What role does the hippocampus play in the memory process?

3. Devise a plan, using the information from the article, that would increase the probability that you could get students to remember something that you want them to be able to recall.

FIGURE 8-21 Circle of Knowledge

Circle of Knowledge

Circle Members:

1. _____   3. _____

2. _____   4. _____

Recorder: _____

The task: List as many memory strategies (internal and external) as you can. You have two (2) minutes to complete the brainstorming. When you have finished your list, attempt to reach a consensus on which five (5) strategies the members of your group believe to be the most powerful.

_____   _____

_____   _____

_____   _____

_____   _____

_____   _____

_____   _____

_____   _____

_____   _____

Our group's top five (5) memory strategies:

1. _____   4. _____

2. _____   5. _____

3. _____

FIGURE 8-22   Sample Role Playing

Role Playing

Group Members		*Roles*	
1.	_____	1.	_____
2.	_____	2.	_____
3.	_____	3.	_____
4.	_____	4.	_____
5.	_____	5.	_____

Either with your group or alone, write the dialog and act out a skit that illustrates the functions of the following brain systems in the development of a memory:

> Sensory memory
> Short-term memory
> Long-term memory
> The hippocampus

Be certain to include a title for your skit and to make arrangements with the inservice coordinator to present the skit.

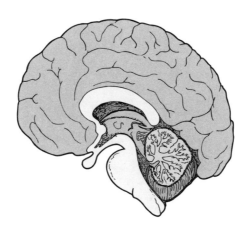

FIGURE 8-23 Sample Alternative Multisensory Resources

Alternative Resources

Books and Magazines

Kelly, E. (1994). *Memory enhancement for educators* (Chapter 3, "What Is Memory?"; Chapter 4, "Memory Principles"). Bloomington, IN: Phi Delta Kappa Educational Foundation.

Kinoshita, J. (1992). Mapping the mind. *New York Times Magazine,* October 18.

Lemonick, M. (1995). Glimpses of the mind. *Time,* July 17.

Sylwester, R. (1995). *A celebration of neurons.* (Chapter 4, "How Our Brain Determines What's Important"; Chapter 5, "How Our Brain Learns, Remembers, and Forgets"). Alexandria, VA: Association Publications.

Video

Memory: Fabric of the mind (1988). Films for the Humanities, Inc. Princeton, New Jersey.

Teacher-Made Resources

Electroboard, Flip Chute, Floor Game, Task Cards, and other tactual and kinesthetic materials found in the Multisensory Instructional Package

Note: Sample CAPs on many topics are available for purchase at reasonable prices from St. John's University's Center for the Study of Learning and Teaching Styles, 8000 Utopia Parkway, Jamaica, NY 11439. Send a stamped, self-addressed envelope when you request a free Resource Brochure.

FIGURE 8-24   Sample Pre- and Posttest

Pre- and Posttest

Answer any nine (9) of the following ten (10) questions. Each correct answer is worth 11.1 (eleven and one-tenth) points.

1. Describe the role of the hippocampus in making memory.
2. Explain why emotional memories are more powerful than other memories.
3. Compare and contrast sensory, short-term, and long-term memory.
4. List two (2) types of brain cells and describe how each functions.
5. On the following drawing of the brain, label the sections involved in the memory process.

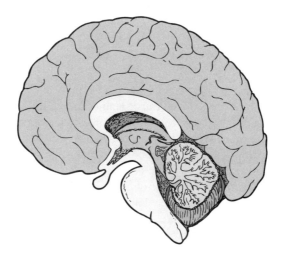

6. List four (4) principles of memory.
7. List and describe six (6) internal memory strategies.
8. List and describe five (5) external memory strategies.
9. Describe a plan that *you* could use to help your students remember things better.
10. Describe (2) strategies that *you* could use to increase your own memory.

9

Designing Programmed Learning Sequences for Inservice

Rita Dunn

Another method for responding to adults' individual learning styles is to program the inservice content so that it can be learned in small, simple steps without the direct instruction of a presenter. Like any other method, programmed instruction is responsive to only certain learning-style characteristics and should not be prescribed for all participants. The special type of programming described in this chapter is called Programmed Learning Sequences (PLS).

Assuming the purpose of inservice is to develop specific information or skills among the participants, that knowledge needs to be translated into objectives to be mastered by all. Therefore, the PLS should be designed to teach to those objectives, and the expectation that each participant will master them should be made clear.

Objectives can range from simple to complex. All participants who use the PLS proceed through the identical sequence but pace themselves and study in the section of the facility that is most responsive to their environmental preferences for sound, light, temperature, and seating.

In the past, programs that were commercially produced had only limited effectiveness because they were solely visual—similar to a workbook—and therefore had only limited appeal to adults who neither enjoyed reading nor retained information easily through the visual modality. People were given programmed information, and, as they completed the various objectives and their related questions, progressed gradually toward mastering the content. Unless they needed and sought assistance, individuals worked through the material by themselves, without much peer or presenter interaction.

There are adults in every inservice session who function better with a colleague or two than they do alone. Therefore, if you are able to test participants with the Productivity Environmental Preference Survey (PEPS) or Building Excellence (BE), identify those individuals who prefer to learn with a colleague, and encourage those persons to work together on a PLS rather then independently.

Learning-Styles Characteristics Responsive to Programmed Learning Sequences (PLS)

Because PLSs originally were designed to be used by people who enjoyed learning alone, participants who used this resource needed to be persistent; they were required to continue working with it until they completed the entire program. If they found the content difficult, they were advised to review each frame until they had mastered the material or to seek assistance from the presenter or colleagues.

In a PLS, everything that should be learned is organized so only one item at a time is presented. Therefore, the sequenced materials in each PLS provide extensive structure. Participants cannot proceed to the next PLS "frame" (page) until the content included on the previous frames has been understood, as demonstrated by correct answers to the questions included in a brief quiz at the bottom of each frame. Adults who are self-structured and prefer to avoid external directions may find the PLS less challenging or irritating.

PLSs are a perfect match with participants who prefer learning (a) alone or in a pair; (b) by reading text supported by illustrations, tactuals, and an accompanying tape recording for those who prefer hearing the material read to them; (c) with structure; and (d) in small steps followed by periodic gamelike reinforcements (see the frames in Figures 9-23 through 9-27). Finally, because a PLS should always have a short story beginning, that part also appeals to global processors.

A PLS can be used in any facility—a classroom, a library, a corridor, or an office. Thus, it accommodates each person's environmental and physiological preferences. For example, it can be taken to a silent area if quiet is desired, or to the center of inservice activity if the participant either prefers sound or wishes to be with a friend or two and can block out noise. The PLS can be taken to a warm section of a facility and used near a sunny window or radiator, or to a cool area. It can be studied at a desk or in an easy chair; in a well-illuminated space or away from bright light. A person may snack—or not—as he or she works, and can use the PLS at any time of day. In addition, participants can take a break whenever mobility is necessary.

Designing a Programmed Learning Sequence

Developing a PLS is not difficult but *does* require organization of the topic into a logical, easy-to-follow sequence. Begin with step 1 and move gradually through each of the remaining steps until you have completed your first PLS. Each consecutive PLS will be easier to design. By the comments they make and the answers they give to the questions at the bottom of the frames, participants provide direct feedback on how to revise and improve your first PLS.

Step 1: Identify the Topic

Begin by identifying the topic, concept, or skill that you want participants to master. A good choice would be a practical strategy or skill that would improve their teaching. It is helpful if staff have read or heard something about the approach and want to know more about it, but that is not always the case. Because all participants are not interested in the same topic or capable of learning at the same time, in the same way, and with the same speed, inform the potential registrants beforehand that this particular inservice program/session will provide alternative resources for learning. A PLS would be one of those resources.

If you are willing to experiment, a PLS permits people to self-pace themselves at the time of day they are best able to concentrate. Thus, some staff may use this resource early in the day; others may use it later. Some will use it to learn *before* their colleagues have been exposed to the material; others will use it to reinforce an idea that the presenter discussed during the inservice session's brief large-group introduction.

Step 2: Create an Analytic and a Global Title

To begin developing the PLS, type the name of the topic, concept, or skill that you want staff to become proficient in as a heading at the top of a blank sheet of paper. Add a subtitle that is humorous or related to the experiences of the people who will participate in the inservice.

Examples of Analytic Titles and Their Humorous Global Counterparts

- Teaching about Memory: How to Plant FORGET-ME-NOTS!
- The Triune Brain Theory: THREE for the Price of One
- Teaching about Insects: Don't BUG Them!
- Teaching about Ecosystems: There's a NICHE for You!
- Teaching about Inference: They Won't Have a CLUE!
- Teaching about Numismatics: A PENNY for Your Thoughts!
- Teaching about Travel: A MOVING Experience!
- Teaching about Aerodynamics: The Wind beneath Their Wings!
- Teaching about Death and Dying: A GRAVE Experience!
- Teaching about Mitosis: BREAKING UP Is Hard to Do!
- Teaching about Learning Styles: No-Fault Insurance
- Teaching Math through Philately: Don't STAMP on Them!

Step 3: Design a Shaped Cover

Design the cover—or the entire PLS—in a shape that represents its content. The shape will appeal to visual/tactual participants. If you can, add humor to appeal further to global participants (see Figures 9-1 and 9-2 on pages 131 and 132).

Inservice Applications

When introducing the PLS, in one or two simple, declarative sentences, explain to all the participants that everyone will be exposed to the identical information and will need to master the identical objectives. However, participants may choose the resources that best match their learning style. Then explain what they will need to do to show they have mastered the content. This information will be stated as inservice objectives and will be included in the PLS, as well as in the other resources you elect to develop, so everyone understands exactly what must be learned.

Step 4: Identify the Objectives

The tactual, kinesthetic, small-group, CAP, and PLS objectives will all be identical for the same topic. Participants will master them differently with style-responsive resources.

Examples of PLS Objectives

For a PLS on Memory (Raupers, 1995):
- List the two (2) types of brain cells and describe how each functions.
- Label the section of the brain involved in the memory process.
- Describe the role of the hippocampus in the development of memories.
- Explain how emotion influences memory.
- Compare and contrast sensory memory, short-term memory, and long-term memory.
- List the four (4) memory principles, and describe six (6) internal memory strategies.
- Create a personal "How-to-Study" plan that you can use to help you maximize your memory.

For a PLS on the Triune Brain Theory (Raupers, 1997):
- List the scientist most responsible for developing the triune brain theory.
- Locate the three (3) separate processing systems in the human brain on a diagram, and sequence them in evolutionary order.
- Name several characteristics of each system.
- Analyze the three (3) systems for their similarities and differences.
- Describe the human behaviors that are controlled by each of the three (3) "brains."

For a PLS on Ecosystems (Scheiring, 1997):
- Describe three (3) ecosystems that exist in your environment.
- Explain the interaction of plants and animals in a specific ecosystem.
- Identify five (5) populations in a single ecosystem.
- If an ecosystem is considered to be a neighborhood, then a habitat is an address in that neighborhood. Name and explain two (2) different habitats in a pond and forest ecosystem.

- Name at least four (4) factors that affect the size of a population.
- Describe how succession occurs.

Step 5: Explain the Directions for Use

List all the necessary directions for using this program effectively. Explain what needs to be done in just a few words, and accompany the directions with a picture or two.

Examples of Directions

- "Answer the questions on the following frames by either filling in the blanks or circling, underlining, or matching answers. Correct answers will be on the back of each frame. You may use an erasable marker or wipe-off crayons to write your answers." **Note:** If the PLS is laminated, add this sentence: "Be certain to go back and wipe off each answer when you have completed this PLS so that someone else can use it."
- "Be certain you begin reading this Programmed Learning Sequence either on or near a large table so you have ample room to use the booklet, its materials, and the tape recorder at the same time—if you wish to use the tape recorder to hear me sing the introductory song on why you ought to take care of your heart! (You would be heart-less *not* to listen to it!) Please rewind the tape when you have completed the entire PLS."

Inservice Application

Because you may realize that certain knowledge or skills are prerequisites to mastering the content objectives in this PLS, after you have moved beyond step 5, leave space on your paper so that you can insert additions as they come to mind.

Step 6: Begin with a Brief Global Opening

Create a global story, fantasy, anecdote, cartoon, poem, or humorous beginning that relates to the participants' interests. The opening need not be more than a paragraph long, but, if you are creative, it *could* weave, story-like, throughout the PLS. Place this global opening just before the teach-and-then-question frames begin.

Examples of Global Openings to the PLS

For a PLS on "Cardiovascular Assessment: Have a Heart" (O'Hare, 1997):

Part of me feels like a warm river flowing calmly downstream. Up, down, through areas with—and without—oxygen. I feel swishing and surges of this wonderful thing called "blood" that keeps me alive. I feel sudden impulses—like electrical surges that rejuvenate me every 60 to 80 times per minute. I can remain alive with the right care and maintenance, but I am likely to stop dead in my tracks when I am not cared for properly. There is so much that I am responsible for that, occasionally, even I get tired. Please read this PLS and find out how to take care of me. I am your heart, and we need each other desperately.

For a PLS on "The Triune Brain Theory: Three for the Price of One" (Raupers, 1997):

Noelle is having a stony relationship with her new boyfriend. It has not been smooth sailing because of their frequent arguments and her parents' disapproval of this young man. Previous boyfriends had been perceived as friends, and her parents had always liked them. Those relationships had been comfortable. Noelle, however, is very attracted to Dan; the first time she met him her heart fluttered just as they describe in romance novels. Despite that attraction, they have little in common and argue often.

Noelle feels that she is being torn between two forces—her heart and her head. Her heart perceives the situation on an emotional level with love songs and poetry; her head recognizes that she and Dan have major differences and admits that her parents aren't all wrong. Sometimes she feels trapped and she has to fight a third force—one that seems to want her to just run away from it all.

Have you ever felt that you were being torn between your heart and your head? In actuality, you were torn between separate processing systems in your brain! The ancients believed that emotions were housed in the heart, but we now know that our emotions are generated and controlled by our brains. Scientists believe that each brain has three systems, and that each system perceives and reacts to the world in different ways. The theory that explains this phenomenon is called the *triune brain theory*. Please explore this theory with me in this Programmed Learning Sequence (PLS).

For a PLS on "Ecosystems: There's a Niche for You" (Schiering, 1997):

Janet and Tom were walking through the forest when suddenly, Janet's foot slipped out from under her. Sitting on the forest floor as Tom looked at her foot, she wondered what she had fallen on—or over. Tom saw what it was. It appeared to be only some moss on a rock.

Janet thought her ankle might swell, so she asked Tom to get some cool water from the clear brook a few yards away. When Tom got the water, he noticed a few fish swimming lazily near the shore line. The pebbly brook bottom with a few strands of seaweed seemed to be a home in which the fish darted around. Tom returned to Janet and wrapped a cool, water-soaked scarf around her ankle.

It was a beautiful day and everything seemed to be perfectly in place. The trees amidst a rocky, often moss-covered forest floor were extraordinary. The fish in the brook, the flowering plants all around, the birds in the trees, and the blue sky overhead made the scene lovely. Even the rabbits, squirrels, and chipmunks seemed to be running around happily among the insect-inhabited berry bushes. Everything "fit" into its own niche in the forest ecosystem.

Step 7: Identify the Specific Content

Describe the specific content that needs to be included in this PLS. What needs to be included is the material to teach to the objectives you established. Teach to those objectives directly and clearly in small segments. A segment is small enough if it fits onto one or two frames without crowding. A "frame" is the space you have on each shaped page that should be cut to reflect the topic of this PLS. Leave room for (a) an illustration or two and (b) one or more questions related to what you have taught on that frame.

Step 8: Develop Questions and Possible Answers or Fill-Ins

At the bottom of the frame, ask one or more questions about whatever was taught on that frame. Turn the frame over and write the answer(s) to the question(s) on the top of the back side. Illustrate the answer. If you can, add a teaser or joke for humor. However, the humor must be directly related to the topic. *Be certain the answers do not have to be read upside down when the participant turns the frame over!*

This type of programming presents material in a highly structured sequence. Each part of the sequence is printed on a frame, and each frame builds on the one immediately preceding it. Each frame ends with an item that requires an answer—either in completion, matching, or multiple-choice format. Prior to the introduction of each subsequent frame, the answer is accompanied by an explanation and a humorous comment or cartoon. Additional comprehension is developed when the incorrect answers also are accompanied by explanations.

Inservice Application

Vary the way participants need to respond to the questions on the frames. Their concentration remains alert when different types of responses are required—for example, "*circle* the correct answer"; "*match* the correct answers to each question by connecting them with lines"; "*pick up* the Velcro heart and place the correct heart onto the phrase that correctly describes it"; "*write* the correct answers"; "*fill in* the missing letters."

Step 9: Outline a Plan

Outline how you plan to teach the topic. Use short, simple sentences, if possible. Most people have two different vocabularies—one for speaking, the other for writing. When you begin to outline your program, pretend you are speaking to the participants who may have the most trouble learning this material. Despite their professional status, use simple words and sentences. Then write exactly the words that you would use if you were actually talking to one of those adults. In other words, use your speaking vocabulary instead of your professional writing vocabulary to develop the PLS.

Step 10: Create Separate Frames

Divide the sentences in your outline into frames. Frames are equivalent to pages, and each frame includes only a brief section of the topic to teach part of the idea, unit, skill, or information of that PLS. After listing the sentences that teach the information, ask a question that relates to that material. Participants' answers will reveal their developing understanding of the subject.

Inservice Application

Think small! Most people who begin to write programs cover too much in one frame. Keep each frame simple, and include only a brief part of the total amount of knowledge that should be included in this PLS.

Pose fairly easy to answer questions in the first two or three frames to: (a) build participants' self confidence, (b) demonstrate to them that they can learn independently with this particular resource, and (c) provide them with successful experiences in at least their first five or six PLS frames.

Step 11: Design an Appropriate Shape

Cut five- by-eight-inch (or larger) index or oaktag cards into an outline of a shape related to the concept of this curriculum unit. Make a pattern for the cover, and cut out as many shaped frames as are needed to teach everything you want the participants to learn (see Figures 9-1 and 9-2 on pages 131 and 132).

Step 12: Proofread the Text Carefully

Reread what you wrote, and refine what will be printed on each index card frame before you actually transfer the teaching material from your papers to the card frames.

Step 13: Check the Sequence of Frames and Personalize Each Frame

Review the sequence you developed to be certain it is logical and does not teach too much on each frame. Add the answers to the questions you posed on the front of each frame to the back of it. After you place the answers on the back of the frame, "talk" to the users. If possible, add a humorous or "corny" comment, joke, or remark to relax them (see Figures 9-7 and 9-11 on pages 137 and 141).

Step 14: Edit

Check the spelling, grammar, and punctuation of each frame.

Step 15: Review Vocabulary

Review the vocabulary you included to be certain that it (1) includes all the important and/or unique words needed for this PLS and (2) is understandable by the least motivated person in the inservice. Avoid colloquialisms that are acceptable in conversation but are less than professional in written form. Remember to use good oral language as opposed to good written language.

Step 16: Reread the Frames

Reread the entire series to be certain that (a) each frame leads to the next one, (b) you did not forget to teach something that you consider important, and (c) the participants can really learn from what you have written.

Step 17: Add Illustrations

When you are satisfied with the content, sequence, and questions on the frames, add colorful illustrations to clarify the main point on each index card. If you do not wish to draw, use magazine cutouts or gift-wrapping paper to supplement the most important sections of the text graphically; or ask a colleague to do the illustrating for you. If colleagues do the illustrations, give them credit as illustrated in Figure 9-2. Remember that the illustrations and humor should relate directly to the PLS content.

Step 18: Audiotape Each Frame for Auditory Learners

When you are satisfied with the text of the PLS, read the written material on each frame onto a cassette so auditory participants can listen to the frames being read to them as they simultaneously read along.

Step 19: Field-Test

Ask three or four of your colleagues to try the PLS, one at a time. Watch these adults as they use the material, and see whether any errors, omissions, or areas of difficulty exist. Correct anything that requires improvement *before* you introduce it at the next inservice session.

Step 20: Revise and Refine

If necessary, revise the PLS based on your observations of your colleagues' usage.

Step 21: Paginate

Paginate the front and back of each frame—for example, "Frame 1."

Step 22: Duplicate

Duplicate the PLS so you have enough copies for approximately 20 percent of the number of people you anticipate signing up for the inservice program in which you will introduce this method. We suggest 20 percent with the assumption that some will choose to listen to the presenter, some will opt for the kinesthetic Floor Game, others will prefer to explore the content with a Team Learning they can share with some colleagues, and some will want the tactual materials.

Step 23: Laminate

Laminate each of the index cards that make up the original PLS—not the copies—or cover them with clear Contac paper. Over time, participants' use will cause the index cards to deteriorate unless they are protected by a covering. Laminated programs last for years and can be cleaned with warm water and detergent. They can be written on with grease pencils or water-soluble felt-tip pens and then erased for use by another participant at another session.

Step 24: Add Tactual Reinforcement Frames

Periodically (every seven or eight frames), add miniature tactual activities (Pic-A-Holes, Task Cards, or Electroboards) for reinforcement of the most important information covered to that point in the PLS (see Figures 9-12 through 9-17 on pages 142 through 147 and 9-22 through 9-26 on pages 152 through 156. These cards would all have been inserted into a single, laminated envelope and attached with Velcro or glue on a single PLS frame.) The PLS, as designed through step 23, will respond only to adults who learn through either visual or auditory perceptual strengths. The tactual reinforcements provide participants who need to learn by touching and handling with a method appropriate for them. The tactual reinforcement also will increase the number of participants who can learn successfully with the PLS.

Step 25: Field-Test Again

Ask additional colleagues to use the PLS. Again, observe their reactions. This time, assess how much they learned as they worked through the PLS.

Step 26: Add Covers

When you are satisfied that all the "bugs" have been eliminated, add an oaktag or cardboard front and back cover to the PLS in the shape related to the topic.

Step 27: Add Global and Analytic Titles

Place the title and global subtitle of the program onto the front cover. Bind the covers to the index card frames. You may use notebook rings, colored yarn, or any other substance that will permit easy turning of the index cards. Again, be certain the answers to each frame, which appear on the back of the previous frame, are easily readable and are not upside down. When the program has been completed, introduce it to those participants whose learning styles would be complemented by it at the next inservice you plan

Sample Programmed Learning Sequence

A sample PLS follows (Figures 9-1 through 9-35).

FIGURE 9-1   Cover (Raupers, 1997)

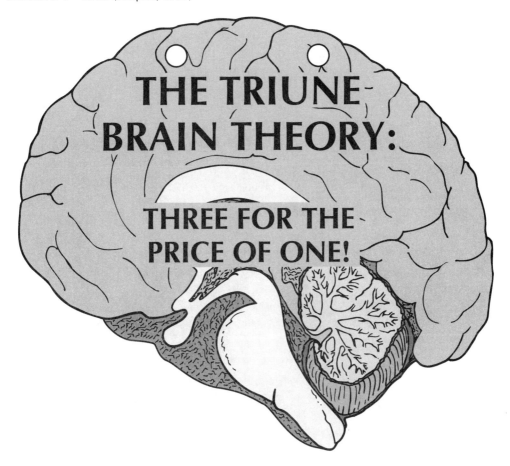

FIGURE 9-2   Inside Cover with Author and Illustrator (Raupers, 1997)

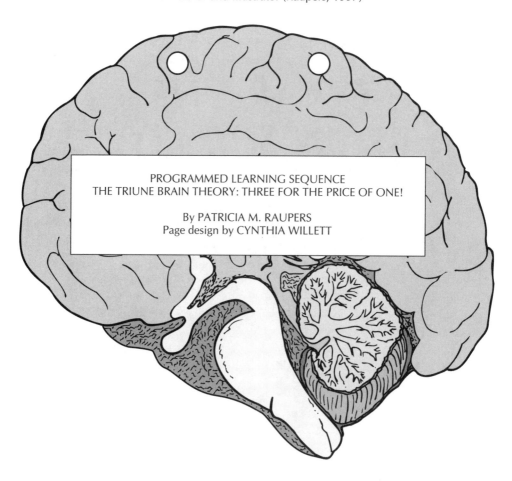

PROGRAMMED LEARNING SEQUENCE
THE TRIUNE BRAIN THEORY: THREE FOR THE PRICE OF ONE!

By PATRICIA M. RAUPERS
Page design by CYNTHIA WILLETT

FIGURE 9-3   Directions for Usage

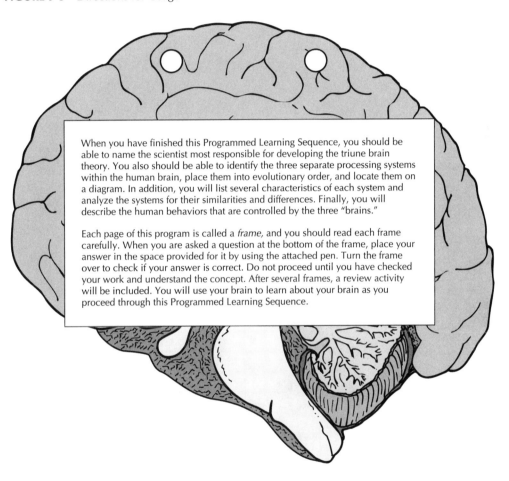

When you have finished this Programmed Learning Sequence, you should be able to name the scientist most responsible for developing the triune brain theory. You also should be able to identify the three separate processing systems within the human brain, place them into evolutionary order, and locate them on a diagram. In addition, you will list several characteristics of each system and analyze the systems for their similarities and differences. Finally, you will describe the human behaviors that are controlled by the three "brains."

Each page of this program is called a *frame,* and you should read each frame carefully. When you are asked a question at the bottom of the frame, place your answer in the space provided for it by using the attached pen. Turn the frame over to check if your answer is correct. Do not proceed until you have checked your work and understand the concept. After several frames, a review activity will be included. You will use your brain to learn about your brain as you proceed through this Programmed Learning Sequence.

FIGURE 9-4 Global Introduction

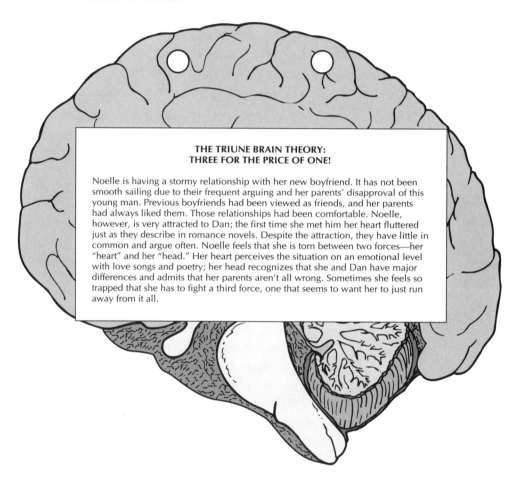

THE TRIUNE BRAIN THEORY:
THREE FOR THE PRICE OF ONE!

Noelle is having a stormy relationship with her new boyfriend. It has not been smooth sailing due to their frequent arguing and her parents' disapproval of this young man. Previous boyfriends had been viewed as friends, and her parents had always liked them. Those relationships had been comfortable. Noelle, however, is very attracted to Dan; the first time she met him her heart fluttered just as they describe in romance novels. Despite the attraction, they have little in common and argue often. Noelle feels that she is torn between two forces—her "heart" and her "head." Her heart perceives the situation on an emotional level with love songs and poetry; her head recognizes that she and Dan have major differences and admits that her parents aren't all wrong. Sometimes she feels so trapped that she has to fight a third force, one that seems to want her to just run away from it all.

FIGURE 9-5   Link between Global Introduction and Teaching Frames

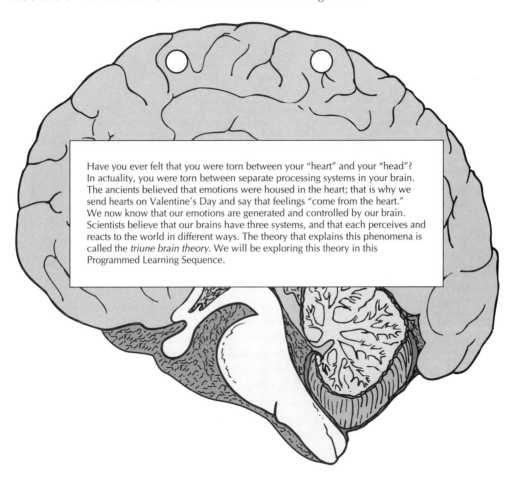

Have you ever felt that you were torn between your "heart" and your "head"? In actuality, you were torn between separate processing systems in your brain. The ancients believed that emotions were housed in the heart; that is why we send hearts on Valentine's Day and say that feelings "come from the heart." We now know that our emotions are generated and controlled by our brain. Scientists believe that our brains have three systems, and that each perceives and reacts to the world in different ways. The theory that explains this phenomena is called the *triune brain theory*. We will be exploring this theory in this Programmed Learning Sequence.

FIGURE 9-6 First Teaching Frame

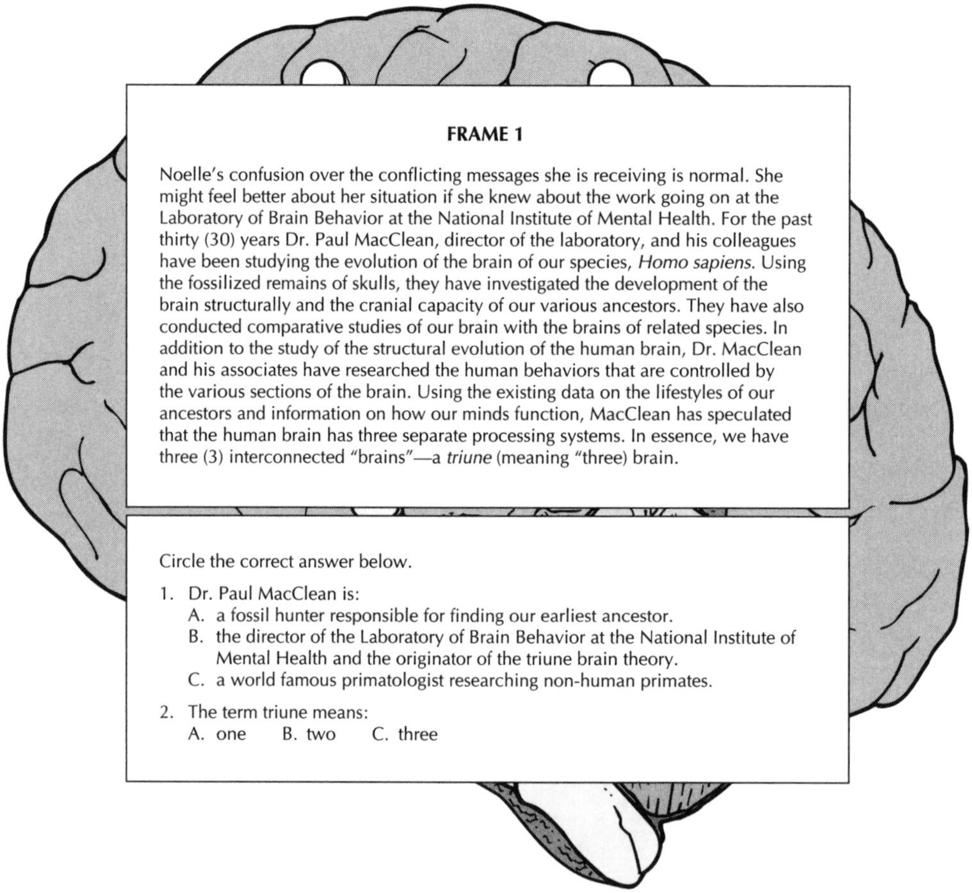

FRAME 1

Noelle's confusion over the conflicting messages she is receiving is normal. She might feel better about her situation if she knew about the work going on at the Laboratory of Brain Behavior at the National Institute of Mental Health. For the past thirty (30) years Dr. Paul MacClean, director of the laboratory, and his colleagues have been studying the evolution of the brain of our species, *Homo sapiens*. Using the fossilized remains of skulls, they have investigated the development of the brain structurally and the cranial capacity of our various ancestors. They have also conducted comparative studies of our brain with the brains of related species. In addition to the study of the structural evolution of the human brain, Dr. MacClean and his associates have researched the human behaviors that are controlled by the various sections of the brain. Using the existing data on the lifestyles of our ancestors and information on how our minds function, MacClean has speculated that the human brain has three separate processing systems. In essence, we have three (3) interconnected "brains"—a *triune* (meaning "three") brain.

Circle the correct answer below.

1. Dr. Paul MacClean is:
   A. a fossil hunter responsible for finding our earliest ancestor.
   B. the director of the Laboratory of Brain Behavior at the National Institute of Mental Health and the originator of the triune brain theory.
   C. a world famous primatologist researching non-human primates.

2. The term triune means:
   A. one   B. two   C. three

FIGURE 9-7   Back of First Teaching Frame

Answers:

1. B. Dr. Paul MacClean is director of the Laboratory of Brain Behavior at the National Institute of Mental Health and the originator of the triune brain theory.

2. C. The term *triune* refers to the number three.

Can you imagine spending thirty (30) years of your life in pursuit of knowledge that will help us better understand ourselves and our world? Many dedicated professionals do just that. Maybe there is a topic out there that intrigues you and that you might pursue!

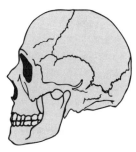
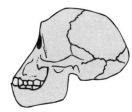
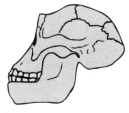

FIGURE 9-8 Second Teaching Frame

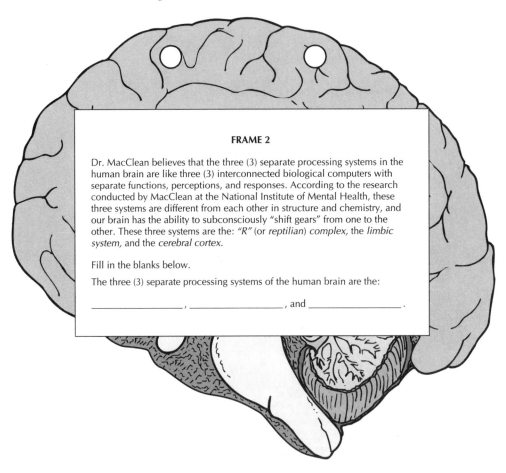

FRAME 2

Dr. MacClean believes that the three (3) separate processing systems in the human brain are like three (3) interconnected biological computers with separate functions, perceptions, and responses. According to the research conducted by MacClean at the National Institute of Mental Health, these three systems are different from each other in structure and chemistry, and our brain has the ability to subconsciously "shift gears" from one to the other. These three systems are the: *"R" (or reptilian) complex,* the *limbic system,* and the *cerebral cortex.*

Fill in the blanks below.

The three (3) separate processing systems of the human brain are the:

_____ , _____ , and _____ .

FIGURE 9-9   Back of Second Teaching Frame

Answers:

The three (3) separate processing systems of the human brain are the *"R" (or reptilian) complex,* the *limbic system,* and the *cerebral cortex.*

You relied on one of the sections of your brain more than the others to answer that last question. In the next frames, you will learn more about your spectacular brain and which section helped you with that last question.

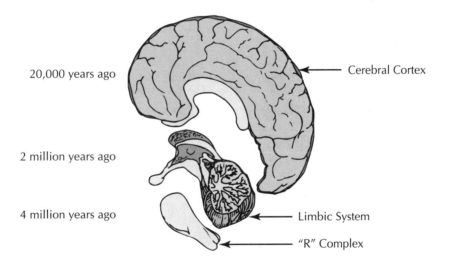

FIGURE 9-10 Third Teaching Frame

FRAME 3

What Noelle was experiencing when she shifted from wanting to flee from her relationship with Dan, to strong emotions and feelings of love for Dan, to analytic thought about the many differences between them that leads to arguments, was the functioning of her triune brain. The flight reaction was the response of her most primitive "brain," the *"R" complex*. The "R" complex was the first formation to develop through evolution. Feelings of love and conflict were the responses of her *limbic system,* the second to evolve in our ancestors. When Noelle was engaged in conscious thought of an analytic nature, she was responding to the world by using her *cerebral cortex*. The cerebral cortex is the most complex "brain" and was the last to evolve, according to Dr. MacClean's theory.

Fill in the blanks below.

According to the triune brain theory, the human brain's three (3) formations or systems evolved in the following order:

The first to evolve was the _____.

The second to evolve was the _____.

The third to evolve was the _____.

Hint: On the diagrams in this PLS, the cerebral cortex will appear in BLUE (for "cool thought"), the limbic system in RED (for "heart"), and the "R" complex in GREEN (for the color of many reptiles).

FIGURE 9-11 Back of Third Teaching Frame

Answers:

According to the triune brain theory, the human brain's three (3) formations or systems evolved in the following order:

> The first to evolve was the *"R" complex.*
> The second to evolve was the *limbic system.*
> The third to evolve was the *cerebral cortex.*

Now don't get "primitive" and run away from this Programmed Learning Sequence just yet; there's still much to learn about your very complex brain!

FIGURE 9-12   Envelope Housing Tactual Task Cards in PLS

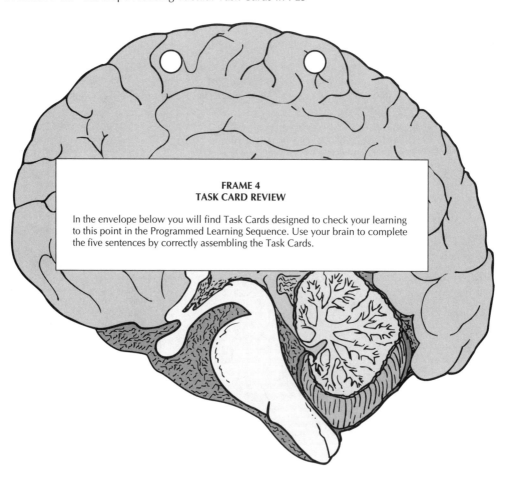

FRAME 4
TASK CARD REVIEW

In the envelope below you will find Task Cards designed to check your learning to this point in the Programmed Learning Sequence. Use your brain to complete the five sentences by correctly assembling the Task Cards.

FIGURE 9-13 Directions for Using Task Cards

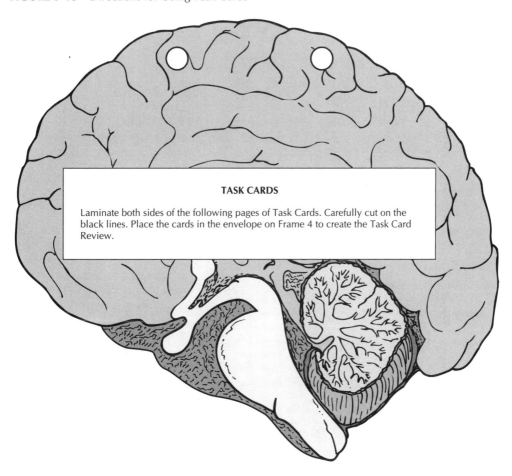

TASK CARDS

Laminate both sides of the following pages of Task Cards. Carefully cut on the black lines. Place the cards in the envelope on Frame 4 to create the Task Card Review.

FIGURE 9-14 Tactual Task Card Set in PLS

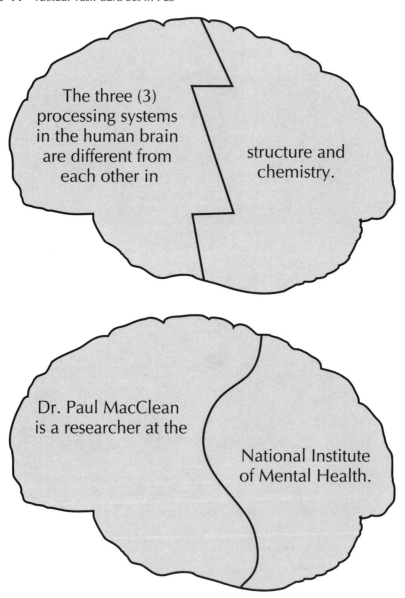

FIGURE 9-15   Tactual Task Cards with Self-Correcting Answers

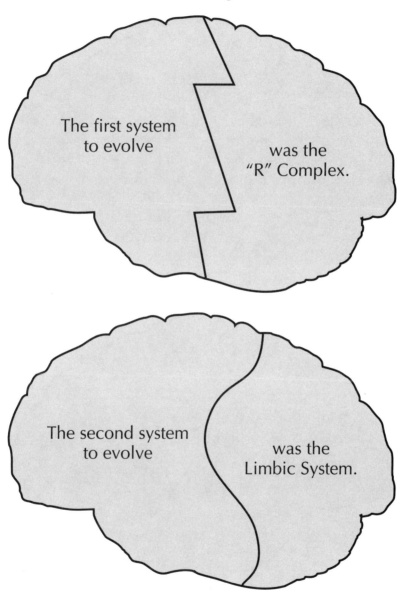

FIGURE 9-16 Tactual Task Card Set in PLS

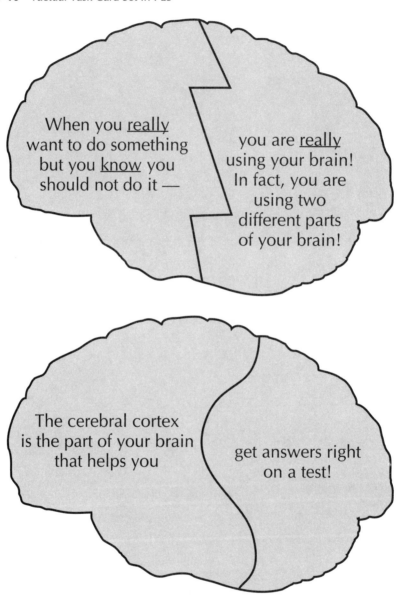

FIGURE 9-17   Tactual Task Cards with Self-Correcting Answers

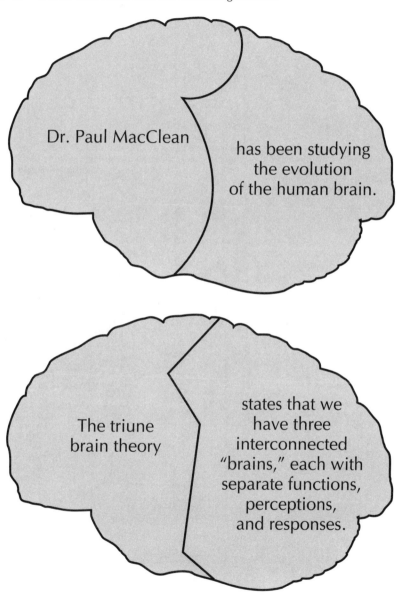

FIGURE 9-18   Fifth Teaching Frame

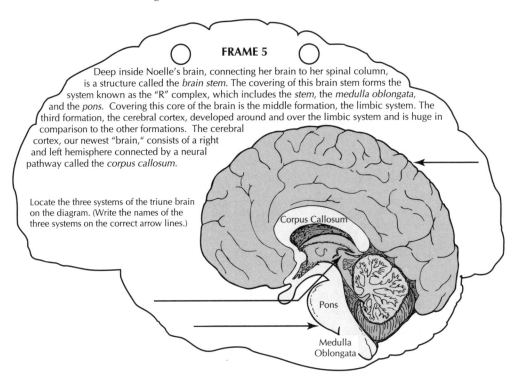

FRAME 5

Deep inside Noelle's brain, connecting her brain to her spinal column, is a structure called the *brain stem*. The covering of this brain stem forms the system known as the "R" complex, which includes the *stem*, the *medulla oblongata*, and the *pons*. Covering this core of the brain is the middle formation, the limbic system. The third formation, the cerebral cortex, developed around and over the limbic system and is huge in comparison to the other formations. The cerebral cortex, our newest "brain," consists of a right and left hemisphere connected by a neural pathway called the *corpus callosum*.

Locate the three systems of the triune brain on the diagram. (Write the names of the three systems on the correct arrow lines.)

Corpus Callosum

Pons

Medulla Oblongata

FIGURE 9-19   Backs of Fifth Teaching Frame

Answers:

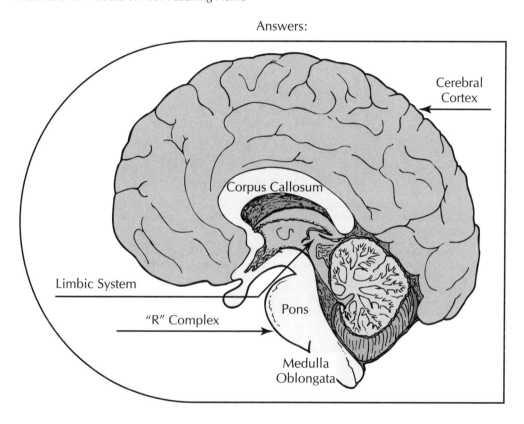

FIGURE 9-20 Sixth Teaching Frame

FRAME 6

Dr. MacClean and his colleagues at the National Institute of Mental Health describe the three (3) processing systems in the following way.

The "R" complex is the least complex; it controls behavior patterns in humans that relate to survival and territoriality. It houses what is left of our instinctive reactions and is believed to be the center of compulsive behaviors. The "R" complex appears to cling to ancient ways and is probably the reason why we like home.

The limbic system is the emotional center of our minds; the raw stuff of emotion is built into the circuitry of this system. It is the center of our feelings. It provides the feelings' base that helps to guard us against a hostile world.

The cerebral cortex is the center of our thought: it needs constant, fresh input because it gets bored easily. The cerebral cortex is enormous in proportion, is divided into two (2) hemispheres, and is our most complex formation. It is the portion of our brain that gets us to take risks. All three (3) perceive the outside world and can react to it.

List two (2) characteristics of the "R" complex:

List two (2) characteristics of the limbic system:

List two (2) characteristics of the cerebral cortex:

FIGURE 9-21   Back of Sixth Teaching Frame

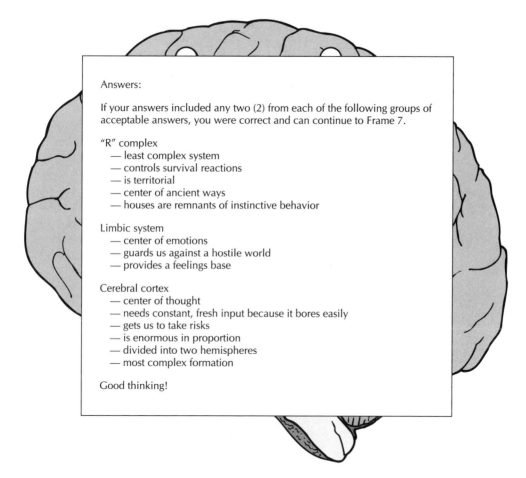

Answers:

If your answers included any two (2) from each of the following groups of acceptable answers, you were correct and can continue to Frame 7.

"R" complex
   — least complex system
   — controls survival reactions
   — is territorial
   — center of ancient ways
   — houses are remnants of instinctive behavior

Limbic system
   — center of emotions
   — guards us against a hostile world
   — provides a feelings base

Cerebral cortex
   — center of thought
   — needs constant, fresh input because it bores easily
   — gets us to take risks
   — is enormous in proportion
   — divided into two hemispheres
   — most complex formation

Good thinking!

FIGURE 9-22   Tactual Pic-A-Hole Reinforcement

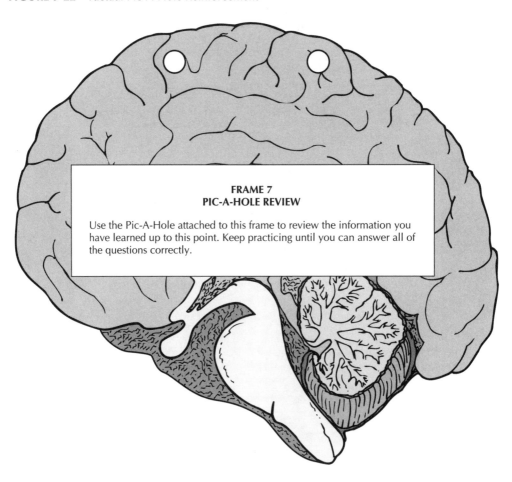

FRAME 7
PIC-A-HOLE REVIEW

Use the Pic-A-Hole attached to this frame to review the information you have learned up to this point. Keep practicing until you can answer all of the questions correctly.

FIGURE 9-23   Tactual Pic-A-Hole Reinforcement Form

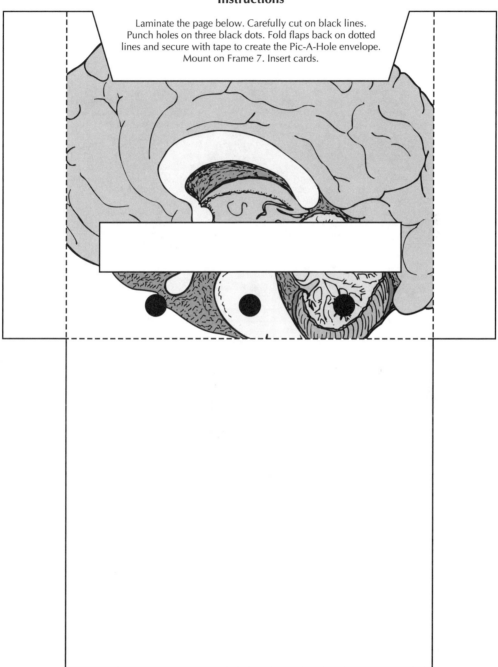

Instructions

Laminate the page below. Carefully cut on black lines.
Punch holes on three black dots. Fold flaps back on dotted
lines and secure with tape to create the Pic-A-Hole envelope.
Mount on Frame 7. Insert cards.

FIGURE 9-24   Sample Pic-A-Hole Self-Correcting Cards

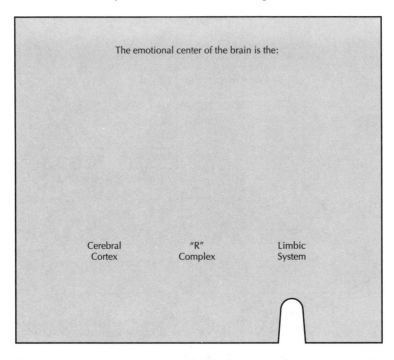

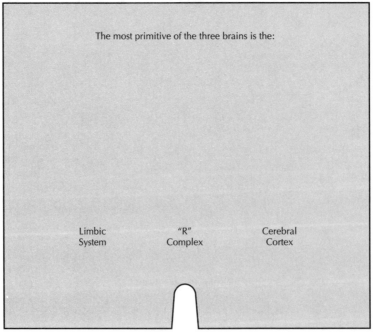

FIGURE 9-25   Additional Sample Pic-A-Hole Self-Correcting Cards

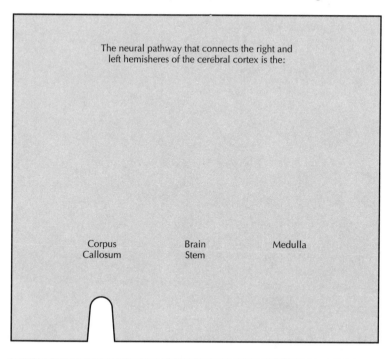

The neural pathway that connects the right and
left hemisheres of the cerebral cortex is the:

Corpus   Brain   Medulla
Callosum   Stem

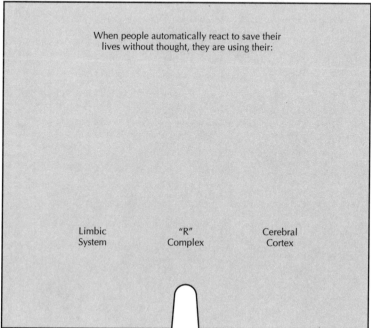

When people automatically react to save their
lives without thought, they are using their:

Limbic   "R"   Cerebral
System   Complex   Cortex

FIGURE 9-26   Additional Pic-A-Hole Self-Correcting Cards

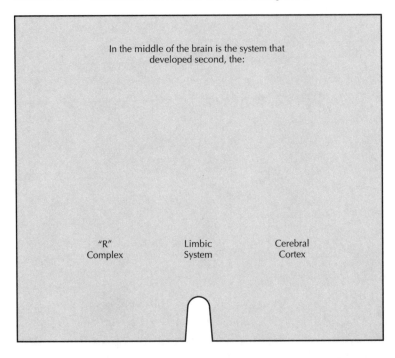

In the middle of the brain is the system that
developed second, the:

"R"
Complex

Limbic
System

Cerebral
Cortex

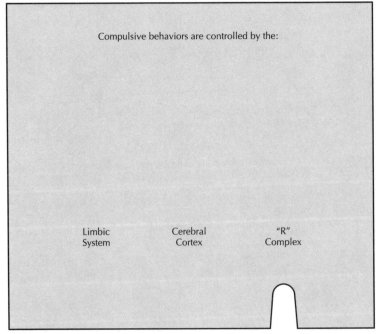

Compulsive behaviors are controlled by the:

Limbic
System

Cerebral
Cortex

"R"
Complex

FIGURE 9-27   Eighth Teaching Frame

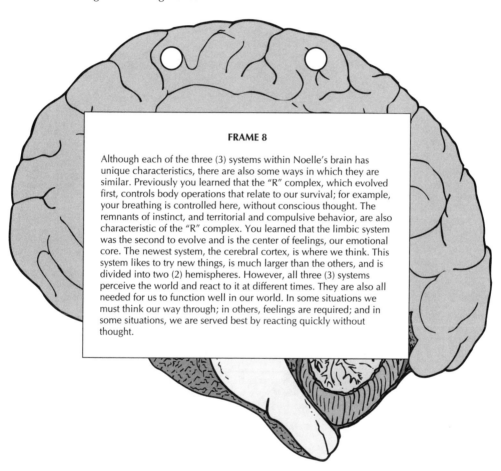

FRAME 8

Although each of the three (3) systems within Noelle's brain has unique characteristics, there are also some ways in which they are similar. Previously you learned that the "R" complex, which evolved first, controls body operations that relate to our survival; for example, your breathing is controlled here, without conscious thought. The remnants of instinct, and territorial and compulsive behavior, are also characteristic of the "R" complex. You learned that the limbic system was the second to evolve and is the center of feelings, our emotional core. The newest system, the cerebral cortex, is where we think. This system likes to try new things, is much larger than the others, and is divided into two (2) hemispheres. However, all three (3) systems perceive the world and react to it at different times. They are also all needed for us to function well in our world. In some situations we must think our way through; in others, feelings are required; and in some situations, we are served best by reacting quickly without thought.

FIGURE 9-28 Self-Testing on PLS Objectives

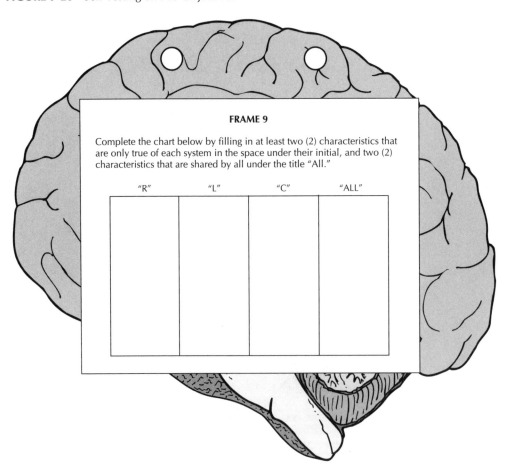

FRAME 9

Complete the chart below by filling in at least two (2) characteristics that are only true of each system in the space under their initial, and two (2) characteristics that are shared by all under the title "All."

"R"	"L"	"C"	"ALL"

FIGURE 9-29   Answers to Self-Testing

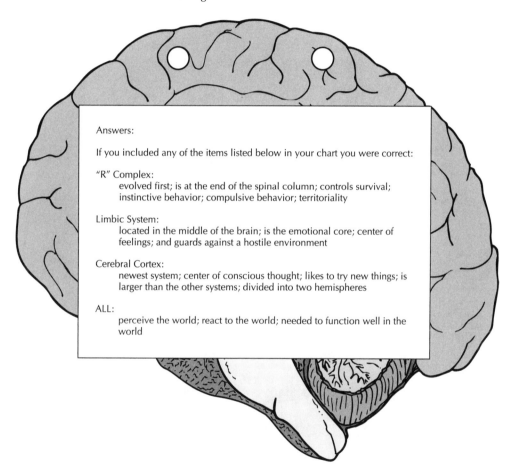

Answers:

If you included any of the items listed below in your chart you were correct:

"R" Complex:
  evolved first; is at the end of the spinal column; controls survival; instinctive behavior; compulsive behavior; territoriality

Limbic System:
  located in the middle of the brain; is the emotional core; center of feelings; and guards against a hostile environment

Cerebral Cortex:
  newest system; center of conscious thought; likes to try new things; is larger than the other systems; divided into two hemispheres

ALL:
  perceive the world; react to the world; needed to function well in the world

FIGURE 9-30 Tenth Teaching Frame

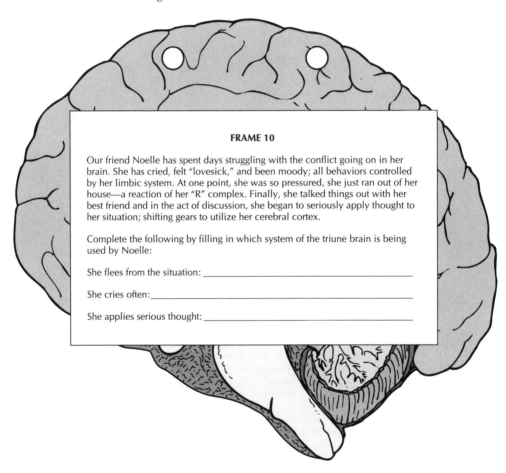

FRAME 10

Our friend Noelle has spent days struggling with the conflict going on in her brain. She has cried, felt "lovesick," and been moody; all behaviors controlled by her limbic system. At one point, she was so pressured, she just ran out of her house—a reaction of her "R" complex. Finally, she talked things out with her best friend and in the act of discussion, she began to seriously apply thought to her situation; shifting gears to utilize her cerebral cortex.

Complete the following by filling in which system of the triune brain is being used by Noelle:

She flees from the situation: _____

She cries often: _____

She applies serious thought: _____

FIGURE 9-31 Answers to Tenth Teaching Frame

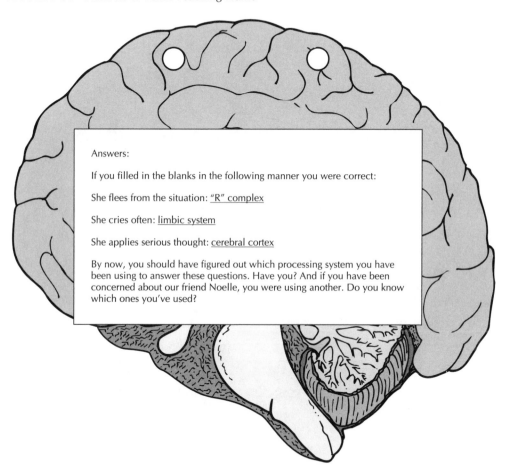

Answers:

If you filled in the blanks in the following manner you were correct:

She flees from the situation: "R" complex

She cries often: limbic system

She applies serious thought: cerebral cortex

By now, you should have figured out which processing system you have been using to answer these questions. Have you? And if you have been concerned about our friend Noelle, you were using another. Do you know which ones you've used?

FIGURE 9-32 Eleventh Teaching Frame

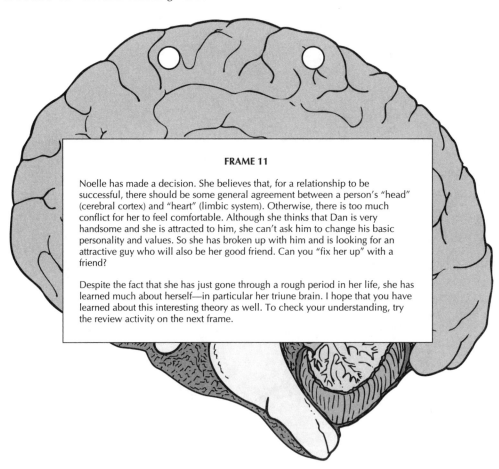

FRAME 11

Noelle has made a decision. She believes that, for a relationship to be successful, there should be some general agreement between a person's "head" (cerebral cortex) and "heart" (limbic system). Otherwise, there is too much conflict for her to feel comfortable. Although she thinks that Dan is very handsome and she is attracted to him, she can't ask him to change his basic personality and values. So she has broken up with him and is looking for an attractive guy who will also be her good friend. Can you "fix her up" with a friend?

Despite the fact that she has just gone through a rough period in her life, she has learned much about herself—in particular her triune brain. I hope that you have learned about this interesting theory as well. To check your understanding, try the review activity on the next frame.

FIGURE 9-33 Review Frame

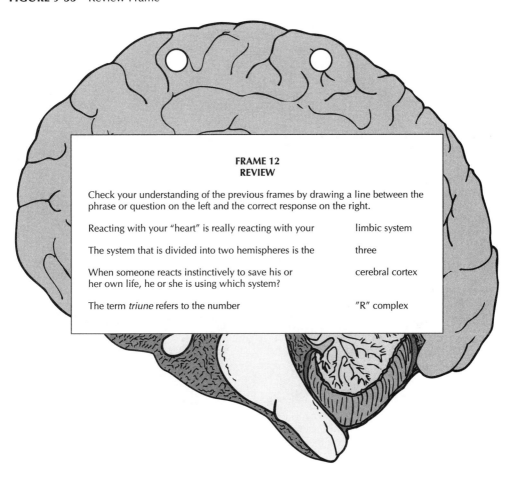

FRAME 12
REVIEW

Check your understanding of the previous frames by drawing a line between the
phrase or question on the left and the correct response on the right.

Reacting with your "heart" is really reacting with your   limbic system

The system that is divided into two hemispheres is the   three

When someone reacts instinctively to save his or   cerebral cortex
her own life, he or she is using which system?

The term *triune* refers to the number   "R" complex

FIGURE 9-34   Answers to Review Frame

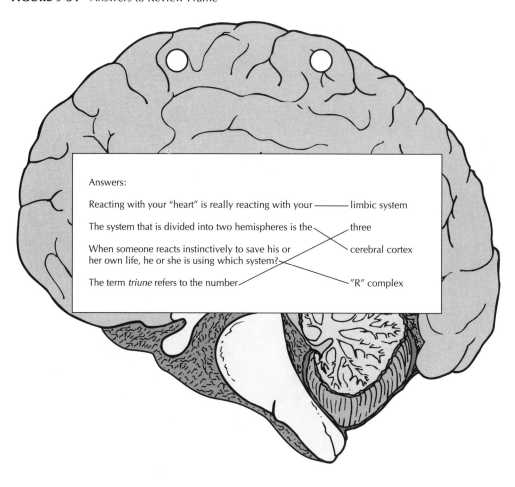

Answers:

Reacting with your "heart" is really reacting with your ——— limbic system

The system that is divided into two hemispheres is the ——— three

When someone reacts instinctively to save his or her own life, he or she is using which system? ——— cerebral cortex

The term *triune* refers to the number ——— "R" complex

FIGURE 9-35 Ending Frame

> **FRAME 13**
> **CONGRATULATIONS!**
>
> Now that you have completed this Programmed Learning Sequence on the Triune Brain Theory, you are ready to take the unit test. You also may wish to use some of the other materials to help review what you have learned.

THE TRIUNE BRAIN

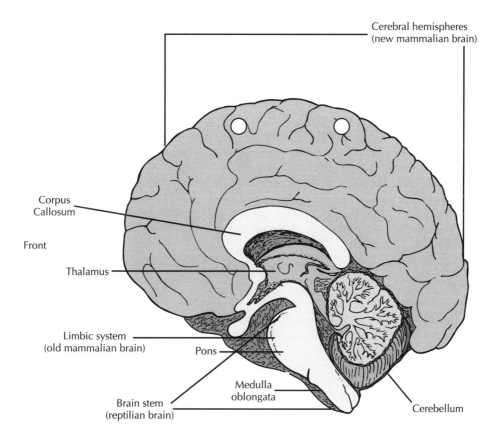

We are not pampering adults when we recommend prescribing a match between their learning-style preferences and the resources they use to learn new and difficult information during inservice. Consider the study conducted in an urban college of allied health sciences at a large New York state university that compared the effects of traditional teaching versus teaching with learning-style instructional resources—the PLS in book format and the PLS on CD Rom (Miller, 1997).

Twenty-three students enrolled in Sonography 1 and 17 students enrolled in Cross-Sectional Anatomy were administered the PEPS (Dunn, Dunn, & Price, 1987) to identify their learning styles. Students alternatively were presented with units of study in PLS book format versus a traditional lecture-supplemented-with-visuals versus a PLS computer format. Considering that the population comprised achieving students in a medical college, wouldn't you anticipate that all would perform equally well, regardless of the instructional approach?

That is *not* what happened! Significant achievement differences emerged between those lessons taught with the PLS and those taught with the conventional presentation—which is how most inservice is delivered. In both classes, achievement *and* attitude scores were statistically higher when the PLS was used. In the Sonography course, achievement was statistically higher with the book PLS (the method described in this chapter) than with the computer PLS!

Interestingly, (a) students who preferred learning with the book PLS required a comparatively more quiet environment than students who preferred working with the computer-version PLS; (b) those who preferred the computer PLS required more quiet and light than students who preferred the book PLS; and (c) an authority figure (the presenter) favored traditional methods more than colleagues did. In addition, the combination of learning independently and using the book PLS approached significance with regard to achievement.

These findings demonstrated that PLSs accommodate individuals' diverse learning styles and, in so doing, become a more effective instructional resource for certain adults than the highly charismatic consultants we often employ to conduct inservice.

Conclusion

Using the PLS will increase the effectiveness of inservice because it responds to the learning styles of adults who require structure and are tactual and/or visual. The tape attached to the PLS may be used to benefit participants who need auditory support but who like to control their exposure by turning the tape on or off.

Notes

The PLSs included in this chapter can be obtained from the following sources:

O'Hare, L. E. (1997) *Cardiovascular assessment: Have a heart!* Jamaica, NY: St. John's University's Center for the Study of Learning and Teaching Styles.

Raupers, M. P. (1995). *Understanding memory: Important things you don't want to forget.* Demaraest, NJ: Northern Valley Schools Curriculum Center.

Raupers, M. P. (1997). *The triune brain theory: Three for the price of one.* Jamaica, NY: St. John's University's Center for the Study of Learning and Teaching Styles.

Scheiring, M. (1997). *Ecosystems: There's a niche for you.* Jamaica, NY: St. John's University's Center for the Study of Learning and Teaching Styles.

10

Learning-Styles Inservice: Managing the Implementation

Rita Dunn

Beginning a learning styles–based inservice program can be either energizing and self-actualizing or exhausting and frustrating. The end result depends on your interest in and commitment to the improvement of inservice and your ability to adapt these guidelines into a practical plan that is relatively easy to implement and is comfortable for you.

There is no specific time or way to begin; implement as gradually as necessary and as quickly as possible. Success depends on combining what we recommend with what makes sense in your professional judgment. The more quickly you introduce learning-style strategies, however, the sooner you will provide quality inservice.

Alternative Stages and Steps

This chapter outlines the stages and steps you can take to revitalize inservice for your organization (see the example in Figure 10-1). Choose what you will do first, second, third, and so forth. Each of the stages should be introduced gradually, over time. But which steps you choose and how long they take to implement depend on your level of comfort, the available resources, administrative support and cooperation, and the learning styles of the participants who attend each program for which you are responsible. No one format is better than another; each merely provides different benefits for different participants (Filipczak, 1995).

Develop a plan that responds to your productivity style and risk-taking tolerance. It is not necessary to implement every stage and step in the plan, and it is wise to proceed slowly so that both you and the participants are comfortable and successful with

FIGURE 10-1   Objectives to Be Mastered during This Session

---

1. Interpret Kim Suh's learning-style strengths.
2. On the basis of Kim's learning style, hypothesize whether, in a traditional classroom, Kim would be perceived as a gifted, highly achieving, average, poorly achieving, or failing student. Explain *why* you decided as you did.
3. Describe the resources through which Kim would be most likely to achieve.
4. Explain whether Kim is global or analytic, and *how* you determined her processing style.
5. Develop a plan outlining how Kim should study new and difficult academic material by using her learning-style strengths.

---

what you initiate. These guidelines are based on what worked well for successful learning-styles inservice leaders in various regions of the United States (Braio, Beasley, Dunn, Quinn, & Buchanan, 1997; Greb, 1997; Klavas, 1993; Klavas, Dunn, Griggs, Gemake, Geisert, & Zenhausern, 1994; Lenehan, Dunn, Ingham, Murray, & Signer, 1994; Raupers, 1996, 1999; Taylor, 1999). They are intended to get you started. You may develop better strategies as you work with these guidelines in your school or district.

Stage 1

Step 1. Identifying participants' learning-style strengths.   The first step toward improving inservice is to identify the learning styles of all the teachers and administrators in the school or district who are likely to take part in any inservice that you plan. Decide whether you will use the Productivity Environmental Preference Survey (PEPS) or Building Excellence (BE) based on the advantages and disadvantages of each described in Chapter 2. Identify the entire professional staff's learning styles at the beginning of the year to make the process efficient. Once you have a database of everyone's style and the resources each will require, you can organize complementary materials or have them prepared quickly—without having to test participants, interpret data, and then begin analyzing required resources under pressure.

If you cannot assess everyone's style, or if some teachers do not participate, identify the styles of those who do. This allows you to provide interested persons with responsive resources and strategies and then move to the next best alternative for those whose styles you have not assessed.

Alternative step 1. When you cannot identify participants' learning-style strengths prior to inservice.   Make an educated guess about the instructional resources that might be most likely to intrigue the inservice participants, based on the information provided in previous chapters. For example, assume that the presenter may attract the relatively few auditory persons in the group. Presenters who are experts in their area may attract authority-oriented adults; those who are teachers who have been successful may attract collegially oriented counterparts. You undoubtedly will need kinesthetic and tactual resources for many of the males and for the highly kinesthetic, highly tactual, or low-auditory females. It also is likely that at least some in the group will enjoy working with other people. For this last group, develop a Team Learning if you are introducing new material. Add a Circle of Knowledge if you are reinforcing something previously introduced (see Chapter 7).

Another way of anticipating the kind of resources you may need for inservice when you have no information concerning the learning styles of the participants is to think of how the same persons behaved in previous sessions. For example, consider developing:

- A Team Learning if, in the past, many participants talked among themselves and fraternized while the presenter was lecturing
- A kinesthetic Floor Game if, in the past, people seemed restless, walked into and out of the presentation, took several breaks, or were relatively nonparticipatory
- Tactual resources if, in past inservice sessions, colleagues seemed to pay attention but afterward evidenced little knowledge of the topic.

If you want your first attempt at learning-style based inservice to be stimulating for the participants, try all three resources. Observe their effectiveness or lack of it, and decide which resources you will try again next time and which you will discard in favor of others—for *these* particular people.

Step 2. Translating participants' learning-style data into practical applications. If you do have data describing the staff's learning styles, process that information with the software package Productivity Disc (Dunn & Ingham, 1990). You then will have two things to share with prospective participants if they want to know about themselves:

1. A complete listing of all the elements that make up each person's learning style
2. A printed prescription for how to capitalize on each individual's strengths.

Alternative step 2. When you cannot provide prescriptions.   If you do not have the participants' data and, therefore, cannot provide them with individual prescriptions for learning new and difficult information, *briefly* address the entire group at the beginning of the inservice session and do the following:

1. Show the clearly stated objectives that each needs to master during that session.
2. Read aloud or paraphrase the objectives as the participants also read them.

3. Describe the various instructional resources they can use to master the objectives while, simultaneously, explaining for whom each resource would be most appropriate. For example, if we were conducting an inservice session on how teachers could use learning-style data to help their students, we would display the following objectives attractively illustrated on a Power-Point-designed transparency (see Figure 10-1 on page 169).

Stage 2

Step 1. Developing a variety of appropriate resources. Design different kinds of resources to teach the exact objectives that you told the participants they would need to master. For example, you might develop a Team Learning for teachers who like to work cooperatively in groups, a Floor Game for kinesthetic teachers who become restless when required to merely sit and listen to a lecture, or an enormous Flip Chute and easy-to-follow directions for tactual teachers who learn through manipulatives. Be certain that you have enough resources for all the people who plan to attend. Some will elect to stay with the presenter. One kinesthetic game can accommodate 8 to 10 adults; one oversized Flip Chute can accommodate 4 or 5 people. Large Task Cards can be used individually, in pairs, or by a group of 3 or 4. Estimate the first time, and gradually you will develop a feel for what is most preferred by the people for whom you are planning inservice.

Step 2. Distributing the resources in different sections of the facility. Mount clearly printed and illustrated directions for using each resource onto a wall adjacent to that resource. Distributing the resources will allow the participants who are willing to use them to move to those areas. Place the presenter in a fourth section of the room so that those who want to hear the information may do so in relative quiet.

Step 3. Allowing choices. Encourage each person to use the resource of his or her choice. Participants need to obtain the information related to the objectives in ways that appeal to them individually. The novelty of the resources will attract their attention and the ease of learning through the "right" (best matched) strategy will help them gain knowledge, acquire new teaching techniques, and hold their interest. At the end of the directions, clearly indicate that if *this* resource doesn't make learning interesting or enjoyable, it probably is not their best choice, and they should move to another section of the room, examine their objectives again, and try to master them with a different resource.

Step 4. Responding to participants' chronobiological differences. Establish inservice classes at two or more different times to complement diverse time-of-day preferences. Permit teachers to sign up for the session of their choice. Take attendance and check on their mastery of the objectives. Thus, participants are given choices and are required to accept responsibility for them.

Stage 3

Step 1. Teaching both globally and analytically.   Experiment with introducing new topics globally and reinforcing the information analytically. Then reverse the sequence the next time you meet with these same people. Explain the difference between the two processing styles so that the participants become aware of their own style and how they react to each session—and why. See Chapter 4 for additional in-service applications.

Step 2. Experimenting with environmental elements.   Try to feel comfortable about introducing at least one or more of the environmental elements of learning style that may be important to many of the participants. Tell them what you are trying to do by labeling different areas of the facility. For example, in one corner, mount a sign indicating "Quiet Corner: No Talking Here Please" but add a humorous illustration or cartoon for global talkers. In that same room or area, if you can add a couch to the traditional chairs, or a pillow to the chairs, add two more signs: "Leisure Lounging" and "Formal Furniture." You might develop these sections in two or more areas of the environment.

Alternative step 2. Solicit participants' aid.   Prior to the inservice meeting, send a note—or start a telephone "chain"—to ask the participants if they could assist by bringing cushions, bean bags, carpet squares, small rugs, summer lawn furniture, a couch, rocking chairs, or easy chairs.

Alternative step 3. "Play" with the lighting.   Try one or more of the following.

- Keep one bank of lights on and the other off. Encourage participants to sit wherever they feel most comfortable.
- Turn the lights off in a single corner of the room to create a softly lit area. Observe differences in behavior and attention spans among the adults in the brightly and softly lit sections.
- Make colored acetates, used for writing on overhead projectors, available for those involved in reading extensively, for example, the peer-oriented persons using a Team Learning or the visual persons using a PLS. Encourage individuals to select a color of their choice—blue, green, lilac, pink, red, or yellow—and to place the acetate on top of each page as they read. Ask them to be aware of any effects that may occur in their ability to attend to, focus on, and absorb the material they are reading.
- Use colored, fireproof Dennison paper, which often is available in greeting card stores, between the light bulb and the glass that covers it in one or more corners of the room to diffuse illumination effects.
- Cover large, bright white surfaces when they are not in use.

Alternative step 4. Address sound preferences.   Individuals vary extensively in their ability to concentrate on difficult cognitive tasks in either quiet or noisy environments. In addition, strongly analytic processors consistently require quiet, whereas strongly global processors think lucidly with sound—music, background talking, ocean waves crashing, or birds singing. Experiment with providing softly played Baroque music for participants who like it, but do have a quiet area for those who cannot tolerate sound while concentrating.

- Establish the quiet area away from traffic and activity patterns. You also might provide earmuffs or earphones that are not connected for those who require quiet.
- Separate the quiet area from the sections with sound or activities. Further subdivide them to provide self-contained spaces that block out the view of the inservice activities for those who may be distracted by visual overstimulation. You will find that more women require quiet than men. Place those who function best with sound near the hub of involvement, for example, close to the kinesthetic Floor Games.

Alternative step 5. Address seating and mobility preferences

- Cover a small section of the quiet area with a donated rug or carpet for participants who are distracted by sound or who might like to sit on the floor.
- Place a few desks and chairs in sections you can call dens, alcoves, "offices," and private spaces where the activity-oriented participants' movements will not disturb their colleagues.
- Scout around and find varied sizes of desks and chairs suitable to adults' diverse heights, weights, and girths.
- Allow participants to stand or lounge while they are concentrating, as long as they do not distract anyone. Do not require that they sit while they complete tasks. Sitting-while-concentrating is extremely difficult for those who require informal seating, mobility, or kinesthetic learning.
- Allow kinesthetic participants—those who rarely sit still for more than a few moments—to walk back and forth quietly in a specifically designated aisle or section on the periphery of the room while they read, complete assignments, or think. Actually create a "Concentration Walkway" replete with a sign designating it as such, and explain its purpose (in one or two sentences only). Most people will not take advantage of your concern for their comfort and achievement, but, although few may use the Walkway in the beginning, within time, a couple may try it and appreciate the opportunity. When teachers see some of their colleagues walking while reading or walking while thinking, they often begin to appreciate the implications of these behaviors for some of their students.

Alternative step 6: Address temperature preferences. Inservice participants who seem either devoid of energy or consistently withdrawn may be revealing their temperature discomfort, among other possibilities. Try to:

- Provide curtains that block out the sun during the warmest hours.
- Provide a fan. Those who feel comfortable with its effects will choose to sit near it.

- Provide water and paper cups for those who need a drink or to wet their faces or wrists.
- Encourage participants to wear layers of clothes that can be removed or kept on—depending on the temperature and their individual reactions to its variations.
- Remember that the warmest part of most rooms—with the exception of areas near a window in warm weather or a radiator in winter—is the center.

Stage 4. Addressing Structure and Persistence Preferences

Step 1. Structuring assignments.   Structure assignments related to the objectives you announced to permit those who need variety, mobility, breaks, and peer interaction to (a) move about the room as they study, (b) go from one activity to another, or (c) migrate purposefully from one section to the next.

Step 2. Designing the inservice area.   Divide the room or facility into subdivisions to permit participants who require a few moments of relaxation between serious work segments to have short concentration periods in which they can change location. Some people, particularly strongly global processors, need to be involved in short-term, instructionally oriented activities that differ from the main tasks in which they have been engaging. These persons often need space away from those who persist in working in one location to avoid distracting them.

Step 3. Designing instructional resources.   Instructional resources should allow global processors to concentrate on many relatively short exercises rather than on a few comparatively long assignments. Thus, different sections of the physical environment are needed for globals to work on objectives, take breaks, be involved in something else for a short interval, and then return to completing their tasks. Those same subdivisions of the room will permit analytics to continue working without interruption. Analytics need to complete their tasks and then relax and engage in alternative activities.

Step 4. Addressing sociological preferences.   Individuals learn best in a variety of patterns—alone, in pairs, in small groups of peers, in a team, with an authoritative or collegial presenter, and/or in a variety of arrangements—sometimes alone, sometimes in cooperative groups, and sometimes highly competitively. Sociological preferences are related to age, achievement level, and experience. Some people consistently learn in one way, others in two or more, others in varied patterns. Still others have no preference at all. However, more global than analytic adults seem to be people-oriented (Dunn, Cavanaugh, Eberle, & Zenhausern, 1982).

- Regardless of the assignment, encourage participants to use the resources they prefer either alone, in pairs, in small groups, or with the presenter, as each chooses. However, all are responsible for mastering the same objectives.

Stage 5

Step 1. Developing style-responsive instructional resources

- Develop a couple of generic kinesthetic Floor Games for which you only have to change the content on the cards for each new inservice session. Introducing Floor Games or Stand-up Board Games is likely to motivate activity-oriented persons (including athletes and athletic coaches) to concentrate on what you would like them to learn.
- Develop a few tactual resources that appeal to *you*. Having these available will win over some of the people who rarely concentrated in previous inservice sessions.
- Develop a Team Learning as an introduction to difficult objectives. If you follow the directions in Chapter 7 *closely,* many participants will enjoy learning in that way.
- If you are planning a follow-up session, develop a Circle of Knowledge to reinforce what was introduced through the Team Learning. Once some of the participants become familiar with these small-group strategies, you will appreciate the relative ease of conducting inservice. After you have tried these resources, consider the following resources.
- Develop a mini–Contract Activity Package (CAP) for an entire inservice series or a single session (see Chapter 8). When using the CAP, participants may choose (a) any of the instructional resources you have introduced previously, because CAPs allow choices of materials; (b) to work in any sociological pattern they select; and (c) to work anywhere in the environment they prefer. By the time you have introduced this step, staff will be crediting you with providing excellent inservice and will become very interested in how you are inservicing them.
- Sometime later, develop a mini–Programmed Learning Sequence (PLS) for a single inservice session (see Chapter 9). When using the PLS, participants will (a) be introduced to the content globally, (b) receive periodic reinforcement tactually and visually, (c) work anywhere in the environment they prefer, and (d) learn either independently or in a pair. By the time you have introduced this step, staff will be clamoring for more inservice than administration will be willing to provide.
- Should you choose to conduct inservice for parents, paraeducators, or substitutes, use the steps described previously. Should you need to conduct inservice for participants who require a great deal of variety and many choices, design a Multisensory Instructional Package (MIP)—a packaged set of all the resources you already have developed. Merely add a brief tape or set of illustrated directions that describe how to use each of the resources, so that participants can work completely on their own and not merely have to sit and listen. From that point on, your professional life will be a delight; all you will need to do is plan the objectives and make them known to the participants, arrange for a learning style–responsive environment, make the MIP and a presenter available, and observe and evaluate what occurs.

Evaluate Your Learning-Style Inservice

Compare the attitudes of participants toward inservice before and after you introduce the learning-style strategies. Question participants about their reactions to what you provided environmentally and instructionally. Compare the number of times they leave early before and after the introduction of learning style–responsive sessions. Submit a questionnaire to staff who attended and ask whether they want you to return to conventional inservice!

Compare the implementation efforts of participants before and after the learning-style inservice. Question staff about the extent to which they used the content related to the objectives. See whether some of them have adopted for use with their students one or more of the learning-style strategies or resources that you introduced. If you have access to their lesson plans, see whether teachers are using the skills or knowledge they gained during the inservice.

Sample Inservice Agenda

The following is a sample inservice agenda you might like to use as a guide.

Inservice Program: The Elements of the Dunn and Dunn Learning-Style Model*

1. General Session: Overview of Learning Styles (8:30–9:30 A.M.)

   BREAK

2. Session 1: Learn the Elements through YOUR Perceptual Strengths (9:45–11:00 A.M.)
   - Auditory Preference Group   (Room 202)
   - Visual Preference Group   (Room 203)
   - Tactual Preference Group   (Room 204)
   - Kinesthetic Preference Group   (Room 205)

   BREAK

3. General Session: Elements of Learning Style: Questions and Answers (11:15 A.M.–12:00 noon)
4. Session 11: Application Activity: Using the Elements to Address Learning-Style Preferences in Your Classroom (1:00–2:15 P.M.)
   (Choose a site based on your sociological preferences)
   - Learning with an Authority   (Room 205)

5. General Sessions: Sharing of Plans; Questions and Answers (2:15–3:00 P.M.)

*This sample inservice program was designed by Patricia M. Raupers.

Conclusion

Until you provide inservice through participants' learning styles, you cannot imagine how well these procedures will be received by teachers. Please make the effort; the results will be well worth your energy and time!

REFERENCES

Alberg, J., Cook, L., Fiore, T., Friend, M., Sano, S., et al. (1992). *Educational approaches and options for integrating students with disabilities: A decision tool.* Triangle Park, NC: Research Triangle Institute.

Andrews, R. H. (1990, July–September). The development of a learning styles program in a low socioeconomic, underachieving North Carolina elementary school. *Journal of Reading, Writing, and Learning Disabilities International, 6*(3), 307–314. New York: Hemisphere.

Andrews, R. H. (1991). Insights into education: An elementary principal's perspective. In *Hands on approaches to learning styles: Practical approaches to successful schooling* (pp. 50–52). New Wilmington, PA: Association for the Advancement of International Education.

Atkinson, S. L. (1988). A longitudinal study: The effect of similar and non-similar student / teacher learning styles on academic achievement in fourth- and fifth-grade mathematics. Doctoral dissertation, Temple University. *Dissertation Abstracts International, 49*(09)A, 2569.

Avise, M. J. (1982). The relationship between learning styles and grades of Dexfield junior and senior high school students in Redfield, Iowa. Doctoral dissertation, Drake University. *Dissertation Abstracts International 43*,(09)A, 2953.

Bailey, G. K. (1988). Examination of the relationship between hemispheric preferences and environmental characteristics of learning styles in college students. Doctoral dissertation, University of Southern Mississippi. *Dissertation Abstracts International, 49*(08)A, 2151.

Bauer, E. (1991). The relationships between and among learning styles perceptual preferences, instructional strategies, mathematics achievement, and attitude toward mathematics of learning disabled and emotionally handicapped students in a suburban junior high school. Doctoral dissertation, St. John's University. *Dissertation Abstracts International, 53*(06), 1378.

Baugh, I. W. (1994). Hypermedia as a performance based assessment tool. *The Computing Teacher, 21*(6), 14–17. Eugene, OR: International Society for Technology Education.

Beaty, S. A. (1986). The effect of inservice training on the ability of teachers to observe learning styles of students. Doctoral dissertation, Oregon State University. *Dissertation Abstracts International, 47*, 1998A.

Billings, D., & Cobb, K. (1992). Effects of learning style preference, attitude, and GPA on learner achievement using computer-assisted interactive videodisc instruction. *Journal of Computer-Based Instruction, 19*(1), 12–16.

Bonham, L. A. (1987). Theoretical and practical differences and similarities among selected cognitive and learning styles of adults: An analysis of the literature (Vols. I, II). Doctoral dissertation, University of Georgia. *Dissertation Abstracts International, 48*, 2530A.

Botroff, S. M. (1993). The impact of group versus individualized classroom activities on the levels of achievement of students in a tenth-grade religious course (group activities, individualized activities, learning style). Doctoral dissertation, La Sierra University. *Dissertation Abstracts International* on disk, January 1993–December 1, 1993.

Boyle, R., & Dunn, R. (in press). Teaching law students through individual learning styles. *Albany Law Review, 62*(1). Albany, NY: Albany Law School.

Braio, A. (1995). Effects of incrementally introducing learning-style strategies on special education and low-achieving general education intermediate students' structural analysis and attitude test scores. Doctoral dissertation, St. John's University.

Braio, A., Beasley, M. T., Dunn, R., Quinn, P., & Buchanan, K. (1997). Effects of incremental implementation of learning-styles strategies among urban low-achievers' structural analysis and attitude test scores. *Journal of Educational Research, 91*(1), 15–25. Washington, DC: Heldref Publications.

Branton, P. (1966). *The comfort of easy chairs.* FIRA Technical Report 22. Hertfordshire, England: Furniture Industry Research Association.

Brennan, P. K. (1984). An analysis of the relationships among hemispheric preference and analytic/global cognitive style, two elements of learning style, method of instruction, gender, and mathematics achievement of tenth-grade geometry students. Doctoral dissertation, St. John's University. *Dissertation Abstracts International, 45*, 3271A.

Brodhead, M. R., & Price, G. E. (1993). The learning styles of artistically talented adolescents in Canada. In R. M. Milgram, R. Dunn, & G. E. Price (Eds.), *Teaching and counseling gifted and talented adolescents: An international learning style perspective* (Chapter 12, pp. 186–195). New York: Praeger.

Brown, M. D. (1991). The relationship between traditional instructional methods, Contract Activity Packages, and mathematics achievement of fourth-grade gifted students. Doctoral dissertation, University of Southern Mississippi. *Dissertation Abstracts International, 52*(6)A, 1999A–2000A.

Brunner, C. E., & Majewski, W. S. (1990, October). Mildly handicapped students can succeed with learning styles. *Educational Leadership, 48*(2), 21–23. Alexandria, VA: Association for Supervision and Curriculum Development.

Brunner, R., & Hill, D. (1992, April). Using learning styles research in coaching. *Journal of Physical Education, Recreation and Dance, 63*(4), 26–61.

Bruno, J. (1988). An experimental investigation of the relationships between and among hemispheric processing, learning style preferences, instructional strategies, academic achievement, and attitudes of developmental mathematics students in an urban technical college. Doctoral dissertation, St. John's University. *Dissertation Abstracts International, 48*(5), 1066A.

Buell, B. G., & Buell, N. A. (1987). Perceptual modality preference as a variable in the effectiveness of continuing education for professionals. Doctoral dissertation, University of Southern California. *Dissertation Abstracts International, 48*, 283A.

The Buffalo Experience Videotape. (1993). New York: State Education Department and the Buffalo City Schools. Available from St. John's University's Center for the Study of Learning and Teaching Styles, 8000 Utopia Parkway, Jamaica, NY 11439.

Buhler, J. (1990). A study of the relationship between selected learning styles and achievement of kindergarten language arts objectives in a local school district. Doctoral dissertation, University of North Texas. *Dissertation Abstracts International, 51*(09)A, 2978.

Burke, K. (1997). Responding to participants' learning style during staff development. *The Clearing House*, 70(6), 299–301.

Burke, K. (1998). Relationship(s) between the consistency scores of an analytic versus a global learning-style assessment for middle-school students (grades 6–8). Doctoral dissertation, St. John's University.

Burke, R., & McCaffery, C. (1988, Fall). A system to relieve the high anxiety of the global adult learner. *Oregon Elementary Principals' Journal, 50*(1), 26–27.

Burkman, T. A. (1994). An analysis of the relationships among achievement, attitude, and the sociological element of individual learning style of students in an interactive television course. Dissertation submitted to the faculty at Western Michigan University, Kalamazoo.

Callan, R. J. (1995). Early-morning challenge: The potential effects of chronobiology on taking the Scholastic Aptitude Test. *The Clearing House, 68*(3), 174–176.

Callan, R. J. (1996, February). Learning styles in the high school: A novel approach. *NASSP Bulletin, 80*(577), 66–72.

Callan, R. (1997). Giving students the right time of day. *Educational Leadership, 55*(4), 85–87.

Callan, R. (1998). An experimental investigation of the relationship(s) among the time-of-day preferences of students taking a comprehensive test in sequential mathematics and achievement in the test. Doctoral dissertation, St. John's University.

Calvano, E. J. (1985). The influence of student learning styles on the mathematics achievement of middle school students. Doctoral dissertation, East Texas State University. *Dissertation Abstracts International, 46*, 10A.

Canfield, A. A., & Lafferty, J. C. (1976). *Learning Style Inventory*. Detroit: Humanica Media.

Carbo, M. (1980). An analysis of the relationship between the modality preferences of kindergartners and selected reading treatments as they affect the learning of a basic sight-word vocabulary. Doctoral dissertation, St. John's University. *Dissertation Abstracts International, 41*, 1389A.

Carbo, M. (1984). *Reading Style Inventory*. New York: St. John's University.

Carbo, M., Dunn, R., & Dunn K. (1986). *Teaching students to read through their individual learning styles*. Englewood Cliffs, NJ: Prentice-Hall.

Carbo, M., & Hodges, H. (1987). Learning style strategies can help students at risk. *Teaching Exceptional Children, 20*(4), 55–58.

Carns, A. W., & Carns, M. R. (1991, May). Teaching study skills, cognitive strategies, and metacognitive skills through self-diagnosed learning styles. *The School Counselor, 38*, 341–346.

Carruthers, S. A., & Young, A. L. (1979). Do time preferences affect achievement or discipline? *Learning Styles Network Newsletter, 1*(2), 1. New York: St. John's University and the National Association of Secondary School Principals.

Cavanaugh, D. (1981, November). Student learning styles: A diagnostic/prescriptive approach to instruction. *Kappan, 64*(3), 202–203.

Cholakis, M. M. (1986). An experimental investigation of the relationships between and among sociological preferences, vocabulary instruction and achievement, and the attitudes of New York urban, seventh and eighth grade underachievers. Doctoral dissertation, St. John's University. *Dissertation Abstracts International, 47*, 4046A.

Clark, W. R. (1993). Effects of computerized instruction on the improvement and transfer of math skills for low and below average performing sophomore students, considering gender, ethnicity, and learning-style preferences. Doctoral dissertation, University of LaVerne. *Dissertation Abstracts International 55*(01), 21.

Clark-Thayer, S. (1987). The relationship of the knowledge of student-perceived learning style preferences, and study habits and attitudes to achievement of college freshmen in a small urban university. Doctoral dissertation, Boston University. *Dissertation Abstracts International, 48*, 872A.

Clay, J. E. (1984). A correlational analysis of the learning characteristics of highly achieving and poorly achieving freshmen at A&M University as revealed through performance on standardized tests. Normal: Alabama A&M University.

Cody, C. (1983). Learning styles, including hemispheric dominance: A comparative study of average, gifted, and highly gifted students in grades five through twelve. Doctoral dissertation, Temple University. *Dissertation Abstracts International, 44*, 1631A.

Cohen, L. (1986). Birth order and learning styles: An examination of the relationships between birth order and middle school students' preferred learning style profiles. Doctoral dissertation, University of Minnesota's Graduate Department of Educational Psychology. *Dissertation Abstracts International, 47*, 2084A.

Coker, C. A. (1995). Learning style consistency across cognitive and motor settings. *Perceptual and Motor Skills, 81,* 1023–1026.

Coleman, S. J. (1988). An investigation of the relationships among physical and emotional learning style preferences and perceptual modality strengths of gifted first-grade students. Doctoral dissertation, Virginia Polytechnic Institute and State University. *Dissertation Abstracts International,* 50(04), 873A.

Cook, L. (1989). Relationships among learning style awareness, academic achievement, and locus of control among community college students. Doctoral dissertation, University of Florida. *Dissertation Abstracts International, 49*(03), 217A.

Coolidge-Parker, J. A. (1989). A comparison of perceived and objectively measured perceptual learning style modality elements of court reporters and court-reporting students. Doctoral dissertation, University of South Florida. *Dissertation Abstracts International, 50*(07)A, 1996.

Cooper, T. J. D. (1991). An investigation of the learning styles of students at two contemporary alternative high schools in the District of Columbia. Doctoral dissertation, The George Washington University, School of Education and Human Development. *Dissertation Abstracts International, 52*(06), 2002.

Cramp, D. C. (1990). A study of the effects on student achievement of fourth- and fifth-grade students' instructional times being matched and mismatched with their particular time preference. Doctoral dissertation, University of Mississippi. *Dissertation Abstracts International, 52*(02)A, 407.

Crampton, N. A. S. (1990). Learning style (modality) preferences for students attending private residential alternative schools (at risk). Doctoral dissertation, University of South Dakota. *Dissertation Abstracts International, 52*(02)A, 407.

Crino, E. M. (1984). An analysis of the preferred learning styles of kindergarten children and the relationship of these preferred learning styles to curriculum planning for kindergarten children. Doctoral dissertation, State University of New York at Buffalo, 1984. *Dissertation Abstracts International, 45,* 1282A.

Currence, J. A. (1991). High school dropouts as learners: A comparative analysis of schooling experiences and school behaviors, school climate perceptions, learning style preferences, and locus-of-control orientation of persisters and high school dropouts in a rural Eastern Shore county school system. Doctoral dissertation, University of Maryland, College Park. *Dissertation Abstracts International, 52*(7)A, 2388A.

Curry, E. R. (1994). Matching chemistry instructional methods with perceptual learning-style preferences of eleventh-grade women: Effects on attitude and achievement. Doctoral dissertation, New York University.

Curry, L. (1987). *Integrating concepts of cognitive learning style: A review with attention to psychometric standards.* Ottawa, Ontario: Canadian College of Health Science Executives.

Davis, M. A. (1985). An investigation of the relationship of personality types and learning style preferences of high school students (Myers-Briggs Type Indicator). Doctoral dissertation, George Peabody College for Teachers of Vanderbilt University. *Dissertation Abstracts International, 46,* 1606A.

Dean, W. L. (1982). A comparison of the learning styles of educable mentally retarded students and learning disabled students. Doctoral dissertation, University of Mississippi. *Dissertation Abstracts International, 43,* 1923A.

DeBello, T. (1985). A critical analysis of the achievement and attitude effects of administrative assignments to social studies writing instruction based on identified, eighth grade students' learning style preferences for learning alone, with peers, or with teachers. Doctoral dissertation, St. John's University. *Dissertation Abstracts International, 47,* 68A.

DeBello, T. (1990, July–September). Comparison of eleven major learning styles models: Variables, appropriate populations, validity of instrumentation, and the research behind them. *Journal of Reading, Writing, and Learning Disabilities International, 6*(3), 203–222. New York: Hemisphere.

DeBello, T., & Guez, R. (1996, November). How parents perceive children's learning styles. *Principal, 76*(2), 38–39.

DeCoux, V. H. (1990). Kolb's Learning Style Inventory: A review of its application in nursing research. *Journal of Nursing Education, 29*(5), 202–207.

DeGregoris, C. N. (1986). Reading comprehension and the interaction of individual sound preferences and varied auditory distractions. Doctoral dissertation, Hofstra University. *Dissertation Abstracts International, 47*, 3380A.

Delbrey, A. (1987, August). The relationship between the Learning Style Inventory and the Gregorc Style Delineator. Doctoral dissertation, University of Alabama. *Dissertation Abstracts International, 49*(02)A, 219.0

Della Valle, J. (1984). An experimental investigation of the word recognition scores of seventh grade students to provide supervisory and administrative guidelines for the organization of effective instructional environments. Doctoral dissertation, St. John's University. *Dissertation Abstracts International, 45*, 359A.

Della Valle, J. (1990, July–September). The development of a learning styles program in an affluent, suburban New York elementary school. *Journal of Reading, Writing, and Learning Styles International, 6*(3), 315–322. New York: Hemisphere.

DiSebastian, J. (1994). Learning in style in Tegucigalpa, Honduras. *International Education, 21*(71), 11, 16. New Wilmington, PA: Association for the Advancement of International Education.

Drew, M. W. (1991). An investigation of the effects of matching and mismatching minority underachievers with culturally similar and dissimilar story content and learning style and traditional instructional strategies. Doctoral dissertation, St. John's University.

Drew, M., Dunn, R., Quinn, P., Sinatra, R., & Spiridakis, J. (1994). Effects of matching and mismatching minority underachievers with culturally similar and dissimilar story content and learning style and traditional instructional practices. *Applied Educational Research Journal, 8*(2), 3–10.

Dunham, H. P. (1999). Effects of sociological preferences and congruent versus incongruent instruction on college students' economic achievement and anxiety. Doctoral dissertation, St. John's University.

Dunn, R. (1984). How should students do their homework? Research vs. opinion. *Early Years, 14*(4), 43–45.

Dunn, R. (1985). A research-based plan for doing homework. *Education Digest, 9*, 40–42.

Dunn, R. (1987, Spring). Research on instructional environments: Implications for student achievement and attitudes. *Professional School Psychology, 2*(1), 43–52.

Dunn, R. (1988). Commentary: Teaching students through their perceptual strengths or preferences. *Journal of Reading, 31*(4), 304–309.

Dunn, R. (1989a, May–June). Can schools overcome the impact of societal ills on student achievement? The research indicates—yes! *The Principal, 34*(5), 1–15. New York: Board of Jewish Education of Greater New York.

Dunn, R. (1989b). Capitalizing on students' perceptual strengths to ensure literacy while engaging in conventional lecture/discussion. *Reading Psychology: An International Quarterly, 9*(4), 431–453.

Dunn, R. (1989c, Summer). Do students from different cultures have different learning styles? *International Education, 16*(50), 40–42. New Wilmington, PA: Association for the Advancement of International Education.

Dunn, R. (1989d). Individualizing instruction for mainstreamed gifted children. In R. R. Milgram (Ed.), *Teaching gifted and talented learners in regular classrooms* (Chapter 3, pp. 63–111). Springfield, IL: Charles C Thomas.

Dunn, R. (1989e). Recent research on learning and seven applications to teaching young children to read. *The Oregon Elementary Principal, 50*(2), 32–39.

Dunn, R. (1989f, February). A small private school in Minnesota. *Teaching K–8, 18*(5), 54–57. Norwalk, CT: Early Years.

Dunn, R. (1989g, Fall). Teaching gifted students through their learning style strengths. *International Education, 16*(51), 6–8. Wilmington, PA: Association for the Advancement of International Education.

Dunn, R. (1990a, January). Bias over substance: A critical analysis of Kavale and Forness' report on modality-based instruction. *Exceptional Children, 56*(4), 354–356. Reston, VA: Council for Exceptional Children.

Dunn, R. (1990b, October). Rita Dunn answers questions on learning styles. *Educational Leadership, 48*(15), 15–19. Alexandria, VA: Association for Supervision and Curriculum Development.

Dunn, R. (1990c, Summer). Teaching young children to read: Matching methods to learning styles perceptual processing strengths, Part 1. *International Education, 17*(54), 2–3. New Wilmington, PA: Association for the Advancement of International Education.

Dunn, R. (1990d, Fall). Teaching young children to read: Matching methods to learning styles perceptual processing strengths, Part 2. *International Education, 17*(55), 5–7. New Wilmington, PA: Association for the Advancement of International Education.

Dunn, R. (1990e, Winter). Teaching underachievers through their learning style strengths. *International Education, 16*(52), 5–7. New Wilmington, PA: Association for the Advancement of International Education.

Dunn, R. (1990f, July–September). Understanding the Dunn and Dunn learning styles model and the need for individual diagnosis and prescription. *Journal of Reading, Writing, and Learning Disabilities International, 6*(3), 223–247. New York: Hemisphere.

Dunn, R. (1990g, Spring). When you really have to lecture, teach students through their perceptual strengths. *International Education, 17*(53), 1, 6–7. New Wilmington, PA: Association for the Advancement of International Education.

Dunn, R. (1991a, Winter). Are you willing to experiment with a tactual/visual/auditory global approach to reading? Part 3. *International Education, 18*(56), 6–8. New Wilmington, PA: Association for the Advancement of International Education.

Dunn R. (1991b). *Hands on approaches to learning styles: A practical guide for successful schooling.* New Wilmington, PA: Association for the Advancement of International Education.

Dunn, R. (1991c). Instructional leadership in education: Limited, diffused, sporadic, and lacking in research. *CSA Leadership* (pp. 30–41). New York: American Federation of School Administrators.

Dunn, R. (Ed.). (1992a, Summer). Initial research findings concerning *adults'* learning styles: Data from college campuses and the corporate world. *Learning Styles Network Newsletter, 13*(1), 1–8. New York: St. John's University and the National Association of Secondary School Principals.

Dunn, R. (1992b, April–June). Strategies for teaching word recognition to disabled readers. *Reading and Writing Quarterly, 8*(2), 157–177. New York: Hemisphere.

Dunn, R. (1992c, Spring). Teaching the "I-was-paying-attention-but-I-didn't-hear-you-say-it" learner. *International Education, 19*(61), 1, 6. New Wilmington, PA: Association for the Advancement of International Education.

Dunn, R. (Ed.). (1993a). Learning styles and the health professions: A literature review, selected abstracts, and suggested future directions. *Learning Styles Network Newsletter, 14*(2), 1–8. New York: St. John's University and the National Association of Secondary School Principals.

Dunn, R. (Ed.). (1993b). Learning styles and the law: Teaching to individuals' strengths to increase achievement, improve behavior, and reduce litigation. *Learning Styles Network Newsletter, 14*(1), 1–8. New York: St. John's University and the National Association of Secondary School Principals.

Dunn, R. (1993c, Winter–Spring). The learning styles of gifted adolescents in nine culturally diverse nations. *International Education, 20*(64), 4–6. New Wilmington, PA: Association for the Advancement of International Education.

Dunn, R. (1993d, March–April). Learning styles of multiculturally diverse students. *Emergency Librarian, 20*(4), 24–35. British Vancouver, CA: Emergency Librarians' Association.

Dunn, R. (1993e). Teaching gifted students through their learning style strengths. In R. M. Milgram, R. Dunn, & G. E. Price (Eds.), *Teaching and counseling gifted and talented adolescents: An international learning style perspective* (pp. 37–67). Westport, CT: Praeger.

Dunn, R. (1993f, September). Teaching the . . . "I don't like school and you can't make me like it" learner. *International Education, 20*(65), 4–5.

Dunn, R. (1994). The Dunn and Dunn learning styles model: Theory, research, and application. In M. F. Shaughnessy (Ed.), *Education in the 21st century* (Chapter 13, pp. 131–141). Las Cruces, NM: Eastern New Mexico University.

Dunn, R. (1995a). *Educating diverse learners: Strategies for improving current classroom practices.* Bloomington, IN: Phi Delta Kappa.

Dunn, R. (1996a). *Everything you need to successfully implement a learning-styles instructional program: Teaching and counseling adolescents.* Westport: CT: Greenwood.

Dunn, R. (1996b). *How to implement and supervise a learning-style program.* Alexandria, VA: Association for Supervision and Curriculum Development.

Dunn, R. (Ed.). (1996c, Winter). *Learning Styles Network Newsletter, 16*(3). New York: St. John's University and the National Association of Secondary School Principals.

Dunn, R. (1997a, Winter). Contract Activity Packages (CAPS): Teaching the way many middle-school students learn. *Michigan Elementary and Middle School Principals' Journal, 73*(1), 8–9, 27–29. East Lansing, MI: Michigan Elementary and Middle School Principals Association.

Dunn, R. (1997b). Multicultural education: Its goals and track record. *Educational Leadership, 54*(7), 74–77. Alexandria, VA: Association for Supervision and Curriculum Development.

Dunn, R., Bauer, E., Gemake, J., Gregory, J., Primavera, L., & Signer, B. (1994). Matching and mismatching junior high school learning disabled and emotionally handicapped students' perceptual preferences on mathematics scores. *Teacher Education Journal, 5*(1), 3–13.

Dunn, R., Beasley, M., & Buchanan, K. (1994). What do you believe about how culturally diverse students learn? *Emergency Librarian, 22*(1), 8–14. Vancouver, B.C.: Emergency Librarian's Association.

Dunn, R., Beaudry, J. A., & Klavas, A. (1989). Survey of research on learning styles. *Educational Leadership, 46*(6), 50–58.

Dunn, R., & Brunner, C. (1997, Summer). International misconceptions about learning: Where did they begin? *International Education, 24*(81), 1, 9–11. Wilmington, PA: Association for the Advancement of International Education.

Dunn, R., & Bruno, A. (1985). What does the research on learning styles have to do with Mario? *The Clearing House, 59*(1), 9–11.

Dunn, R., Bruno, J., Sklar, R. I., & Beaudry, J. (1990, May–June). Effects of matching and mismatching minority developmental college students' hemispheric preferences on mathematics scores. *Journal of Educational Research, 83*(5), 283–288. Washington, DC: Heldref Publications.

Dunn, R., & Buchanan, K. (1996). Whose fault is it anyway? Middle school teachers' perceptions of why students fail. *Michigan Principal, 72*(1), 21–23. East Lansing: Michigan Elementary and Middle School Principals' Association.

Dunn, R., Carbo, M., & Burton, E. (1981, May). Breakthrough: How to improve early reading instruction. *Kappan*, pp. 675–680. Bloomington, IN: Phi Delta Kappa.

Dunn, R., Cavanaugh, D., Eberle, B., & Zenhausern, R. (1982). Hemispheric preference: The newest element of learning style. *American Biology Teacher, 44*(5), 291–294.

Dunn, R., DeBello, T., Brennan, P., Krimsky, J., & Murrain, P. (1981). Learning style researchers define differences differently. *Educational Leadership, 38*(5), 382–392. Alexandria, VA: Association for Supervision and Curriculum Development.

Dunn, R., Deckinger, E. L., Withers, P., & Katzenstein, H. (1990, Winter). Should college students be taught how to do homework? The effects of studying marketing through individual perceptual strengths. *Illinois School Research and Development Journal, 26*(3), 96–113. Normal: Illinois Association for Supervision and Curriculum Development.

Dunn, R., Della Valle, J., Dunn, K., Geisert, G., Sinatra, R., & Zenhausern, R. (1986). The effects of matching and mismatching students' mobility preferences on recognition and memory tasks. *Journal of Educational Research, 79*(5), 267–272.

Dunn, R. & Dunn, K. (1972). *Practical approaches to individualizing instruction: Contracts and other effective strategies.* Englewood Cliffs, NJ: Prentice-Hall.

Dunn, R., & Dunn K. (1975). *Educator's self-teaching guide to individualizing instructional programs.* Nyack, NJ: Parker Publishing Company, A Prentice-Hall Division.

Dunn, R., & Dunn K. (1977a). *Administrator's guide to new programs for faculty management and evaluation.* Nyack, NY: Parker Publishing Company, A Prentice-Hall Division.

Dunn, R., & Dunn, K. (1977b). *How to raise independent and professionally successful daughters.* Englewood Cliffs, NJ: Prentice-Hall.

Dunn, R., & Dunn, K. (1978). *Teaching students through their individual learning styles: A practical approach.* Reston, VA: Reston Publishing Company, A Prentice-Hall Division.

Dunn, R., & Dunn, K. (1983). *Situational leadership for principals: The school administrator in action.* Englewood Cliffs, NJ: Prentice-Hall.

Dunn, R., & Dunn, K. (1992). *Teaching elementary students through their individual learning styles.* Boston: Allyn and Bacon.

Dunn, R., & Dunn K. (1993). *Teaching secondary students through their individual learning styles.* Boston: Allyn and Bacon.

Dunn, R., & Dunn, K. (1998). *Practical approaches to individualizing staff development for adults.* Westport, CT: Greenwood.

Dunn, R., Dunn, K., & Freeley, M. E. (1984). Practical applications of the research: Responding to students' learning styles—Step one. *Illinois State Research and Development Journal, 21*(1), 1–21.

Dunn, R., Dunn, K., & Freeley, M. E. (1985). Tips to improve your inservice training. *Early Years,* 15(8), 43–45. Darien, CT: Allen Raymond.

Dunn, R., Dunn, K., & Perrin, J. (1994). *Teaching young children through their individual learning styles.* Boston: Allyn and Bacon.

Dunn, R., Dunn, K., & Price, G. E. (1977). Diagnosing learning styles: Avoiding malpractice suits against school systems. *Phi Delta Kappan, 58*(5), 418–420.

Dunn, R., Dunn, K., & Price, G. E. (1979). *Learning Style Inventory.* Available from Price Systems, Box 1818, Lawrence, KS 66044-1818.

Dunn, R., Dunn, K., & Price, G. E. (1982). *Productivity Environmental Preference Survey.* Lawrence, KS: Price Systems.

Dunn, R., Dunn, K., & Price, G. E. (1985). *Learning Style Inventory.* Available from Price Systems, Box 1818, Lawrence, KS 66044-1818.

Dunn, R., Dunn, K., & Price, G. E. (1987). *Learning Style Inventory.* Available from Price Systems, Box 1818, Lawrence, KS 66044-1818.

Dunn, R., Dunn, K., & Price, G. E. (1989a). *Learning Style Inventory.* Available from Price Systems, Box 1818, Lawrence, KS 66044-1818.

Dunn, R., Dunn, K., & Price, G. E. (1989b). *Productivity Environmental Preference Survey.* Lawrence, KS: Price Systems.

Dunn, R., Dunn, K., Primavera, L., Sinatra, R., & Virostko, J. (1987). A timely solution: A review of research on the effects of chronobiology on children's achievement and behavior. *The Clearing House, 61*(1), 5–8.

Dunn, R., Dunn, K., & Treffinger, D. (1992). *Bringing out the giftedness in every child: A guide for parents.* New York: Wiley.

Dunn, R., Gemake, J., Jalali, F., Zenhausern, R., Quinn, P., & Spiridakis, J. (1990, April). Cross-cultural differences in the learning styles of elementary-age students from four ethnic backgrounds. *Journal of Multicultural Counseling and Development, 18*(2), 68–93.

Dunn, R., Gemake, J., & Zenhausern, R. (1990, January). Cross-cultural differences in learning styles. *Missouri Association for Supervision and Curriculum Development Journal, 1*(2), 9–15.

Dunn, R., Giannitti, M. C., Murray, J. B., Geisert, G., Rossi, I., & Quinn, P. (1990, August). Grouping students for instruction: Effects of individual vs. group learning style on achievement and attitudes. *Journal of Social Psychology, 130*(4), 485–494.

Dunn, R., & Gremli, J. (1998–1999). Teaching urban students with contract activity packages: Rap, rock, and ragtime—a rational approach. *The National Forum of Teacher Education Journal, 9*(1), 27–35. Monroe: Louisiana University.

Dunn, R., & Griggs, S. A. (1988a). High school dropouts: Do they learn differently from those who remain in high school? *The Principal, 34*(1), 1–8. New York: Jewish Board of Education of Greater New York.

Dunn, R., & Griggs, S. (1988b). *Learning styles: Quiet revolution in American secondary schools.* Reston, VA: National Association of Secondary School Principals.

Dunn, R., & Griggs, S. A. (1989a, January). Learning styles: Key to improving schools and student achievement. *Curriculum report.* Reston, VA: National Association of Secondary School Principals.

Dunn, R., & Griggs, S. A. (1989b, October). The learning styles of multicultural groups and counseling implications. *Journal of Multicultural Counseling and Development, 7*(4), 146–155. Alexandria, VA: American Association for Multicultural Counseling and Development.

Dunn, R., & Griggs, S. A. (1989c). Learning styles: Quiet revolution in American secondary schools. *Momentum, 63*(1), 40–42. Washington, DC: Heldref Publications.

Dunn, R., & Griggs, S. A. (1989d, September). Learning styles: Quiet revolution in American secondary schools. *The Clearing House, 32*(1), 40–42. Washington, DC: Heldref Publications.

Dunn, R., & Griggs, S. A. (1989e, April). A matter of style. *Momentum, 20*(2), 66–70. Washington, DC: National Catholic Education Association.

Dunn, R., & Griggs, S. A. (1989f). A quiet revolution: Learning styles and their application to secondary schools. *Holistic Education, 2*(4), 14–19. Greenfield, MA: Holistic Education Review.

Dunn, R., & Griggs, S. A. (1989g, January). A quiet revolution in Hempstead. *Teaching K–8, 18*(5), 54–57. Norwalk, CT: Early Years.

Dunn, R., & Griggs, S. A. (1990). Research on the learning style characteristics of selected racial and ethnic groups. *Journal of Reading, Writing, and Learning Disabilities, 6*(3), 261–280. Washington, DC: Hemisphere Press.

Dunn, R., & Griggs, S. A. (1995a). Hispanic-Americans and learning styles. *Emergency Librarian, 23*(2), 11–16.

Dunn, R., & Griggs, S. A. (1995b). *Multiculturalism and learning style: Teaching and counseling adolescents.* Westport, CT: Praeger.

Dunn, R., & Griggs, S. A. (Eds). (1988). *Learning styles and the nursing profession.* New York: National League of Nursing.

Dunn, R., Griggs, S. A., Milgram, R. M., & Price, G. E. (1997–98). Learning styles of gifted adolescents in nine culturally diverse nations. *Applied Educational Research Journal, 10*(2), 3–18.

Dunn, R., Griggs, S. A., Olson, J., Gorman, B., & Beasley, M. (1995). A meta analytic validation of the Dunn and Dunn learning styles model. *Journal of Educational Research, 88*(6), 353–361.

Dunn, R., Griggs, S. A., & Price, G. E. (1993a). The learning styles of gifted adolescents in the United States. In R. M. Milgram, R. Dunn, & G. E. Price (Eds.), *Teaching and counseling gifted and talented adolescents: An international learning style perspective* (Chapter 7, pp. 119–136). Westport, CT: Praeger.

Dunn, R., Griggs, S. A., & Price, G. E. (1993b, October). Learning styles of Mexican-American and Anglo elementary school students. *Journal of Multicultural Counseling and Development, 21*(4), 237–247.

Dunn, R., & Ingham, J. (1990). *Productivity Disc.* Jamaica, NY: St. John's University's Center for the Study of Learning and Teaching Styles.

Dunn, R., Ingham, J., & Deckinger, L. (1995). Effects of matching and mismatching corporate employees' perceptual preferences and instructional strategies on training achievement and attitudes. *Journal of Applied Business Research, 11*(3), 30–37.

Dunn, R., & Klavas, A. (1996). *Productivity disk.* Jamaica, NY: St. John's University.

Dunn, R., Krimsky, J., Murray, J., & Quinn, P. (1985). Light up their lives: A review of research on the effects of lighting on children's achievement. *The Reading Teacher, 38*(9), 863–869.

Dunn, R., & Milgram, R. (1993). Learning styles and gifted students in diverse cultures. In R. M. Milgram, R. Dunn, & G. E. Price (Eds.), *Teaching and counseling gifted and talented adolescents: An international learning style perspective* (Chapter 1, pp. 3–23). Westport, CT: Praeger.

Dunn, R., & Nelson, B. (1996). Introducing educational administration candidates to learning-styles approaches. *Educational Considerations, 24*(1), 45–47.

Dunn, R., Pizzo, J., Sinatra, R., & Barretto, R. A. (1983, Winter). Can it be too quiet to learn? *Focus: Teaching English Language Arts, 9*(2), 92.

Dunn, R., & Price, G. E. (1980). The learning style characteristics of gifted children. *Gifted Child Quarterly, 24*(1), 33–36.

Dunn, R., Price, G. E., Dunn, K., & Griggs, S. A. (1981). Studies in students' learning styles. *Roeper Review, 4*(2), 38–40.

Dunn, R., Shea, T. C., Evans, W., & MacMurren, H. (1991). Learning style and equal protection: The next frontier. *The Clearing House, 65*(2), 93–96. Washington, DC: Heldref Publications.

Dunn, R., & Smith, J. B. (1990). Learning styles and library media programs. In J. B. Smith (Ed.), *School library media annual* (Chapter 4, pp. 32–49). Englewood, CO: Libraries Unlimited.

Dunn, R., & Waggoner, B. (1995). Comparing three innovative instructional systems. *Emergency Librarian, 23*(1), 9–15.

Dunn, R., White, R. M., & Zenhausern, R. (1982). An investigation of responsible versus less responsible students. *Illinois School Research and Development, 19*(1), 19–24.

Elliot, I. (1991, November–December). The reading place. *Teaching K–8, 21*(3), 30–34. Norwalk, CT: Early Years.

Ettington, N. J. (1989). A comparison of learning styles of freshmen with high and low reading achievement in the Community Scholars Liberal Studies Program at Georgetown University. *Dissertation Abstracts International, 50*(05)A, 1285.

Ewing, N., & Yong, L. F. (1992). A comparative study of the learning style preferences among gifted African-American, Mexican-American, and American-born, Chinese middle-grade students. *Roeper Review, 14*(3), 120–123.

Faulkner, D. L. (1994). An investigation of modality preferences, musical aptitude, and attitude toward music at the third-grade level. Doctoral dissertation, University of Mississippi.

Ferdenzi, A. (1998). Effects of modality-responsive home-learning treatments on parental attitudes and efficacy in helping children succeed in school and their first-grade children's word recognition achievement and attitudes. Doctoral dissertation, St. John's University.

Ferrell, B. G. (1981). Factor analytic validation of the learning styles paradigm. Doctoral dissertation, Southern Illinois University of Carbondale. *Dissertation Abstracts International, 42*(07)A, 3069.

Filipczak, B. (1995, March). Different strokes: Learning styles in the classroom. *Training,* 43–49.

Flanary, D. (1997). *Computer shopping strategies: Don't take a BITE out of your wallet!* Jamaica, NY: St. John's University's Center for the Study of Learning and Teaching Styles.

Fleming, V. J. (1989, August). Vocational classrooms with style. *Vocational Education Journal, 10*(1), 36–39. Alexandria, VA: American Vocational Association.

Fourqurean, J. M., Meisgeier, C., & Swank, P. (1990). The link between learning style and Jungian psychological type: A finding of two bipolar preference dimensions. *Journal of Experimental Education, 58*(3), 225–237.

Frazier, E. R. (1992). An analysis of and comparison between self-assessed, individualized learning-style based teaching practices and behaviors within selected dimensions of the instructional process and individuals' beliefs about student learning. *Dissertation Abstracts International, 53*(10).

Frazier, E. R., Primavera, L. H., & Dunn, K. J. (1995). Toward a reliable teaching style instrument. *Educational Administration and Supervision Journal, 12*(2), 16–29.

Freeley, M. E. (1984). An experimental investigation of the relationships among teachers' individual time preferences, inservice workshop schedules, and instructional techniques and the subsequent implementation of learning style strategies in participants' classrooms. Doctoral dissertation, St. John's University. *Dissertation Abstracts International, 46*, 403A.

French, S. B. (1991). The relationship between congruent and incongruent instructional methods and first-grade reading vocabulary achievement and learning styles. Doctoral dissertation, University of Southern Mississippi. *Dissertation Abstracts International*, 52(04)A, 1192.

Gadwa, K., & Griggs, S. A. (1985). The school dropout: Implications for counselors. *The School Counselor, 33*, 9–17.

Gallucci, A. K. (1991). The relationship(s) among the academic achievement, learning style preferences, and creativity of gifted and normal intermediate students in a suburban New York school district. Doctoral dissertation, St. John's University. *Dissertation Abstract International, 53*(02), 389.

Galvin, A. J. (1992). An analysis of learning and productivity styles across occupational groups in a corporate setting (learning styles, corporate training). Doctoral dissertation. Boston University. *Dissertation Abstracts International, 53*(04)A, 1027.

Garcia-Otero, M. (1987). Knowledge of learning styles and the effect on the clinical performance of nurse anesthesiology students. Doctoral dissertation, University of New Orleans, 1987. *Dissertation Abstracts International, 49*(05B), 1602.

Garcia-Otero, M., & Teddlie, C. (1992). The effect of knowledge of learning styles on anxiety and clinical performance of nurse anesthesiology students. *American Association of Nursing Anesthesiology Journal, 60*(3), 257–260.

Gardiner, B. (1983). Stepping into a learning styles program. *Roeper Review, 6*(2), 90–92.

Gardiner, B. (1986). An experimental analysis of selected teaching strategies implemented at specific times of the school day and their effects on the social studies achievement test scores and attitudes of fourth grade, low achieving students in an urban school setting. Doctoral dissertation, St. John's University. *Dissertation Abstracts International, 47*, 3307A.

Garger, S. (1990, October). Is there a link between learning style and neurophysiology? *Educational Leadership, 48*(2), 63–65. Alexandria, VA: Association for Supervision and Curriculum Development.

Garrett, S. L. (1992). The effects of perceptual preference and motivation on vocabulary and attitude test scores among high school students. Doctoral dissertation, University of La Verne, California. *Dissertation Abstracts International, 53*(02)A, p. 389.

Geiser, W. F. (1998). Effects of learning-style awareness and responsive study strategies on achievement, incidence of study, and attitudes of suburban eighth-grade students. Doctoral dissertation, St. John's University.

Geisert, G., & Dunn, R. (1991a, January). Computer and learning style, *70*(4), 47–49. *Principal*. Reston, VA: National Association of Elementary School Principals.

Geisert, G., & Dunn, R. (1991b, March). Effective use of computers: Assignments based on individual learning style. *The Clearing House, 64*(4), 219–224. Washington, DC: Heldref Publications.

Geisert, G., Dunn, R., & Sinatra, R. (1990). Reading, learning styles, and computers. *Journal of Reading, Writing, and Learning Disabilities, 6*(3), 297–306. Washington, DC: Hemisphere Press.

Giannitti, M. C. (1988). An experimental investigation of the relationships among the learning style sociological preferences of middle-school students (grades 6, 7, 8), their attitudes and achievement in social studies, and selected instructional strategies. Doctoral dissertation, St. John's University. *Dissertation Abstracts International, 49*, 2911A.

Glasner, J., & Ingham, J. (1993). Learning styles and literacy. *The Bookmark, 50*(111), 218–223. Albany State Education Department, New York State Library, 50.

Gordon, R. B. (1993). The effects of computerized instruction on the improvement and transfer of writing skills for low-skilled and below average–skilled sophomore students. Doctoral dissertation, University of LaVerne. *Dissertation Abstracts International, 55*(01), 23.

Gould, B. J. (1987). An investigation of the relationships between supervisors' and supervisees' sociological productivity styles on teacher evaluations and interpersonal attraction ratings. Doctoral dissertation, St. John's University. *Dissertation Abstracts International, 48*, 18A.

Greb, F. M. (1997, Spring). Learning styles study group: Program for change. *Education Viewpoints: A New Movement in Education, 17*(1), 22–24. Jamesburg: New Jersey Principals and Supervisors Association.

Gregorc, A. F. (1985). *Inside styles: Beyond the basics.* Columbia, CT: Gregorc Associates.

Gremli, J. (1996, November). Tuned into learning styles. *Music Educators Journal, 83*(3), 24–27.

Gremli, J. (1999). Effects of traditional versus contract activity package and programmed learning sequence instruction on the short- and long-term achievement and attitudes of seventh- and eighth-grade general music students. Doctoral dissertation, St. John's University.

Griggs, D., Griggs, S. A., Dunn, R., & Ingham, J. (1994). A challenge for nurse educators: Accommodating nursing students' diverse learning styles. *Nurse Educator, 19*(6), 41–45.

Griggs, S. A. (1989, November). Students' sociological grouping preferences of learning styles. *The Clearing House, 63*(3), 135–139. Washington, DC: Heldref Publications.

Griggs, S. A. (1991a). Counseling gifted children with different learning-style preferences. In R. M. Milgram (Ed.), *Counseling talented and gifted children: A guide for teachers, counselors, and parents* (pp. 53–74). Greenwich, CT: Ablex JAI Press.

Griggs, S. A. (1991b). *Counseling students through their individual learning styles.* Ann Arbor: University of Michigan. Obtainable from Center for the Study of Learning and Teaching Styles, St. John's University, Jamaica, NY 11439.

Griggs, S. A., & Dunn, R. (1995). Hispanic-American students and learning styles. *Emergency Librarian, 23*(2), 11–16. Vancouver, BC: Canadian Association of School Librarians.

Griggs, S. A., & Dunn, R. (1996). Learning styles of Asian-American adolescents. *Emergency Librarian, 24*(1), 8–13. Vancouver, BC: Canadian Association of School Librarians.

Griggs, S. A., & Price, G. E. (1980). A comparison between the learning styles of gifted versus average junior high school students. *Phi Delta Kappan, 61*, 361.

Griggs, S. A., & Price, G. E. (1982). A comparison between the learning styles of gifted versus average junior high school students. *Creative and Gifted Child Quarterly, 7*, 39–42.

Griggs, S. A., Price, G. E., Kopel, S., & Swaine, W. (1984). The effects of group counseling with sixth-grade students using approaches that are compatible versus incompatible with selected learning style elements. *California Personnel and Guidance Journal, 5*(1), 28–35.

Guastello, F. (1998). Reliability and concurrent validity of an interactive, global learning-style assessment for elementary-school students. Doctoral dissertation, St. John's University.

Guild, P. O'R. (1980). Learning styles: Knowledge, issues and applications for classroom teachers. Oral dissertation, University of Massachusetts. *Dissertation Abstracts International, 41*, 1033A.

Guinta, S. F. (1984). Administrative considerations concerning learning style and the influence of instructor/student congruence on high schoolers' achievement and educators' perceived stress. Doctoral dissertation, St. John's University. *Dissertation Abstracts International, 45*, 32A.

Guzzo, R. S. (1987). Dificuldades de apprenddizagem: Modalidade de attencao e analise de tarefas em materials didaticos. Doctoral dissertation, University of São Paulo, Institute of Psychology, Brazil.

Hall, L. A. (1993). A critical exploration of learning-style preferences and the mathematical achievement of Chapter 1 middle-school students: Administrative and instructional implications. Doctoral dissertation, Syracuse University.

Hanna, S. J. (1989). An investigation of the effects on achievement test scores of individual time preferences and time of training in a corporate setting. Doctoral dissertation, St. John's University.

Harp, T. Y., & Orsak, L. (1990, July–September). One administrator's challenge: Implementing a learning style program at the secondary level. *Journal of Reading, Writing, and Learning Disabilities International, 6*(3), 335–342. New York: Hemisphere.

Harty, P. M. (1982). Learning styles: A matter of difference in the foreign language classroom. Unpublished master's dissertation, Wright State University.

Hawk, T. D. (1983). A comparison of teachers' preference for specific inservice activity approaches and their measured learning styles. Doctoral dissertation, Kansas State University, 1983. *Dissertation Abstracts International, 44*(12)A, 3557.

Hickerson-Roberts, V. L. (1983). Reading achievement, reading attitudes, self-concept, learning styles and estimated high school grade-point average as predictions of academic success for 55 adult learners at Kansas State University. Doctoral dissertation, Kansas State University, 1983. *Dissertation Abstracts International, 44*(05)A, 1295.

Hill, G. D. (1987). An experimental investigation into the interaction between modality preference and instructional mode in the learning of spelling words by upper-elementary learning disabled students. Doctoral dissertation, North Texas State University, 1987. *Dissertation Abstracts International, 48*, 2536A.

Hills, J. S. (1976). Cognitive Style Interest Inventory. Available from Oakland Community College, 2480 Opdyke Road, Bloomfield Hills, MI 48013.

Hodges, H. (1985). An analysis of the relationships among preferences for a formal/informal design, one element of learning style, academic achievement, and attitudes of seventh and eighth grade students in remedial mathematics classes in a New York City junior high school. Doctoral dissertation, St. John's University. *Dissertation Abstracts International, 45*, 2791A.

Hodgin, J., & Wooliscroft, C. (1997, March). Eric learns to read: Learning styles at work. *Educational Leadership, 54*(6), 43–45.

Hong, E., Milgram, R. M., & Perkins, P. G. (1995). Homework style and homework behavior of Korean and American children. *Journal of Research and Development in Education, 28*, 197–207.

Hong, E., & Suh, B. (1995). An analysis of change in Korean-American and Korean students' learning styles. *Psychological Reports, 76*, 691–699.

Hunt, D. (1979). Learning style and student needs: An introduction to conceptual level. In *Student learning styles: Diagnosing and prescribing programs* (pp. 27–38). Reston, VA: National Association of Secondary School Principals.

Hutto, J. R. (1982). The association of teacher manipulation of scientifically acquired learning styles information to the achievement and attitudes of second and third grade remedial students. Doctoral dissertation, University of Southern Mississippi. *Dissertation Abstracts International, 44*(01)A, 30.

Ignelzi-Ferraro, D. M. (1989). Identification of the preferred conditions for learning among three groups of mildly handicapped high school students using the Learning Style Inventory. Doctoral dissertation, University of Pittsburgh. *Dissertation Abstracts International, 51*(3), 796A.

Ingham, J. (1990). An experimental investigation of the relationships among learning style perceptual preference, instructional strategies, training achievement, and attitudes of corporate employees. Doctoral dissertation, St. John's University. *Dissertation Abstracts International, 51*(02)A.

Ingham, J. (1991). Matching instruction with employee perceptual preferences significantly increases training effectiveness. *Human Resource Development Quarterly, 2*(1), 53–64.

Ingham, J. (1993). Learning styles and the law: A review of important cases. *Learning Styles Network Newsletter, 14*(1), 2. New York: St. John's University and the National Association of Secondary School Principals.

Ingham, J., & Dunn, R. (1993). The Dunn and Dunn model of learning styles: Addressing learning diversity. *1993 Annual: Developing Human Resources.* London: Phieffer.

Ingham, J., Dunn, R., Deckinger, L., & Geisert, G. (1995). Impact of perceptual preferences on adults' corporate training and achievement. *Educational Administration and Supervision Journal, 12*(2), 3–15. Dayton, OH: Wright State University.

Ingham, J., & Price, G. E. (1993). The learning styles of gifted adolescents in the Philippines (Chapter 9, pp. 149–160). In R. M. Milgram, R. Dunn, & G. E. Price, (Eds.), *Teaching and counseling gifted and talented adolescents: An international learning style.* New York: Praeger.

Jacobs, R. L. (1987). An investigation of the learning style differences among Afro-American and Euro-American high, average, and low achievers. Doctoral dissertation, George Peabody University. *Dissertation Abstracts International, 49*(01), 39A.

Jadid, R. (1998). Analysis of the learning styles, gender, and creativity of Bruneian elite-, high performing-, and non-performing primary- (elementary) and secondary-school students and their teachers' teaching styles. Doctoral dissertation, St. John's University.

Jalali, F. (1988). A cross cultural comparative analysis of the learning styles and field dependence/independence characteristics of selected fourth-, fifth-, and sixth-grade students of Afro, Chinese, Greek, and Mexican heritage. Doctoral dissertation, St. John's University. *Dissertation Abstracts International, 50*(62), 344A.

Jarsonbeck, S. (1984). The effects of a right-brain and mathematics curriculum on low achieving fourth grade students. Doctoral dissertation, University of South Florida. *Dissertation Abstracts International, 45*, 2791A.

Jenkins, C. (1991). The relationship between selected demographic variables and learning environmental preferences of freshman students of Alcorn State University. Doctoral dissertation, University of Mississippi. *Dissertation Abstracts International, 92*, 16065.

Johnson, C. D. (1984). Identifying potential school dropouts. Doctoral dissertation, United States International University. *Dissertation Abstracts International, 45*, 2397A.

Johnston, R. J. (1986). A comparative analysis between the effectiveness of conventional and modular instruction in teaching students with varied learning styles and individual differences enrolled in high school industrial arts manufacturing. Doctoral dissertation, North Carolina State University. *Dissertation Abstracts International, 47*(08)A, 2923.

Kahre, C. J. (1985). Relationships between learning styles of student teachers, cooperating teachers, and final evaluations. Doctoral dissertation, Arizona State University. *Dissertation Abstracts International, 45*, 2492A.

Kaley, S. B. (1977). Field dependence/independence and learning styles in sixth graders. Doctoral dissertation, Hofstra University. *Dissertation Abstracts International, 38*, 1301A.

Karlova, U., Lekarska, F., & Kralove, H. (1994). Dotaznik stylu ucenti pro zaky zakladnich a strednich skol/LSI—the questionnaire of learning styles for pupils of basic and middle education schools. *Psychologia-a-Patopsychologia-Dietat, 29*(3), 248–264.

Keefe, J. W. (1979). Foreword. In *Student learning styles: diagnosing and prescribing programs* (pp. i–ii). Reston. VA: National Association of Secondary School Principals.

Keefe, J. (1982). Foreword. In *Student learning style and brain behavior* (pp. 1–2). Reston, VA: National Association of Secondary School Principals.

Kelly, A. P. (1989). Elementary principals' change-facilitating behavior as perceived by self and staff when implementing learning styles instructional programs. Doctoral dissertation, St. John's University. *Dissertation Abstracts International, 51*(06), 1852.

Kennedy, M. D. (1995, Spring). The effects of an individual's learning style preference on psychomotor achievement for college students. Florida State University College of Education.

Kirby, P. (1979). *Cognitive styles, learning style, and transfer skill acquisition* (Information Series No. 195). National Center for Research in Vocational Education). Columbus: Ohio State University.

Kizilay, P. E. (1991). The relationship of learning style preferences and perceptions of college climate and performance on the National Council Licensure Examination for registered nurses in associate degree nursing programs. Doctoral dissertation, University of Georgia.

Klavas, A. (1991). Implementation of the Dunn and Dunn learning styles model in United States elementary schools: Principals' and teachers' perceptions of factors that facilitated or impeded the process. Doctoral dissertation, St. John's University.

Klavas, A. (1993). In Greensboro, North Carolina: Learning style program boosts achievement and test scores. *The Clearing House, 67*(3), 149–151.

Klavas, A., Dunn, R., Griggs, S. A., Gemake, J. Geisert, G., & Zenhausern, R. (1994). Factors that facilitated or impeded implementation of the Dunn and Dunn learning style model. *Illinois School Research and Development Journal, 31*(1), 19–23.

Kleinfeld, J., & Nelson, P. (1991). Adapting instruction to Native Americans' language styles: An iconoclastic view. *Journal of Cross Cultural Psychology, 22*(2), 273–282.

Kolb, D. (1976). *Learning Style Inventory: Technical manual.* Boston: McBer.

Koshuta, V., & Koshuta, P. (1993, April). Learning styles in a one-room school. *Educational Leadership, 50*(7), 87.

Kreitner, K. R. (1981). Modality strengths and learning styles of musically talented high school students. Unpublished master's dissertation, Ohio State University.

Krimsky, J. (1982). A comparative analysis of the effects of matching and mismatching fourth grade students with their learning style preference for the environmental element of light and their subsequent reading speed and accuracy scores. Doctoral dissertation, St. John's University. *Dissertation Abstracts International, 43*, 66A.

Kroon, D. (1985). An experimental investigation of the effects on academic achievement and the resultant administrative implications of instruction congruent and incongruent with secondary, industrial arts students' learning style perceptual preference. Doctoral dissertation, St. John's University. *Dissertation Abstracts International, 46*, 3247A.

Kulp, J. J. (1982). A description of the processes used in developing and implementing a teacher training program based on the Dunns' concept of learning style. Doctoral dissertation, Temple University. *Dissertation Abstracts International, 42*, 5021A.

Kussrow, P. G. (1994). Learning styles research and the community educator. *Michigan Principal, 70*(1), 9–12.

Kussrow, P. G., & Dunn, K. (1992, Summer). Learning styles and the community educator. *Community Education Journal, 19*(4), 16–19. Alexandria, VA: National Community Education Association.

Kuznar, E., Falciglia, G. A., Grace, A., Wood, L., & Frankel, J. (1991). Learning style preferences: A comparison of younger and older adult females. *Journal of Nutrition for the Elderly, 10*(3), 213–233.

Kyriacou, M., & Dunn, R. (1994). Synthesis of research: Learning styles of students with learning disabilities. *Special Education Journal, 4*(1), 3–9.

LaMothe, Billings, D. M., Belcher, A., Cobb, K., Nice, A., & Richardson, V. (1991). Reliability and validity of the productivity environmental preference survey (PEPs). *Nurse Educator, 16*(4), 30–34.

Lam-Phoon, S. (1986). A comparative study of the learning styles of southeast Asian and American Caucasian college students of two Seventh-Day Adventist campuses. Doctoral dissertation, Andrews University. *Dissertation Abstracts International, 48*(09), 2234A.

Lan Yong, F. (1989). Ethnic, gender, and grade differences in the learning style preferences of gifted minority students. Doctoral dissertation, Southern Illinois University at Carbondale.

Lau, L. (1997). The perceptual preferences of a group of Malaysian kindergarten children and the effects of tactile and kinesthetic teaching methods on their learning of Bahasa Melayu as a second language. Master's thesis, Massey University, Australia.

LeClair, T. J. (1986). The preferred perceptual modality of kindergarten-aged children. Master's thesis, California State University. *Master's Abstracts, 24*, 324.

Lemmon, P. (1985). A school where learning styles make a difference. *Principal, 64*(4), 26–29.

Lenehan, M. (1994). Effects of learning style knowledge on nursing majors' achievement, anxiety, anger, and curiosity. Doctoral dissertation, St. John's University.

Lenehan, M. C., Dunn, R., Ingham, J., Murray, W., & Signer, B. (1994, November). Learning style: Necessary know-how for academic success in college. *Journal of College Student Development, 35*, 461–466.

Lengal, O. (1983). Analysis of the preferred learning styles of former adolescent psychiatric patients. Doctoral dissertation, Kansas State University. *Dissertation Abstracts International, 44*, 2344A.

Li, T. C. (1989). The learning styles of the Filipino graduate students of the Evangelical seminaries in metro Manila. Doctoral dissertation, Asia Graduate School of Theology, Philippines.

Lieuthwaite, B. (1999). The Productivity Environmental Preference Survey and Building Excellence: A statistical comparison of two adult learning-style diagnostic instruments applied to a college population. Doctoral dissertation, St. John's University.

Listi, A. (1998). Effects of Programmed Learning Sequences versus traditional instruction on the social studies achievement and attitudes among urban third graders. Doctoral dissertation, St. John's University, New York.

Lux, K. (1987). Special needs students: A qualitative study of their learning styles. Doctoral dissertation, Michigan State University. *Dissertation Abstracts International, 49*(3), 421A.

Lynch, P. K. (1981). An analysis of the relationships among academic achievement, attendance, and the learning style time references of eleventh and twelfth grade students identified as initial or chronic truants in a suburban New York school district. Doctoral dissertation, St. John's University. *Dissertation Abstracts International, 42*, 1880A.

MacMurren, H. (1985). A comparative study of the effects of matching and mismatching sixth-grade students with their learning style preferences for the physical element of intake and their subsequent reading speed and accuracy scores and attitudes. Doctoral dissertation, St. John's University. *Dissertation Abstracts International, 46*, 3247A.

MacMurren, H. (Spring, 1992). Learning style and state law. *The Learning Consultant Journal, 13*, 21–24.

Madison, M. B. (1984). A study of learning style preferences of specific learning disability students. Doctoral dissertation, University of Southern Mississippi. *Dissertation Abstracts International, 46*, 3320A.

Marcus, L. (1977). How teachers view learning styles. *NASSP Bulletin, 61*(408), 112–114.

Mares, J., & Skalska, H. (1994). LSI—The questionnaire of learning styles for pupils of basic and middle-education schools. *Metodiky a konsultacie*, University Karlova, Czech Republic, *3*(S), 248–266.

Mariash, L. J. (1983). Identification of characteristics of learning styles existent among students attending school in selected northeastern Manitoba communities. Unpublished master's dissertation, University of Manitoba, Winnipeg, Canada.

Marino, J. (1993). Homework: A fresh approach to a perennial problem. *Momentum, 24*(1), 69–71.

Martin, M. M. (1993). A study of anxiety levels experienced by student nurses in a psychiatric clinical setting. Doctoral dissertation, University of Idaho. *Dissertation Abstracts International, 54*(6), 2069A.

Martini, M. (1986). An analysis of the relationships between and among computer-assisted instruction, learning style perceptual preferences, attitudes, and the science achievement of seventh grade students in a suburban, New York school district. Doctoral dissertation, St. John's University. *Dissertation Abstracts International, 47*, 877A.

McCabe, D. L. (1992). The underachieving gifted student: An evaluation of the relationship of learning style and academic self-concept to academic achievement and case study of one gifted high-school student. Doctoral dissertation, Virginia Polytechnic Institute and State University. *Dissertation Abstracts International, 54*(1), 92A.

McEwen, P. (1985). Learning styles, intelligence, and creativity among elementary school students. Unpublished master's dissertation, State University of New York at Buffalo, Center for Studies on Creativity.

McFarland, M. (1989). An analysis of the relationship between learning style perceptual preferences and attitudes toward computer assisted instruction. Doctoral dissertation, Portland State University. *Dissertation Abstracts International, 50*(10), 3143A.

Meighan, S. (1991). We put learning styles to work in our school, and you can too. *American School Board Journal, 172*(7), 30–31.

Mein, J. R. (1986). Cognitive and learning style characteristics of high school gifted students. Doctoral dissertation, University of Florida. *Dissertation Abstracts International, 48*(04), 880A.

Melone, R. A. (1987). The relationship between the level of cognitive development and learning styles of the emerging adolescent. Doctoral dissertation, State University of New York at Buffalo. *Dissertation Abstracts International, 38*, 607A.

Mickler, M. L., & Zippert, C. P. (1987). Teaching strategies based on learning styles of adult students. *Community/Junior College Quarterly, 11*, 33–37.

Miles, B. (1987). An investigation of the relationships among the learning style sociological preferences of fifth and sixth grade students, selected interactive classroom patterns, and achievement in career awareness and career decision-making concepts. Doctoral dissertation, St. John's University. *Dissertation Abstracts International, 48*, 2527A.

Milgram, R. M., & Dunn, R. (1993). Identifying learning styles and creativity in gifted learners: Subjects, instrumentation, administration, reliability, validity. In R. M. Milgram, R. Dunn, & G. E. Price (Eds.), *Teaching and counseling gifted and talented adolescents: An international learning style perspective* (Chapter 2, pp. 25–36). New York: Praeger.

Milgram, R. M., Dunn, R., & Price, G. E. (Eds.). (1993). *Teaching and counseling gifted and talented adolescents: An international learning style perspective*. Westport, CT: Praeger.

Milgram, R. M., Price, G. E., & Dunn, R. (1995). Learning styles of highly creative Israeli adolescents. *National Forum of Special Education Journal, 5*(1), 3–11.

Miller, J. (1997). The effects of traditional versus learning-style presentations of course content in ultrasound and anatomy on the achievement and attitudes of college students. Doctoral dissertation, St. John's University.

Miller, J., & Edgar, G. (1994). The Learning Style Inventory and the Learning Style Profile: Concurrent validity and the ability to discriminate among class rankings. *Illinois School Research and Development Journal, 31*(1), 14–18.

Miller, L. M. (1985). Mobility as an element of learning style: The effect its inclusion or exclusion has on student performance in the standardized testing environment. Unpublished master's dissertation, University of North Florida.

Monheit, S. L. (1987). An analysis of learning based upon the relationship between the learning style preferences of parents and their children. Doctoral dissertation, The Fielding Institute. *Dissertation Abstracts International, 50*(2), 395A.

Monsour, S. E. M. (1991). The relationship between a prescribed homework program considering learning style preferences and the mathematics achievement of eighth-grade students. Doctoral dissertation, The University of Southern Mississippi. *Dissertation Abstracts International, 52*(6)A, 1630A.

Montgomery L. F. (1993). A comparison of learning styles of traditional high school students and adult students in Missouri area vocational technical schools. Doctoral dissertation, University of Missouri–Columbia. *Dissertation Abstracts International 54*(10), 3725.

Moore, R. C. (1991). Effects of computer assisted instruction and perceptual preference(s) of eighth-grade students on the mastery of language arts and mathematics (CAI, perceptual preferences). Doctoral dissertation, South Carolina State University. *Dissertation Abstracts International, 53*(06), 1876.

Morgan, H. L. (1981). Learning styles: The relation between need for structure and preferred mode of instruction for gifted elementary students. Doctoral dissertation, University of Pittsburgh. *Dissertation Abstracts International, 43*, 2223A.

Morris, V. J. P. (1983). The design and implementation of a teaching strategy for language arts at Chipley High School that brings about predictable learning outcomes. Doctoral dissertation, Florida State University. *Dissertation Abstracts International, 44*, 3231A.

Moss, V. B. (1981). The stability of first-graders' learning styles and the relationship between selected variables and learning style. Doctoral dissertation, Mississippi State University. *Dissertation Abstracts International, 43*(3), 665A.

Murrain, P. G. (1983). Administrative determinations concerning facilities utilization and instructional grouping: An analysis of the relationships between selected thermal environments and preferences for temperature, an element of learning style, as they affect word recognition scores of secondary students. Doctoral dissertation, St. John's University. *Dissertation Abstracts International, 44*, 1749A.

Murray, C. A. (1980). The comparison of learning styles between low and high reading achievement subjects in the seventh and eighth grades in a public middle school. Doctoral dissertation, United States International University. *Dissertation Abstracts International, 41*, 1005.

Murray-Harvey, R. (1994). Learning styles and approaches to learning: Distinguishing between concepts and instruments. *British Journal of Educational Psychology, 63*(3), 373–388.

Myers, I. (1962). *Myers-Briggs Type Indicator*: Palo Alto, CA: Consulting Psychologists Press.

Naden, R. C. (1992). Prescriptions and/or modality-based instruction on the spelling achievement of fifth-grade students. Doctoral dissertation, Andrews University. *Dissertation Abstracts International, 53*(04)A, 1051.

Nahamoni, M. (1995). Learning style and homework style of gifted and nongifted adolescents. Master's thesis, Tel Aviv University School of Education (under the supervision of Professor Roberta M. Milgram).

Napolitano, R. A. (1986). An experimental investigation of the relationships among achievement, attitude scores, and traditionally, marginally, and underprepared college students enrolled in an introductory psychology course when they are matched and mismatched with their learning style preferences for the element of structure. Doctoral dissertation, St. John's University. *Dissertation Abstracts International, 47*, 435A.

Natale, S. M., Callan, R. J., Ford, J., & Sora, S. (1992, Winter). Social control, efficiency control, and ethical control in different political institutions: Education. *International Journal of Applied Philosophy*, pp. 25–32. New York: International Association of Applied Philosophy.

Nations-Miller, B. R. (1993, February). A profile analysis of the learning styles of tenth-through twelfth-grade at-risk, vocational and gifted students in a suburban Georgia public school. Doctoral dissertation, Georgia State University. *Dissertation Abstracts International, 53*(08)A, 2784.

Neely, R. O., & Alm, D. (1992, November–December). Meeting individual needs: A learning styles success story. *The Clearing House, 2*, 109–113. Washington, DC: Heldref Publications.

Neely, R. O., & Alm, D. (1993). Empowering students with styles. *Principal, 72*(4), 32–35. Reston, VA: National Association of Elementary School Principals.

Nelson, B. N. (1991). An investigation of the impact of learning style factors on college students' retention and achievement. Doctoral dissertation, St. John's University.

Nelson, B., Dunn, R., Griggs, S. A., Primavera, L., Fitzpatrick, M., Bacillious, Z., & Miller, R. (1993). Effects of learning style intervention on students' retention and achievement. *Journal of College Student Development, 34*(5), 364–369.

Nganwa-Bagumah, M. (1986). Learning styles: The effects of matching and mismatching pupils' design preferences on reading comprehension tests. Bachelor's dissertation, University of Transkei, South Africa.

Nganwa-Bagumah, M., & Mwamwenda, T. S. (1991). Effects on reading comprehension tests of matching and mismatching students' design preferences. *Perceptual and Motor Skills, 72*(3), 947–951.

Nides, A. G. (1984). The effect of learning style preferences on achievement when an advanced organizer is employed. Doctoral dissertation, Georgia State University College of Education. *Dissertation Abstracts International, 45*(05)A, 1288.

Ogato, B. G. (1991). A correlational examination of perceptual modality preferences of middle school students and their academic achievement. Doctoral dissertation, Virginia Polytechnic Institute, Northern Virginia Graduate Center. *Dissertation Abstracts International, 52*(12), 4210.

O'Hare, L. E. (1997). *Cardiovascular assessment: Have a heart!* New York: St. John's University's Center for the Study of Learning and Teaching Styles.

Orsak, L. (1990, October). Learning styles versus the Rip Van Winkle syndrome. *Educational Leadership, 48*(2), 19–20. Alexandria, VA: Association for Supervision and Curriculum Development.

Ostoyee, C. H. (1988). The effects of teaching style on student writing about field trips with concrete experiences. Doctoral dissertation, Teachers College, Columbia University. *Dissertation Abstracts International, 49*, 2916A.

Paskewitz, B. U. (1985). A study of the relationship between learning styles and attitudes toward computer programming of middle school gifted students. Doctoral dissertation, University of Pittsburgh. *Dissertation Abstracts International, 47*(03), 697A.

Pederson, J. K. (1984). The classification and comparison of learning disabled students and gifted students. Doctoral dissertation, Texas Tech University. *Dissertation Abstracts International, 45*(09)A, 2810.

Perkins, P., & Milgram, R. M. (in press). Parent involvement in homework: A double-edged sword. *International Journal of Adolescence and Youth.*

Perrin, J. (1983). *Learning Style Inventory: Primary Version.* Jamaica, NY: St. John's University's Center for the Study of Learning and Teaching Styles.

Perrin, J. (1984). An experimental investigation of the relationships among the learning style sociological preferences of gifted and non-gifted primary children, selected instructional strategies, attitudes, and achievement in problem solving and rote memorization. Doctoral dissertation, St. John's University. *Dissertation Abstracts International, 46*, 342A.

Perrin, J. (1990, October). The learning styles project for potential dropouts. *Educational Leadership, 48*(2), 23–24. Alexandria, VA: Association for Supervision and Curriculum Development.

Pizzo, J. (1981). An investigation of the relationships between selected acoustic environments and sound, an element of learning style, as they affect sixth grade students' reading achievement and attitudes. Doctoral dissertation, St. John's University. *Dissertation Abstracts International, 42*, 2475A.

Pizzo, J. (December, 1982). Breaking the sound barrier: Classroom noise and learning style. *Orbit 64, 13*(4), 21–22. Ontario Canada: Ontario Institute for Studies in Education.

Pizzo, J., Dunn, R., & Dunn, K. (1990, July–September). A sound approach to reading: Responding to students' learning styles. *Journal of Reading, Writing, and Learning Disabilities International, 6*(3), 249–260. Washington, DC: Hemisphere.

Ponce Meza, R. M. (1997, July). Talent search identification model: A detection system of learning style and creativity talents of undergraduate students. Paper presented at the Twelfth World Conference of the World Council for Gifted and Talented Children, Seattle.

Ponder, D. (1990). An analysis of the changes and gender differences in preferences of learning styles at adolescence and the relationship of the learning styles of adolescents and their parents when matched and mismatched according to gender. Doctoral dissertation, East Texas State University. *Dissertation Abstracts International, 64*(4), 1170A.

Price, G. E. (1980). Which learning style elements are stable and which tend to change over time? *Learning Styles Network Newsletter, 1*(3), 1.

Price, G. E., Dunn, K., Dunn, R., & Griggs, S. A. (1981). Studies in students' learning styles. *Roeper Review, 4,* 223–226.

Price, G. E., & Milgram, R. M. (1993). The learning styles of gifted adolescents around the world: Differences and similarities. In R. M. Milgram, R. Dunn, & G. E. Price (Eds.), *Teaching and counseling gifted and talented adolescents: An international learning-styles perspective* (Chapter 16, pp. 229–247). Westport, CT: Praeger.

Quindag, S. R. (1992). The effects of guided aural versus guided aural-visual modeling on the performance achievement of beginning string instrumentalists (guided aural modeling). Doctoral dissertation, University of North Carolina at Greensboro. *Dissertation Abstract International, 54*(02), 455.

Quinn, R. (1993). The New York State compact for learning and learning styles. *Learning Styles Network Newsletter, 15*(1), 1–2. New York: St. John's University and the National Association of Secondary School Principals.

Quinn, T. (1995, May). Goals 2000 and the Learning-Styles Connection. *NYC Challenge, 10,* 21–24. New York: New York City Association for Supervision and Curriculum Development.

Ragsdale, C. S. (1991). The experiences and impressions of tenth-grade students in a modern European history class designed as a collaborative, heuristic learning environment. Doctoral dissertation, Union Institute. *Dissertation Abstracts International, 52*(03)A. 796.

Rahal, B. F. (1986). The effects of matching and mismatching the diagnosed learning styles of intermediate level students with their structure preferences in the learning environment. Doctoral dissertation, West Virginia University. *Dissertation Abstracts International, 47*(06)A, 2010.

Ramirez, A. I. (1982). Modality and field dependence/independence: Learning components and their relationship to mathematics achievement in the elementary school. Doctoral dissertation, Florida State University. *Dissertation Abstracts International, 43,* 666.

Ramirez, M., & Castenada, A. (1974). *Cultural democracy: Bicognitive development and education.* New York: Academic Press.

Raupers, P. M. (1995). *Understanding memory: How to plant a FORGET-ME-NOT!* Demaraest, NJ: Northern Valley Schools Curriculum Center.

Raupers, P. M. (1996). A learning styles approach to staff development. *Focus in Education, 40,* 38–40. Bayonne, NJ: New Jersey Association for Supervision and Curriculum Development.

Raupers, P. M. (1997). *The triune brain theory: Three for the price of one.* New York: St. John's University's Center for the Study of Learning and Teaching Styles.

Raupers, P. M. (1999). Effects of accommodating perceptual learning-style preferences on long-term retention and attitudes toward technology of elementary and secondary teachers in professional development training. Doctoral dissertation, St. John's University.

Raviotta, C. F. (1988). A study of the relationship between knowledge of individual learning style and its effect on academic achievement and study orientation in high school mathematics students. Doctoral dissertation, University of New Orleans. *Dissertation Abstracts International, 50*(05)A, 1204.

Rea, D. C. (1980). Effects on achievement of placing students in different learning environments based upon identified learning styles. Doctoral dissertation, University of Missouri.

Reid, J. M. (1987, March). The learning style preferences of ESL students. *TESOL Quarterly, 21*, 87–105. Available to members only from TESP, 1118 22nd Street, N.W., Georgetown University, Suite 205, Washington, DC 20037.

Research on the Dunn and Dunn model. (1998). Jamaica, NY: St. John's University's Center for the Study of Learning and Teaching Styles.

Restak, R. (1979). *The brain: The last frontier.* New York: Doubleday.

Reynolds, J. (1988). A study of the pattern of learning style characteristics for adult dependent decision-makers. Doctoral dissertation, Virginia Polytech Institute and State University. *Dissertation Abstracts International, 50*(04)A, 854.

Reynolds, J. (1991, December). Learning style characteristics of adult dependent decision makers: Counseling and instructional implications. *Career Development Quarterly, 40*, 145–154.

Reynolds, J., & Werner, S. C. (1993–1994). An alternative paradigm for college reading and study skills courses. *Journal of Reading, 37*(4), 272–277.

Ricca, J. (1983). Curricular implications of learning style differences between gifted and nongifted students. Doctoral dissertation, State University of New York at Buffalo. *Dissertation Abstracts International, 44*, 1324A.

Roberts, O. A. (1984). Investigation of the relationship between learning style and temperament of senior high students in the Bahamas and Jamaica. Graduate dissertation, Andrews University.

Rodrigo, R. A. (1989). A comparison of the profiles of the learning styles of first-grade pupils at the Ateneo DeManila Grade School for the school year 1988–1989. Master's dissertation, Graduate School Atteneo de Manila University.

Rundle, S., & Dunn, R. (1996). *Building excellence.* Pittsford, NY: Performance Concepts.

Sage, C. O. (1984). The Dunn and Dunn learning style model: An analysis of its theoretical, practical, and research foundations. Doctoral dissertation, University of Denver. *Dissertation Abstracts International, 45*(12), 3537A.

Sawyer, E. (1995). The need for structure among high school students: When is enough, enough? *NASSP Principal, 79*(569), 85–92. Reston, VA: National Association of Secondary School Principals.

Schiering, M. (1997). *Ecosystems: There's a niche for you.* New York: St. John's University's Center for the Study of Learning and Teaching Styles.

Schmeck, R. R., Ribich, F. D., & Ramanaiah, N. (1977). Development of a self-report inventory for assisting individual differences in learning processes. *Applied Psychological Measurement, 1*(3), 413–431.

Sedgwick, C. B. (1992). The effects of auditory subliminal messages on weight, pre-conscious processing, and self-esteem. Doctoral dissertation, University of Georgia. *Dissertation Abstracts International, 54*(2), 429A.

Shands, R., & Brunner, C., (1989, Fall). Providing success through a powerful combination: Mastery learning and learning styles. *Perceptions, 25*(1), 6–10. New York: New York State Educators of the Emotionally Disturbed.

Shea, T. C. (1983). An investigation of the relationship among preferences for the learning style element of design, selected instructional environments, and reading achievement with ninth grade students to improve administrative determinations concerning effective educational facilities. Doctoral dissertation, St. John's University. *Dissertation Abstracts International, 44*, 2004A.

Siebenman, J. B. (1984). An investigation of the relationship between learning style and cognitive style in non-traditional college reading students. Doctoral dissertation, Arizona State University. *Dissertation Abstracts International, 45*, 1705A.

Sims, J. E. (1988). Learning styles: A comparative analysis of the learning styles of Black-American, Mexican-American, and White-American third and fourth grade students in traditional public schools. Doctoral dissertation, University of Santa Barbara.

Sims, J. (1989, Winter). Learning style: Should it be considered? *Oregon Elementary Principal, 50*(2), 28. Salem: Oregon Elementary Principals' Association.

Sinatra, C. (1990, July–September). Five diverse secondary schools where learning style instruction works. *Journal of Reading, Writing, and Learning Disabilities International, 6*(3), 323–342. New York: Hemisphere.

Sinatra, R., Hirshoren, A., & Primavera, L. H. (1987). Learning style, behavior ratings and achievement interactions for adjudicated adolescents. *Educational and Psychological Research, 7*(1), 21–32.

Sinatra, R., Primavera L., & Waked, W. J. (1986). Learning style and intelligence of reading disabled students. *Perceptual and Motor Skills, 62*, 243–252.

Sinatra, R., Sazo de Mendez, E., & Price, G. E. (1993). The learning styles and creative performance accomplishments of adolescents in Guatemala. In R. M. Milgram, R. Dunn, & G. E. Price (Eds.), *Teaching and counseling gifted and talented adolescents: An international learning style perspective* (Chapter 10, pp. 161–173). Westport, CT: Praeger.

Singleton, N. (1993). Learning style assessment. Doctoral dissertation, University of Portland.

Smith, S. (1987). An experimental investigation of the relationship between and among achievement, preferred time of instruction, and critical-thinking abilities of tenth- and eleventh-grade students in mathematics. Doctoral dissertation, St. John's University. *Dissertation Abstracts International, 47*, 1405A.

Smith, T. D. (1988). An assessment of the self-perceived teaching style of three ethnic groups of public school teachers in Texas. Doctoral dissertation, East Texas University. *Dissertation Abstracts International, 49*(08), 2062A.

Snider, K. P. (1985). A study of learning preferences among educable mentally impaired, emotionally impaired, learning disabled, and general education students in seventh, eighth, and ninth grades as measured by response to the Learning Styles Inventory. Doctoral dissertation, Michigan State University. *Dissertation Abstracts International, 46*(05), 1251.

Solberg, S. J. (1987). An analysis of the Learning Style Inventory, the Productivity Environmental Preference Survey, and the Iowa Test of Basic Skills. Doctoral dissertation, Northern Arizona University. *Dissertation Abstracts International, 48*, 2530A.

Soliman, A. S. (1993). The learning styles of adolescents in Egypt. In R. M. Milgram, R. Dunn, & G. E. Price (Eds.), *Teaching and counseling gifted and talented adolescents: An international learning style perspective* (Chapter 14, pp. 210–218). Westport, CT: Praeger.

Spires, R. D. (1983). The effect of teacher inservice about learning styles on students' mathematics and reading achievement. Doctoral dissertation, Bowling Green State University. *Dissertation Abstracts International, 44*, 1325A.

Spiridakis, J. (1993). The learning styles of adolescents in Greece. In R. M. Milgram, R. Dunn, & G. E. Price (Eds.), *Teaching and counseling gifted and talented adolescents: An international learning style perspective* (Chapter 15, pp. 219–227). Westport, CT: Praeger.

Stahlnecker, R. K. (1988). Relationships between learning style preferences of selected elementary pupils and their achievement in math and reading. Doctoral dissertation, Loma Linda University. *Dissertation Abstracts International, 50*(11)A, 3471.

Steinauer, M. H. (1981). Interpersonal relationships as reflected in learning style preferences: A study of eleventh grade students and their English teachers in a vocational school. Doctoral dissertation, Southern Illinois University. *Dissertation Abstracts International, 43*, 305A.

Stiles, R. (1985). Learning style preferences for design and their relationship to standardized test results. Doctoral dissertation, University of Tennessee. *Dissertation Abstracts International, 46*, 2551A.

Stokes, B. M. (1989). An analysis of the relationship between learning style, achievement, race, and gender. Doctoral dissertation, University of Akron. *Dissertation Abstracts International, 49,* 757A.

Stone, P. (1992, November). How we turned around a problem school. *The Principal, 71*(2), 34–36. Reston, VA: National Association of Elementary School Principals.

Studd, M. (1995). Learning-style differences. *The Clearing House, 69*(1), 38–39. Washington, DC: Heldref.

Suh, B., & Price, G. E. (1993). The learning styles of gifted adolescents in Korea. In R. M. Milgram, R. Dunn, & G. E. Price (Eds.), *Teaching and counseling gifted and talented adolescents: An international learning style perspective* (Chapter 11, pp. 174–185). New York: Praeger.

Sullivan, M. (1993). A meta-analysis of experimental research studies based on the Dunn and Dunn learning styles model and its relationship to academic achievement and performance. Doctoral dissertation, St. John's University. *Dissertation Abstracts International 51*(98), 2976.

Sullivan, M. (1996–1997). A meta-analysis of experimental research studies based on the Dunn and Dunn learning styles model and its relationship to academic achievement and performance. *National Forum of Applied Educational Research, 10*(1), 3–10. Monroe: Northeast Louisiana University, College of Education.

Svreck, L. J. (1990). Perceived parental influence, accommodated learning style preferences, and students' attitudes toward learning as they relate to reading and mathematics achievement. Doctoral dissertation, St. John's University. *Dissertation Abstracts International, 53*(02), 395.

Sykes, S., Jones, B., & Phillips, J. (1990, October). Partners in learning styles at a private school. *Educational Leadership, 48*(2), 24–26. Alexandria, VA: Association for Supervision and Curriculum Development.

Tanenbaum, R. (1982). An investigation of the relationships between selected instructional techniques and identified field dependent and field independent cognitive styles as evidenced among high school students enrolled in studies of nutrition. Doctoral dissertation, St. John's University. *Dissertation Abstracts International, 43,* 68A.

Tanzman, J., & Dunn, K. (1971). *Using instructional media effectively.* Englewood Cliffs, NJ: Parker Publishing Company, A Prentice-Hall Division.

Tappenden, V. J. (1983). Analysis of the learning styles of vocational education and nonvocational education students in eleventh and twelfth grades from rural, urban, and suburban locations in Ohio. Doctoral dissertation, Kent State University. *Dissertation Abstracts International, 44,* 1326A.

Taylor, R. G. (1999). Effects of learning style responsive versus traditional staff development on the knowledge and attitudes of urban and suburban elementary school teachers. Doctoral dissertation, St. John's University.

Tendy, S. (1998a). Effects of matching and mismatching sociological and perceptual learning-style preferences on achievement and attitudes of individuals in a group exercise leadership instructor training program. Doctoral dissertation, St. John's University.

Tendy, S. (1998b). Teaching aerobics: Don't hold your breath! In *Effects of matching and mismatching sociological and perceptual learning-style preferences on achievement of individuals in a group exercise leadership instructor training program.* Jamaica, NY: St. John's University's Center for the Study of Learning and Teaching Styles.

Thies, A. (1979). A brain–behavior analysis of learning styles. In *Student learning styles: Diagnosing and prescribing programs* (pp. 55–62). Reston, VA: National Association of Secondary School Principals.

Thomson, F. L. (1994). Mazapan't learning styles: Phase 11. *Inter Ed, 21*(70), 17. New Wilmington, PA: Association for the Advancement of International Education.

Thomson, B. S. (1994). Fruits, bats, cats, and naked mole rats: Lifelong learning at the zoo. *Digest,* EDO-SE-94-2. Columbus, OH: ERIC Clearinghouse for Science, Mathematics, and Environmental Education.

Tiller, R. W. (1991). An investigation into the extent of congruency between general and music-specific learning style preferences. Doctoral dissertation, Michigan State University. *Dissertation Abstracts International, 52*(5), 1677A.

Torres, P. L. (1992). *The identification of second-grade students' learning styles.* Master's thesis, University of Brasillia, 1992.

Trautman, P. (1979). An investigation of the relationship between selected instructional techniques and identified cognitive style. Doctoral dissertation, St. John's University. *Dissertation Abstracts International, 40*, 1428A.

Tseng, H. L. (1993). Differences in learning styles among Chinese-American, Anglo-American, and Hispanic-American students. Doctoral dissertation, University of Houston. *Masters Abstracts International, 31*(4), 145.

Turner, N. D. (1992). A comparative study of the effects of learning style prescriptions and/or modality-based instruction on the spelling achievement of fifth-grade students. Doctoral dissertation, Andrews University. *Dissertation Abstracts International, 53*(04), 1051.

Van Wynen, E. A. (1997). Information processing styles: One size doesn't fit all. *Nurse Educator, 22*(5), 44–50.

Van Wynen, E. (in progress). Analysis of current and previous learning styles of older adults and the effects of congruent and incongruent instruction on their achievement and attitudes. Doctoral dissertation, St. John's University.

Vaughan, J. L., Underwood, V. L., House, G. L., Weaver, S. W., & Dotson, S. (1992). *Learning styles and TAAS scores: Preliminary results.* Research Report No. 3. Commerce: Texas Center for Learning Styles, East Texas State University.

Vaughan, J. L., Weaver, S. L., Underwood, V. L., Binversie, N., House, G., Durkin, M., & Schroth, G. (1992). *The learning style characteristics of Tohono O'Odham students: An executive summary.* Research Report No. 1. Commerce: Texas Center for Learning Styles, East Texas State University.

Vaughan, J. L., Weaver, S. L., Underwood, V. L., & House, G. L. (1992). *A comparison of students' learning styles as determined by the Learning Style Inventory and Personal Learning Power.* Research Report No. 2. Commerce: Texas Center for Learning Styles, East Texas State University.

Vazquez, A. W. (1985). Description of learning styles of high risk adult students taking courses in urban community colleges in Puerto Rico. Doctoral dissertation, Union for Experimenting Colleges and Universities, Puerto Rico. *Dissertation Abstracts International, 47*, 1157A.

Vignia, R. A. (1983). An investigation of learning styles of gifted and non-gifted high school students. Doctoral dissertation, University of Houston. *Dissertation Abstracts International, 44*, 3653A.

Virostko, J. (1983). An analysis of the relationships among academic achievement in mathematics and reading, assigned instructional schedules, and the learning style time preferences of third, fourth, fifth, and sixth grade students. Doctoral dissertation, St. John's University. *Dissertation Abstracts International, 44*, 1683A.

Wallace, J. (1990). The relationship among preferences for learning alone or with peers, selected instructional strategies, and achievement of third-, fourth-, and fifth-grade social studies students. Doctoral dissertation, Syracuse University. *Dissertation Abstracts International, 51*(11), 3626A.

Weaver, S. (1992). Learning style profile for Tohono O' Odaham elementary students with implications for literacy programs. Doctoral dissertation, East Texas State University. *Dissertation Abstracts International, 53*(12), 4255-A.

Wechsler, S. (1993). The learning styles of creative adolescents in Brazil. In R. M. Milgram, R. Dunn, & G. E. Price (Eds.), *Teaching and counseling gifted and talented adolescents: An international learning style perspective* (Chapter 13, pp. 197–209). Westport, CT: Praeger.

Wegner, W. A. (1980). Opsimathic styles of adults. Doctoral dissertation, University of Southern Mississippi. *Dissertation Abstracts International, 41*(05)A, 1898.

Weinberg, F. (1983). An experimental investigation of the interaction between sensory modality preference and mode of presentation in the instruction of arithmetic concepts to third grade underachievers. Doctoral dissertation, St. John's University. *Dissertation Abstracts International, 44,* 1740A.

Wheeler, R. (1983). An investigation of the degree of academic achievement evidenced when second grade, learning disabled students' perceptual preferences are matched and mismatched with complementary sensory approaches to beginning reading instruction. Doctoral dissertation, St. John's University. *Dissertation Abstracts International, 44,* 2039A.

White, R. (1981). An investigation of the relationship between selected instructional methods and selected elements of emotional learning style upon student achievement in seventh grade social studies. Doctoral dissertation, St. John's University. *Dissertation Abstracts International, 42,* 995A.

White, R. H. (1993). A study of the relationship between teachers' learning styles preferences and their use of the microcomputer at home and at school in Medfield, Massachusetts. Doctoral dissertation, Boston College. *Dissertation Abstracts International, 54*(6), 2124A.

Whitefield, D. (1994). An analysis of the relationships of academic achievement in examinations and the learning-style preferences of design and structure of second-year accounting students. MBA dissertation, Victoria University of Technology.

Wiebe, R. D. (1992). A learning style profile of physics students in comparison with non-physics students. Masters thesis, Gonzaga University, Spokane, Washington.

Wilburn, H. R. (1991). An investigation of interaction among learning styles and computer-assisted instruction with synthetic speech. Doctoral dissertation, The University of Texas at Austin. *Dissertation Abstracts International, 52*(7)A, 2398A–2399A.

Wild, J. B. (1979). A study of the learning styles of learning disabled students and non-learning students at the junior high school level. Unpublished master's dissertation, University of Kansas.

Williams, G. L. (1984). The effectiveness of computer assisted instruction and its relationship to selected learning style elements. Doctoral dissertation, North Texas State University. *Dissertation Abstracts International, 45,* 1986A.

Williams, G. J. (1989). A study of the learning styles of urban black middle school learning-disabled and non-learning-disabled students. Doctoral dissertation, Southern Illinois University. *Dissertation Abstracts International, 51*(6)A.

Williams, H. S. (1994). The differences in cumulative grade point averages among African-American freshman college learning styles: A preliminary investigation. *National Forum of Applied Educational Research Journal, 8*(1), 36–40.

Willis, M. G. (1989). Learning styles of African-American children: A review of the literature and interventions. *Journal of Black Psychology, 16*(1), 47–65.

Wingo, L. H. (1980). Relationships among locus of motivation, sensory modality and grouping preferences of learning style to basic skills test performance in reading and mathematics. Doctoral dissertation, Memphis State University. *Dissertation Abstracts International, 41,* 2923.

Witkin, H. A. (1971). Embedded Figures Test, *Myers-Briggs Type Indicator.* Palo Alto, CA: Consulting Psychologists Press.

Wittenberg, S. K. (1984). A comparison of diagnosed and preferred learning styles of young adults in need of remediation. Doctoral dissertation, University of Toledo. *Dissertation Abstracts International, 45,* 3539A.

Wittig, C. (1985). Learning style preferences among students high or low on divergent thinking and feeling variables. Unpublished master's dissertation, State University of New York College at Buffalo, Center for Studies in Creativity.

Wolfe, G. (1983). Learning styles and the teaching of reading. Doctoral dissertation, Akron University. *Dissertation Abstracts International, 45,* 3422A.

Yeap, L. L. (1987). Learning styles of Singapore secondary students. Doctoral dissertation, University of Pittsburgh. *Dissertation Abstracts International, 48,* 936A.

Yong, F. L. A. (1992). Comparative study on the learning styles among gifted African-American, Mexican-American, and American-born Chinese middle-grade students. Doctoral dissertation, Southern Illinois University. *Dissertation Abstracts International, 53*(6), 1796A.

Yong, F. L. A., & McIntyre, J. D. (1992). A comparative study of the learning styles preferences of students with learning disabilities and students who are gifted. *Journal of Learning Disabilities, 25*(2), 124–132.

Young, B. M. P. (1985). Effective conditions for learning: An analysis of learning environments and learning styles in ability-grouped classes. Doctoral dissertation, University of Massachusetts. *Dissertation Abstracts International, 46,* 708A.

Young, D. B., Jr. (1986). Administrative implications of instructional strategies and student learning style preferences of science achievement on seventh-grade students. Doctoral dissertation, University of Hawaii. *Dissertation Abstracts International, 48*(01)A, 27.

Young, D. B., Jr. (1993). Science achievement and thinking skills: The effects of a sequence of instructional strategies and learning style preferences with seventh grade students. *Pacific-Asian Education, 5*(1).

Zak, F. (1989). Learning style discrimination between vocational and nonvocational students. Doctoral dissertation, University of Massachusetts. *Dissertation Abstracts International, 50*(12)A, 3843A.

Zenhausern, R. (1980). *Differential Hemispheric Activation Test.* New York: St. John's University Department of Psychology.

Zikmund, A. B. (1988). The effect of grade level, gender, and learning style on responses to conservation type rhythmic and melodic patterns. Doctoral dissertation, University of Nebraska. *Dissertation Abstracts International, 50*(1), 95A.

Zikmund, A. B. (1992, April). The effects of perceptual mode preferences and other selected variables on upper-elementary school students' response to conservation-type rhythmic and melodic tasks. *Psychology of Music, 20*(1), 57–69.

APPENDIX A

Research Award Winners

Carbo, M. (1980). An analysis of the relationship between the modality preferences of kindergartners and selected reading treatments as they affect the learning of a basic sight-word vocabulary. Doctoral dissertation, St. John's University, New York. *Dissertation Abstracts International, 41*(04)A, 1389. **Recipient:** Association for Supervision and Curriculum Development National Award for Best Doctoral Research, 1980.

White, R. (1980). An investigation of the relationship between selected instructional methods and selected elements of emotional learning style upon student achievement in seventh-grade social studies. Doctoral dissertation, St. John's University, New York. *Dissertation Abstracts International, 42*(03)A, 995. **Recipient:** Delta Kappa Gamma International Award for Best Research Prospectus, 1980.

Lynch, P. K. (1981). An analysis of the relationships among academic achievement, attendance, and the learning style time preferences of eleventh- and twelfth-grade students identified as initial or chronic truants in a suburban New York school district. Doctoral dissertation, St. John's University, New York. *Dissertation Abstracts International, 42*A, 1980. **Recipient:** Association for Supervision and Curriculum Development. National Recognition for Best Doctoral Research (Supervision), 1981.

Pizzo, J. (1981). An investigation of the relationships between selected acoustic environments and sound, an element of learning style, as they affect sixth-grade students' reading achievement and attitudes. Doctoral dissertation, St. John's University, New York. *Dissertation Abstracts International, 42,* 2475A. **Recipient:** Association for Supervision and Curriculum Development. National Recognition for Best Doctoral Research (Supervision) 1981.

Krimsky, J. (1982). A comparative analysis of the effects of matching and mismatching fourth-grade students with their learning style preferences for the environmental element of light and their subsequent reading speed and accuracy scores. Doctoral dissertation, St. John's University, New York. *Dissertation Abstracts International, 43*(01)A, 66. **Recipient:** Association for Supervision and Curriculum Development First Alternate National Recognition for Best Doctoral Research (Curriculum), 1982.

Virostko, J. (1983). An analysis of the relationships among academic achievement in mathematics and reading, assigned instructional schedules, and the learning style time preferences of third-, fourth-, fifth-, and sixth-grade students. Doctoral dissertation, St. John's University, New York. *Dissertation Abstracts International, 4*(06)A, 1683. **Recipient:** Kappa Delta Pi International Award for Best Doctoral Research, 1983.

Shea, T. C. (1983). An investigation of the relationships among preferences for the learning style element of design, selected instructional environments, and reading achievement of ninth-grade students to improve administrative determinations concerning effective educational facilities. Doctoral dissertation, St. John's University, New York. *Dissertation Abstracts International, 44*(07)A, 2004. **Recipient:** National Association of Secondary School Principals Middle School Research Finalist Citations, 1984.

DellaValle, J. (1984). An experimental investigation of the relationship(s) between preference for mobility and the word recognition scores of seventh-grade students to provide supervisory and administrative guidelines for the organization of effective instructional environments. Doctoral dissertation, St. John's University, New York. *Dissertation Abstracts International, 45*(02)A, 359. **Recipient:** (a) Phi Delta Kappa National Award for Outstanding Doctoral Research, 1984; (b) National Association of Secondary School Principals Middle School Research Finalist Citation, 1984; and (c) Association of Supervision and Curriculum Development Finalist Award for Best National Research, (Supervision), 1984.

Perrin, J. (1984). An experimental investigation of the relationships among the learning style sociological preferences of gifted and non-gifted primary children, selected instructional strategies, attitudes, and achievement in problem solving and rote memorization. Doctoral dissertation, St. John's University, New York. *Dissertation Abstracts International, 46*(02)A, 342. **Recipient:** American Association of School Administrators (AASA) National Research Finalist Recognition, 1984.

Hodges, H. (1985). An analysis of the relationships among preferences for a formal/informal design, one element of learning style, academic achievement, and attitudes of seventh- and eighth-grade students in remedial mathematics classes in a New York City junior high school. Doctoral dissertation, St. John's University, New York. *Dissertation Abstracts International, 45,* 2791A. **Recipient:** Phi Delta Kappa National Award for Outstanding Doctoral Research, 1986.

Martini, M. (1986). An analysis of the relationships between and among computer-assisted instruction, learning style perceptual preferences, attitudes, and the science achievement of seventh-grade students in a suburban New York school district. Doctoral dissertation, St. John's University, New York. *Dissertation Abstracts International, 47*(03)A, 877. **Recipient:** American Association of School Administrators (AASA) National Research Finalist, 1986; AASA First Prize National Award for Best Doctoral Research, 1987.

Miles, B. (1987). An investigation of the relationships among the learning style sociological preferences of fifth- and sixth-grade students, selected interactive classroom patterns, and achievement in career awareness and career decision-making concepts. Doctoral dissertation, St. John's University, New York. *Dissertation Abstracts International, 48,* 2527A. **Recipient:** Phi Delta Kappa Eastern Regional Research Award, 1988.

Ingham, J. (1989). An experimental investigation of the relationships among learning style perceptual strengths, instructional strategies, training achievement, and attitudes of corporate employees. Doctoral dissertation, St. John's University, New York, 1989. **Recipient:** (a) American Society of Training and Development Donald Bullock Dissertation Award (1989) and (b) Phi Delta Kappa Eastern Regional Research Award, 1990.

Quinn, T. (1995). **Recipient:** American Association of School Administrators and Convention Exhibitors Research Award (1994) for best doctoral proposal.

Callan, R. (1996). **Recipient:** American Association of School Administrators and Convention Exhibitors Research Award (1995) for best doctoral proposal.

Listi, A. L. (1996). **Recipient:** Delta Kappa Gamma Society International Scholarship for best doctoral proposal.

Geiser, W. P. (1998). **Recipient:** St. John's University's (first) Outstanding Graduate Award for doctoral dissertation (Dean's Convocation, May 1998). **Recipient:** Northeast PDK Regional Award for best doctoral dissertation (1998).

Van Wynen, E. (1999). **Recipient:** Sigma Theta Tau International Honor Society of Nursing for 1998 doctoral proposal.

___ APPENDIX B ___

Research Concerned with Learning Styles and Environmental Preferences

Researcher and Date	Sample	Subject Examined	Aspect Examined	Significance
Pizzo, J. 1981 St. John's University	Sixth graders	Reading achievement and attitudes	Sound vs. quiet preference and gender	*

Findings: The reading comprehension and attitude scores of students tested in their preferred acoustic environment were significantly higher than those of their peers tested in an incongruent environment. There was a significant interaction between learning-style preferences and gender. Males and females who were tested in acoustic environments matching their learning-style preferences achieved significantly higher reading comprehension scores than their peers tested in a mismatched environment. There were no significant interactions evidenced between acoustic environment and gender, or among acoustic environment, learning style, and gender.

Krimsky, J. 1982 St. John's University	Fourth graders	Reading speed and accuracy	Bright vs. low light preferences	*

Findings: Scores on both reading speed and accuracy were significantly higher when illumination was matched with the students' learning-style preference for light, as opposed to when it was mismatched. It was found also that there was no significant difference in reading speed and accuracy scores between students with a learning-style preference either for bright or dim light.

Researcher and Date	Sample	Subject Examined	Aspect Examined	Significance
Murrain, P. 1983 St. John's University	Seventh graders	Word recognition and memory	Temperature preferences	*

Findings: All subjects were tested twice with a word recognition test, once in an instructional setting that was congruent with their preference for temperature and once in a dissonant environment. Higher scores were attained in an environment congruent with students' identified thermal preferences, and nearly four times as many students preferred a warm, rather than a cool, room in which to learn.

Researcher and Date	Sample	Subject Examined	Aspect Examined	Significance
Shea, T. C. 1983 St. John's University	Ninth graders	English reading comprehension	Formal vs. informal design preferences	*

Findings: Students were randomly and equally assigned to learning environments that either matched or mismatched their design preferences. The mean reading comprehension scores of the youngsters tested in an environment congruent with their preferences for an informal design were significantly higher than those of their peers tested in an incongruent setting. Those who preferred a formal design performed almost as well in the informal environment because of their ability to adapt by sitting on the floor with their backs against the wall while taking the test.

Researcher and Date	Sample	Subject Examined	Aspect Examined	Significance
Della Valle, J. 1984 St. John's University	Seventh graders	Word recognition, memory, achievement	Mobility/ passivity preferences	*

Findings: Students performed significantly better when their mobility/passivity needs were matched rather than mismatched. No single environment—neither the one that required passivity nor the one that allowed for mobility—generated greater overall achievement scores. However, students who preferred a mobile environment achieved the highest scores of all groups when they were permitted to move around, whereas students with a strong passivity preference scored considerably lower when instructed to move while learning. The interaction between learning-style preference and environmental condition revealed statistical significance beyond the .001 level!

Researcher and Date	Sample	Subject Examined	Aspect Examined	Significance
Hodges, H. 1985 St. John's University	Seventh and eighth graders	Mathematics, achievement and attitudes	Formal/ informal design preferences	*

Findings: Students who were taught and tested in their preferred seating environment achieved significantly higher mean test scores, and demonstrated statistically more positive attitudes, than those who were instructed and tested in the mismatched condition. The youngsters who preferred the informal design evidenced higher achievement when permitted to learn and take their test informally than the youngsters who preferred the traditional classroom but were taught and tested in an informal environment.

MacMurran, H. 1985 St. John's University	Sixth graders	Reading speed and accuracy	Need for intake while learning	*

Findings: No statistical differences were found between the scores of students with either strong positive or strong negative preferences for intake. However, students with a strong learning-style preference for intake demonstrated significantly higher reading speed, accuracy, and attitude scores when their testing environment was congruent with their preferences, and significantly lower scores in all areas when their preferences were not matched.

Miller, L. M. 1985 University of North Florida	Second graders	Reading	Mobility/ passivity	*

Findings: This study corroborated Della Valle's findings. Students demonstrated significantly higher achievement test scores and improved behavior when their mobility/ passivity preferences were matched with congruent instructional environments. It was found that students previously labeled as hyperactive or nonconforming performed significantly better when their high mobility needs were accommodated through activity-oriented instruction.

Stiles, R. 1985 University of Tennessee	Fifth graders	Mathematics tests	Formal vs. informal design preferences	*

Findings: Learning-style preferences for design and their relationship to standardized test results were analyzed. Unlike the Shea (1983) and Hodges (1985) studies with secondary students, no significant differences were demonstrated between matched and mismatched groups, but *students* with an informal preference scored higher in both designs.

Researcher and Date	Sample	Subject Examined	Aspect Examined	Significance
DeGregoris, C. N. 1986 Hofstra University	Sixth, seventh, and eighth graders	Reading comprehension	Kinds of sounds preferred	*

Findings: DeGregoris tested sixth, seventh, and eighth graders to determine their learning-style preferences. She then tested their reading comprehension ability and collected test data through a repeated measures design. Acoustical setting was the sole variable responsible for significant differences in scores. It was evidenced that those students who achieved highest scores with music in the background were sound-preferred individuals, when the music had no lyrics.

Researcher and Date	Sample	Subject Examined	Aspect Examined	Significance
Nganwa-Bagumah, M. 1986 University of Transkei, South Africa	High schoolers	English reading comprehension	Formal vs. informal design preferences	*

Findings: In Transkei, South Africa, it was revealed that 63 students had strong preferences for a particular seating design, either formal or informal. These students were then tested for reading comprehension in both formal and informal environments—conventional classroom seating and relaxed, comfortable alternatives. Significantly higher effects were revealed in matched, rather than mismatched treatments.

Researcher and Date	Sample	Subject Examined	Aspect Examined	Significance
Nganwa-Bagumah, M., & Mwamenda, T. S. 1991	Elementary students	Reading comprehension	Formal vs. informal preferences	*

Findings: The learning styles of children in grades 2 through 5 were identified with the Learning Styles Inventory (Dunn, Dunn, & Price, 1991). Sixty-three who indicated strong preferences for the element of design were given a reading comprehension test in both a formal and an informal seating. Children achieved significantly higher test scores when tested in their preferred rather than in their nonpreferred environment.

Source: Table created by Dr. Rita Dunn and Andrea Honigsfeld.
Note: * indicates statistical significance.

APPENDIX C

Research Concerned with the Emotional Elements of Learning Styles

Researcher and Date	Sample	Subject Examined	Aspect Examined	Significance
White, R. 1980 St. John's University	Seventh graders	Social studies	Responsibility Persistence	*

Findings: Students identified as more persistent and responsible achieved higher test scores on specific behavioral objectives than did students who were less persistent and responsible. A positive correlation was evidenced between responsibility and conformity. Persistent and responsible students also tended to manifest conformity, whereas students with low responsibility scores were usually nonconforming.

Napolitano, R. A. 1986 St. John's University	College students	Psychology	Structure	*

Findings: This study investigated differences among the academic achievement and attitudes of traditionally marginally and underprepared college students when the degree of structure was either matched or mismatched with their learning-style preferences for structure.

    The study revealed that students who needed a highly structured environment received significantly higher achievement and attitude test scores when their preferences were accommodated. All students achieved higher test scores when the course was taught under highly structured conditions. However, students who did not prefer structure demonstrated lower attudinal scores in the mismatched environment.

Researcher and Date	Sample	Subject Examined	Aspect Examined	Significance
Rahal, B. F. 1986 West Virginia University	Junior high school students	Science	Structure	*

Findings: Intermediate level students' learning-style preferences for structure were identified. It was evidenced that when the instructional environment was congruent with the students' structure preferences, they performed significantly better on a unit test on energy resources than when the environment was dissonant from the learners' diagnosed structure preferences.

Researcher and Date	Sample	Subject Examined	Aspect Examined	Significance
Clark-Thayer, S. 1987 Boston University	College students	Mathematics	Motivation Homework	*

Findings: This study examined relationships among first-year students' learning style study habits and their college achievement. Both study habits and learning style correlated significantly with achievement. Successful students were Motivated, Responsible (Conforming), and Learning Alone, rather than Peer-Oriented, preferents, and required Varied instructional experiences rather than routines and patterns. They were not Tactual learners. High achievers also engaged in specific study habits and had positive attitudes toward their educational experiences.

Researcher and Date	Sample	Subject Examined	Aspect Examined	Significance
Reynolds, J. 1988 Virginia Polytechnic Institute and State University	Adults	Decision making	Learning-styles characteristics of "dependent" learners	*

Findings: Reynolds used identified characteristics and their associated instructional strategies to suggest instructional interventions for dependent decision makers. The results of the study suggested that any model of instructional strategies designed for dependent decision makers should take into account the four PEPS elements: (1) sound (2) motivation, (3) persistence, and (4) responsibility. Instructional strategies used to assist dependent decision makers should stress motivational factors such as a supportive learning environment. Reynolds concluded that special emphasis should be placed on ways to help dependent decision makers become more persistent and responsible for their own learning.

Researcher and Date	Sample	Subject Examined	Aspect Examined	Significance
Sawyer, E 1995	High school students	All subject areas	Structure	*

Findings: Sawyer reported research that verified the importance of knowing which students preferred structure and which did not. In a typical classroom, 20 to 30 percent of the students needed a great deal of structure; 20 to 30 percent needed minimal structure, and the remainder of the student population operated well either way. Teachers need to adapt their instructional methods to provide structure for those who need it and choices for those who do not.

Source: This table was created by Andrea Honigsfeld, Instructional Leadership doctoral student, St. John's University, Jamaica, NY.
Note: * indicates statistical significance.

_____APPENDIX D_____

Experimental Research Concerned with Learning Styles and Sociological Preferences

Researcher and Date	Sample	Subject Examined	Aspect Examined	Significance
Perrin, J. 1984 St. John's University	First and second grades	Problem solving Word recognition	Sociological	*

Findings: All first- and second-grade students' achievement and attitude scores were significantly higher when they were taught through approaches that matched their sociological preferences for learning alone or with peers. Gifted children preferred to learn alone and performed significantly better when working alone. However, some gifted children performed best when working with their gifted classmates.

DeBello, T. 1985 St. John's University	Eighth graders	Social studies Composition	Sociological	*

Findings: Students received statistically higher scores when their compositions were revised in their preferred sociological mode (alone, with peers, or with a teacher). In addition, those who preferred to learn alone or with a teacher showed statistically better attitudes when matched with congruent revision techniques.

Cholakis, M. 1986 St. John's University	Seventh and eighth graders	Vocabulary development	Sociological	*

Findings: Those who preferred learning alone scored significantly higher than those who preferred learning either with peers or with the teacher. All students attained significantly higher achievement and attitude scores when learning with an authority figure. Results may have been related to this parochial school population.

Researcher and Date	Sample	Subject Examined	Aspect Examined	Significance
Miles, B. 1987 St. John's University	Fifth and sixth graders	Career awareness Career decision making	Sociological	*

Findings: Matching students' sociological preferences with congruent grouping patterns (learning alone or with peers) resulted in significantly higher achievement and attitude scores in both career awareness and decision making. With the exception of career decision making, neither of the two sociologically preferenced groups performed better than the other, although students matched with their preferences for learning alone scored statistically higher than their peer-oriented classmates.

Giannitti, M. C. 1988 St. John's University	Sixth, seventh, and eighth graders	Social CAP, Team Learning	Sociological	*

Findings: Peer-oriented students achieved significantly higher scores and demonstrated statistically better attitudes when learning through Team Learning. Learning-alone preferents performed significantly better when taught through a mini-CAP. Although their attitudes were equally positive in both treatments, nonpreferenced students achieved better when the mini-CAP was used in the learning-alone treatment.

Botroff, S. M. 1993 LaSierra University	Tenth graders	Religion	Sociological	*

Findings: Students whose sociological preferences were matched during group or individualized class activities achieved significantly higher than those whose preferences were mismatched. In addition, students' attitudes were statistically better with the congruent treatment.

Catuogno, J. A. 1996 St. John's University	Ninth graders	Spelling	Sociological	*

Findings: Highly achieving high school students were exposed to four treatments: (1) learning alone, (2) learning in pairs, (3) learning in groups, and (4) learning with a teacher. Lessons were either congruent or incongruent with their sociological preferences. Although there was no significant increase in achievement test scores in the matched treatment, students revealed significantly more positive attitudes when the learning condition was congruent with their sociological styles.

Source: This table was created by Andrea Honigsfeld, Instructional Leadership doctoral student, St. John's University, Jamaica, NY.

Note: * indicates statistical significance.

_____APPENDIX E_____

Experimental Research Concerned with Perceptual Preferences

Researcher and Date	Sample	Subject Examined	Aspect Examined	Significance
Urbschat, K. 1977 Wayne State University	First grade	Reading	Auditory Visual	*

Findings: The majority of first graders revealed few auditory or visual strengths; most were labeled "other" (than auditory or visual). Auditory students learned consonant-vowel-consonant (CVC) words best with phonics; visual students learned word recognition best with linguistics.

Carbo, M. 1980 St. John's University	Kindergartners	Vocabulary	Auditory Visual "Other"	*

Findings: Carbo corroborated Urbschat's findings and revealed, for the first time, that low-auditory (A) and low-visual (V) students were tactual (T) learners. Each group (A,V,T) performed best when introduced to new words through its perceptual strength in both short- and long-term memory tests.

Wheeler, R. 1980 St. John's University	LD second graders	Reading	Auditory Visual Tactual Sequenced	*

Findings: When introduced to new words through their strongest modality (matched) and reinforced through their secondary modality, learning-disabled (LD) students achieved significantly better (at normal B level) than when mismatched. They also retained significantly longer.

Researcher and Date	Sample	Subject Examined	Aspect Examined	Significance
Weinberg, F. 1983 St. John's University	Third-grade under- achievers	Mathematics	Auditory Visual Tactual	*

Findings: Mathematics underachievers taught with tactual/visual resources (Flip Chutes, Task Cards, and Electroboards) achieved significantly higher test scores than when taught with auditory/visual resources.

Wheeler, R. 1983 St. John's University	LD second graders	Reading	A, V, T Without	*

Findings: When introduced to new words through their strongest modality but *not* reinforced through their secondary modality, learning-disabled students achieved significantly better on short-term testing but retained few words over time.

Jarsonbeck, S. 1984 University of South Florida	Fourth-grade under- achievers	Mathematics	Auditory Visual Tactual	*

Findings: Poor mathematics students tended to be tactual learners and achieved statistically higher test scores when taught math tactually (using Flip Chutes, Task Cards, and other manipulatives) than when taught through combined auditory/visual methods.

Kroon, D. 1985 St. John's University	Ninth and tenth graders	Industrial arts	Auditory Visual Tactual Sequenced	*

Findings: Auditory students performed best when taught auditorially, visual students performed best when taught visually, and tactual students performed best when taught tactually—all at significantly higher levels. Each group also achieved statistically higher test scores when introduced through its strongest modality and reinforced through its secondary or tertiary modality—and significantly less well when mismatched with unresponsive resources. For the first time, Kroon demonstrated (1) the value of modality-strength teaching at the secondary level and (2) how few secondary males had auditory or visual strengths.

Researcher and Date	Sample	Subject Examined	Aspect Examined	Significance
Gardiner, B. 1986 St. John's University	Fourth-grade under-achievers	Social studies	Multisensory vs. Traditional resources and time of day	*

Findings: Underachievers tended to be tactual and kinesthetic, rather than auditory and visual. When taught traditionally (by lecture combined with visual pictures and readings) as opposed to through a MIP,[a] all students achieved significantly better with the MIP. When taught in the morning versus in the afternoon, most students achieved significantly better in the afternoon. Higher scores were obtained by underachievers with the MIP in the afternoon than through any other combination.

[a]Multisensory Instructional Package (Dunn & Dunn, 1992, 1993).

Martini, M. 1986 St. John's University	Seventh graders	Science	Auditory Visual Tactual (Computer)	*

Findings: All students studied three science lessons—one heard on a tape, a second read, and the third learned with a computer program. Auditory students performed statistically better with the tape than the visual or tactual students did with the tape. Visual students performed statistically better by reading the chapter than the auditory or tactual students did by reading the chapter. Tactual students performed statistically better with the computer program than the auditory or visual students did with the computer program. However, all students performed better with the computer program than either listening to the tape or reading the chapter. The computer program was both visual and tactual—multisensory!

Buell, B. G., & Buell, N. A. 1987 University of Southern California	Nurses, teachers instructors	Staff develop-ment	Auditory Visual Tactual	

Findings: The closer the match between the perceptual strengths of the instructors and their students, the higher the students' achievement and attitude test scores.

Hill, G. 1987 North Texas State University	Upper elementary LD students	Spelling	Auditory Visual Tactual	

Findings: LD students actually identified their learning-style preferences. They preferred learning kinesthetically (first), followed by tactually, followed by auditorially, and then visually—which differed from usual developmental patterns of tactual, kinesthetic, visual, and then auditory. They achieved statistically higher spelling scores when matched with their preferred modality than when mismatched. Traditional teaching, which begins with the auditory and visual, may be the cause of many of these students' problems.

Researcher and Date	Sample	Subject Examined	Aspect Examined	Significance
Ingham, J. 1989 St. John's University	Adult truck drivers	Safety regulations	Auditory/ visual Tactual/ visual	*

Findings: Among 1,000 truck drivers, 10 percent were auditory, 1 percent were visual, and the remainder were tactual/kinesthetic. Individuals achieved statistically higher test scores when matched, rather than when mismatched, with their perceptual strengths.

Researcher and Date	Sample	Subject Examined	Aspect Examined	Significance
Bauer, E. 1991 St. John's University	LD + EMH junior high school poor achievers	Mathematics	Auditory Visual Tactual	*

Findings: Special education students performed significantly better when introduced to match with tactual/visual—and reinforced with tactual/kinesthetic instructional resources than in any other format.

Researcher and Date	Sample	Subject Examined	Aspect Examined	Significance
Drew, M. 1991 St. John's University	38 Cajun and 29 Louisiana Indians	Reading culturally similar and dissimilar stories	MIP vs. traditional teaching	

Findings: Matching and mismatching minority Title I students with culturally similar and dissimilar story content in traditional versus learning-style instructional teaching (PLS and tactual resources) produced statistically higher test scores with learning-style instruction rather than with traditional instruction regardless of cultural story content.

Researcher and Date	Sample	Subject Examined	Aspect Examined	Significance
Garrett, S. 1991 University of LaVerne, California	Ninth, tenth, eleventh, and twelfth graders	Vocabulary	Auditory Visual Tactual	

Findings: Motivation contributed, but perceptual strength matching produced statistically higher test scores than perceptual mismatching.

Researcher and Date	Sample	Subject Examined	Aspect Examined	Significance
Callan, R. 1995 St. John's University	High school students	Across-subject achievement	Students' homework prescription	

Findings: Students were capable of developing their own homework prescriptions based on their identified perceptual preferences.

Note: * indicates statistical significance.

_____ APPENDIX F_____

Experimental Research Concerned with Learning Styles and Time of Day, Intake, and Mobility Preference

Researcher and Date	Sample	Subject Examined	Aspect Examined	Significance
Carruthers, S., & Young, A. 1980 *Learning Styles Network Newsletter*	Eighth graders	Mathematics	Time of day	*

Findings: Junior high school underachievers who preferred learning in the afternoon but were assigned to morning mathematics classes revealed significant improvement in their behavior, motivation, and academic achievement when they were assigned to afternoon classes.

Researcher and Date	Sample	Subject Examined	Aspect Examined	Significance
Lynch, P. 1981 St. John's University	Eleventh and twelfth graders	English	Time of day, teacher assignment	*

Findings: Chronically truant students achieved significantly higher test scores and attended classes more frequently when their learning-style, time-of-day preference was matched with their English course period schedule. Matched, rather than mismatched, teacher assignments also reduced truancy, but the greatest single influence on the reduction of truancy was accommodating students' time preferences.

Researcher and Date	Sample	Subject Examined	Aspect Examined	Significance
Virostko, J. 1983 St. John's University	Third, fourth, fifth, and sixth graders	Math	Time of day	*

Findings: This two-year longitudinal study demonstrated that when students' time preferences were congruent with their mathematics and reading class schedules, they achieved significantly higher scores; when time preferences and class schedules were incongruent, students achieved significantly lower scores.

Freeley, M. 1984 St. John's University	Teachers	Inservice training	Time of day	*

Findings: Teachers implemented newly acquired instructional strategies in their classrooms to a significantly higher level when their inservice training sessions were held at their preferred time of day, either in the morning or in the afternoon.

Gardiner, B. 1986 St. John's University	Fourth graders	Social studies	Time of day and instructional	*

Findings: Students scored significantly higher on achievement tests when Multisensory Instructional Packages were used, as opposed to traditional instruction, during both morning and afternoon time-of-day periods. Most students achieved significantly higher in the afternoon with either method, but the highest achievement and attitude scores were evidenced with the MIPs in the afternoon.

Smith, S. 1987 St. John's University	Tenth and eleventh graders	Mathematics	Time of day Critical thinking	*

Findings: All students achieved at a higher level when their chronobiological preferences were matched. Attitude scores indicated that average to above-average students were able to adapt to instructional conditions incongruent with their learning-style preferences for time of day. It was evidenced also that students who preferred learning in the morning were significantly better critical thinkers than those who preferred afternoon learning.

Cramp, D. C. 1991 Southeast Missouri State University	Fourth and fifth graders	Reading/math	Time of day	*

Findings: This study corroborated Virostko's findings. In both reading and mathematics, students achieved statistically higher test scores when their time-of-day preferences (late morning or afternoon) were congruent with the instructional time periods for those subjects, as opposed to when they were incongruent.

Researcher and Date	Sample	Subject Examined	Aspect Examined	Significance
Callan, R. 1998 St. John's University	High school students	Math	Time of day	*

Findings: Morning-preferenced students performed statistically better on Regents tests administered in the morning than morning-preferenced students did in the afternoon. The majority of students were *not* morning preferenced. Instead, the later the time of day, the more students evidenced responsive preferences to it.

Researcher and Date	Sample	Subject Examined	Aspect Examined	Significance
MacMurran, H. 1985 St. John's University	Sixth graders	Reading speed and accuracy	Intake	*

Findings: No statistical differences were found between the scores of students with either strong positive or strong negative preferences for intake. However, students with a strong learning-style preference for intake demonstrated significantly higher reading speed, accuracy, and attitude scores when their testing environment was congruent with their preferences and significantly lower scores when their preferences were not matched.

Researcher and Date	Sample	Subject Examined	Aspect Examined	Significance
Della Valle, J. 1984 St. John's University	Seventh graders	Word recognition and memory	Mobility/ passivity	*

Findings: Students performed significantly better when their mobility/passivity needs were matched. No single environment, neither the one that required passivity nor the one that allowed for mobility, generated greater overall achievement scores. However, students who preferred a mobile environment achieved the highest scores of all groups when they were permitted to move around, whereas students with a strong passivity preference scored considerably lower when instructed to move while learning. The interaction between learning style preference and environmental condition was significant beyond the .001 level!

Researcher and Date	Sample	Subject Examined	Aspect Examined	Significance
Miller, L. M. 1985 University of North Florida	Second graders	Reading	Mobility/ passivity	*

Findings: Students demonstrated significantly higher achievement scores and improved behavior when their mobility/passivity preferences were matched with a complementary instructional environment. Students previously labeled as hyperactive or nonconforming performed significantly better when their high mobility needs were accommodated through activity-oriented instruction.

Source: This table was by Andrea Honigsfeld.
Note: * indicates statistical significance.

INDEX